Freedom, God, and Worlds

# Freedom, God, and Worlds

Michael J. Almeida

UNIVERSITY PRESS

**UNIVERSITY PRESS**

Great Clarendon Street, Oxford, OX2 6DP,
United Kingdom

Oxford University Press is a department of the University of Oxford.
It furthers the University's objective of excellence in research, scholarship,
and education by publishing worldwide. Oxford is a registered trade mark of
Oxford University Press in the UK and in certain other countries

British Library Cataloguing in Publication Data
Data available

Library of Congress Cataloging in Publication Data
Data available

ISBN 978–0–19–964002–7

Printed in Great Britain by
MPG Books Group, Bodmin and King's Lynn

For Sam, Zoe, and Yvette

# Contents

# Acknowledgments

Many of the chapters in this book were presented, at various stages of development, in various forums including the University of Texas at San Antonio, Texas A & M University, the American Philosophical Association, and the Annual Baylor Philosophy of Religion Conference. I'd like to express my gratitude to Robert Audi, Adam Barnard, Lara Buchak, Eric Buitron, Robert Burch, Dan Conway, Garrett Dyer, Thomas Flint, Robert Garcia, Luke Gelinas, Michael Hand, David Hunt, Claire Katz, Jon Kvanvig, Brian Leftow, Felipe Leon, Clayton Littlejohn, Hugh McCann, Chris Menzel, Brad Monton, Wes Morriston, Matt Mullins, Kenny Pearce, Alvin Plantinga, Alex Pruss, James Reeves, Robin Smith, James E. Taylor, Kevin Timpe, Patrick Todd, Dale Tuggy, David Vander Laan, Vlastimil Vohánka, Ed Wierenga, and two anonymous referees at Oxford University Press. Apologies to those I may have omitted. I thank everyone for their comments and criticisms.

# Introduction

## 0.1. The Aims and Structure of this Book

It is a principal aim of this book to show that several widely believed and largely undisputed principles in philosophical theology are in fact just philosophical dogmas. The well-entrenched principles have served as basic assumptions in some of the most powerful apriori atheological arguments. But most theists also maintain that the principles express apriori necessary truths. The philosophical dogmas include principles that are presumed to follow apriori from the nature of an essentially omnipotent, essentially omniscient, essentially perfectly good and necessarily existing being. Among the prominent dogmas is D1.

D1. Necessarily, God can actualize the best possible world only if God does actualize the best possible world.

D1 entails that there is no possible world in which it is non-trivially true that God can actualize the best possible world and he does not actualize the best possible world. The principle is advanced as an apriori necessary truth entailed by the nature of God as an essentially omnipotent and essentially perfectly good being. The intuition is presumably that, necessarily, God is essentially omnipotent, essentially perfectly good, and God can actualize the best possible world only if God does actualize the best possible world. But contrary to D1 it is possible that God does not actualize the best possible world despite the fact that God is essentially omnipotent, essentially perfectly good, and able to actualize the best possible world. Another prominent philosophical dogma is D2.

D2. Necessarily, God can actualize a morally perfect world only if God does actualize a morally perfect world.

The principle entails that there is no possible world in which it is true that God can actualize a morally perfect world and God does not actualize a morally perfect world. Morally perfect worlds are possible worlds in which every significantly free being always acts in ways that are morally right. A morally perfect world includes no morally bad states of affairs. But a morally perfect world might not be among the best possible worlds. So, the principle does not entail that there is no possible world in which it is true that God can actualize a best possible world and God does not actualize a best possible world. Even if there is no best possible world, according to this principle, God must actualize a morally perfect world. But D2 is also false. Contrary to D2 it is possible that God does not actualize a morally perfect world despite the fact that God is able to actualize such a world.

Even if D1 and D2 are false, it might reasonably be expected that an Anselmian God must actualize a good enough world. But D3 too is a dogma of philosophical theology.

> D3. Necessarily, God can actualize a good enough world only if God does actualize a good enough world.

The principle D3 entails that there is no possible world at which it is true that God can actualize a good enough world and God does not actualize a good enough world. Good enough worlds are possible worlds whose overall value exceeds N for some positive N. The exact value of N is of course a matter of dispute, but D3 is false for any value of N. Good enough worlds have an overall positive value, but a good enough world might not be morally perfect. So, D3 entails D2 only if all morally perfect worlds are good enough worlds. And it is not clear that this is so. Even if there are no morally perfect worlds, according to principle D3, God must actualize some world that is among the good enough worlds. But D3 is also false. For any positive N whatsoever, it is possible that God can actualize a world whose overall value is N and God does not actualize such a world.

I offer a set of *Impossibility Arguments* that aim to show that the prominent principles, D1–D3, are necessarily false. The arguments share a common structure. Each impossibility argument assumes for reductio that, necessarily, God can actualize the relevant kind of world—the best world or a morally perfect world or a good enough world. Each argument concludes that it's possible that God does not actualize the relevant kind of world. The impossibility arguments show that the prominent principles in philosophical theology are simply entrenched falsehoods. These principles can no longer serve any theological or atheological purposes.

The impossibility arguments also show that many of the most serious apriori atheological arguments are unsound. Many of the most serious atheological arguments assume D1–D3. Included among the most problematic atheological arguments are the *Logical Problem of Evil*, the *Logical Problem of the Best Possible World*, the *Logical Problem of Good Enough Worlds*, the *Logical Problem of Naturally Perfect Worlds*, the *Problem of Divine Freedom*, the *Problem of Gratuitous Evil*, the *Problem of No Best World*, *Heller's Worst World*, the *Darwinian Problem of Evil*, and the *Evidential Problem of Evil*. Solutions to several less serious atheological problems are also forthcoming. It is among the principal conclusions of the book that these atheological arguments present no important challenge to the existence of an Anselmian God.

The argument for the principal conclusions begins in Chapter 1, "A Moderate Anselmian Plea." In Chapter 1, I show that the traditional Anselmian project does not have the resources to explain the persistence of modal intuitions evincing the broad epistemic possibility that, for instance, rabbits suffer pointlessly, people endure pointless abuse, fawns die painful and pointless deaths, and so on. The apriori necessity of divine attributes does afford the traditional Anselmian an unexpectedly straightforward and valid ontological argument. But traditional Anselmianism cannot accommodate the broad conceivability of countless states of affairs incompatible with the view that God's attributes are apriori necessary.

I introduce *Moderate Anselmianism*. Moderate Anselmianism rejects the traditional position that, for the most important essential properties of God, it is apriori necessary that God has those properties. It is not apriori necessary, for instance, that God instantiates the essential properties of omnipotence, omniscience, perfect goodness or necessary existence.[1] Moderate Anselmianism can accommodate the broad conceivability of states of affairs incompossible with the traditional Anselmian God. Moderate Anselmians concede the epistemic possibility that rabbits suffer pointlessly and that people endure pointless abuse. These broad epistemic

---

[1] Moderate Anselmianism is consistent with it being apriori true that God instantiates the trivial essential properties such as being identical to God or not being a prime number. It's worth noting that there is some doubt about whether these trivial properties are essential properties of anything. See, for instance, Kit Fine, "Senses of Essence" in Walter Sinnott-Armstrong, Diana Raffman, and Nicholas Asher (eds.) *Modality, Morality, and Belief: Essays in Honor of Ruth Barcan Marcus* (Cambridge: Cambridge University Press, 1995); and "Reference, Essence, and Identity" in his *Modality and Tense: Philosophical Papers* (Oxford: Oxford University Press, 2005).

possibilities constitute either genuinely possible states of affairs (ultimately) compossible with the Anselmian God or *Anselmian Illusions*.

A state of affairs is an Anselmian illusion only if it is not metaphysically compossible with the Anselmian God and obtains in (at least) some apriori consistent maximal states of affairs that include an Anselmian God.[2] Anselmian illusions are epistemically compossible with the Anselmian God though not metaphysically compossible with the Anselmian God. I argue that many apriori atheological arguments appeal to states of affairs that are nothing more than Anselmian illusions. I defend moderate Anselmianism against several incompossibility arguments. I conclude that moderate Anselmianism is the most promising Anselmian response to apriori atheological arguments.

Moderate Anselmianism is consistent with the apriori possibility of states of affairs that are inconsistent with traditional Anselmianism. Atheological arguments against moderate Anselmianism are more difficult to generate. Such argument must show that there are non-illusory, genuinely possible states of affairs—not merely conceivable states of affairs—that are inconsistent with the moderate Anselmian God. I call these *metaphysical atheological arguments*. Merely conceivable states of affairs inconsistent with the moderate Anselmian God might be nothing more than Anselmian illusions.

In Chapter 2, I introduce the metaphysical atheological arguments against moderate Anselmianism. The best known metaphysical atheological argument is the *Logical Problem of Evil*. Alvin Plantinga famously urged that there is no cogent formulation of the logical problem of evil.[3] In *God and Other Minds* he concludes exactly that.

...we have not been able to find a proposition, necessarily true or an essential part of theism or a consequence of such propositions, which in conjunction with [(1) God is omnipotent, omniscient and wholly good and (2) evil exists] entails a contradiction. Indeed we have not so much as produced a plausible candidate. If this does not show that there is *no* such proposition, it suggests that finding one is much more difficult than most atheologians seems to suppose.[4]

---

[2] As elaborated in Chapter 1, apriori consistent states of affairs need not be metaphysically consistent.

[3] See Alvin Plantinga, *God and Other Minds* (Ithaca: Cornell University Press, 1967); *God, Freedom, and Evil* (Grand Rapids: Eerdmans Publishing, 1974); and *The Nature of Necessity* (Oxford: Oxford University Press, 1974).

[4] See *God and Other Minds*, op. cit. p. 128 ff. The modifications to this passage include an inserted abbreviation in (1) and (2). There are no substantial modifications.

And in *God, Freedom and Evil* he arrives at a similar conclusion.

To summarize our conclusions so far: although many atheologians claim that the theist is involved in a contradiction when he asserts the members of set A, this set, obviously, is neither explicitly nor formally contradictory; the claim, presumably, must be that it is implicitly contradictory. To make good this claim the atheologian must find some necessarily true proposition p . . . such that the addition of p to set A yields a set that is formally contradictory. No atheologian has produced even a plausible candidate for this role, and it is certainly not easy to see what such a proposition might be.[5]

But I argue in Chapter 2 that there are three cogent reconstructions of the logical problem of evil that appeal to principles many believe are metaphysically necessary. The principles vary in strength and differ in implications but each is sufficient to generate a valid logical problem of evil. The propositions (1) God is omnipotent, omniscient, and wholly good and (2) evil exists, are inconsistent with each of (3.3)–(3.5).

3.3. Necessarily, an omnipotent, omniscient, wholly good being brings about *the best possible world* and the best possible world includes no evil states of affairs at all.

3.4. Necessarily, an omnipotent, omniscient, wholly good being brings about *the best actualizable world* and the best actualizable world includes no evil states of affairs.

3.5. Necessarily, an omnipotent, omniscient, wholly good being brings about *a good enough world* and a good enough actualizable world includes no evil states of affairs.

The best known response to the logical problem of evil is surely Alvin Plantinga's free will defense. But the free will defense is also the most frequently misunderstood and misconstrued argument in the literature on the logical problem of evil.[6] The misunderstanding is due in large part to a

[5] See *God, Freedom, and Evil*, op. cit. p. 24. The set A = {God is omnipotent, God is wholly good, Evil exists}.
[6] For discussion of some of these errors see Michael Bergmann, "Review of R. Douglas Geivett's *Evil and the Evidence for God: The Challenge of John Hick's Theodicy*" *Faith and Philosophy* (1996) 436–41; and his "Might-Counterfactuals, Transworld Untrustworthiness and Plantinga's Free Will Defense" *Faith and Philosophy* 16 (1999) 336–51. The misunderstandings occur consistently. Some prominent examples occur in Douglas Geivett, *Evil and the Evidence for God: The Challenge of John Hick's Theodicy* (Philadelphia: Temple University Press,

less-than-cautious assessment of the structure and aim of the argument. But it is also due to a less than perspicuous presentation of the argument.[7] Given the prominence of the free will defense in the literature on the logical problem of evil, I take special care in Sections 2.3–2.6 to present the argument as clearly as possible. The thesis of universal transworld depravity is generally taken to be the cornerstone of Plantinga's solution to the logical problem of evil, but I show in Section 2.7 that it cannot resolve the logical problem of evil on its own. The argument needs additional assumptions. But I underscore that nothing as strong as universal transworld depravity is necessary to resolve the logical problem of evil.

I show in this chapter that the three well-known objections to the free will defense severely underestimate the resources available to that argument. The *Problem of Sanctified Agents* introduces the modal thesis that, possibly, it is necessary that some essence or other is transworld sanctified. Transworld sanctified essences are such that there are some worlds in which their instantiations *might* always go right.[8] So, it is possible that, necessarily, some essence or other is transworld sanctified only if the thesis of universal transworld depravity is false. Indeed, it is possible that, necessarily, some essence or other is transworld sanctified only if the thesis of universal transworld depravity is *necessarily* false.

The *Problem of Sanctified Agents* is seriously hampered by the implicit assumption that there is a single proposition R suitable to the consistency

1993); John Hick, *Evil and the God of Love* (revised edition) (San Francisco: Harper and Row, 1978); and even J. L. Mackie, *The Miracle of Theism* (Oxford: Clarendon Press, 1982).

[7] Plantinga acknowledges that the most frequently cited version of the argument in *The Nature of Necessity* (Oxford: Oxford University Press, 1974) does not contain an especially perspicuous presentation. But he offers the free will defense argument in several places. See especially *God, Freedom, and Evil* (Grand Rapids: Eerdmans Publishing Company, 1974); and H. Tomberlin and Peter van Inwagen (eds.) *Profiles: Alvin Plantinga* (Dordrecht-Holland: D. Reidel Publishing Co., 1985).

[8] What we might have expected is that transworld sanctified essences are such that God could not actualize a world in which they go wrong. That would be the natural analogue for transworld depravity and would be defined as follows.

TS⁺. An essence E enjoys transworld sanctity iff. for every world W such that E instantiates the properties *is significantly free* in W and *does at least one thing wrong* in W, and for every state of affairs T and action A such that,

(1) T is the largest state of affairs God strongly actualizes in W
(2) A is morally significant for E's instantiation in W
(3) if God had strongly actualized T, E's instantiation would not have gone wrong with respect to A.

proof in the free will defense. The objection focuses on a single proposition R as though R alone is suitable to show that God's existence is consistent with the existence of evil. In fact there are several modal theses available to the free will defense that are much weaker than the thesis of universal transworld depravity and that are sufficient to resolve the logical problem of evil. The thesis of *intraworld depravity*, for instance, and the thesis of *multiworld depravity* are sufficient to resolve the logical problem of evil. The theses of intraworld depravity and multiworld depravity are much weaker than the thesis of universal transworld depravity and, in addition, are consistent with the thesis of transworld sanctity. They are also consistent with the theses of multiworld sanctity and intraworld sanctity. So the *Problem of Sanctified Agents* has no hope of making it reasonable to refrain from believing that the existence of God is inconsistent with the existence of evil.

The *Problem of Transworld Untrustworthy Agents* advances the stronger modal thesis that some essence is necessarily not transworld depraved. The thesis is incompatible with the thesis of universal transworld depravity, but it is consistent with the thesis of partial intraworld depravity and partial multiworld depravity. The objection again sorely underestimates the resources available to the free will defense. We can agree that some essence is necessarily not transworld depraved and easily retain the resources to show that the existence of God is consistent with the existence of evil.

The *Problem of Selective Freedom* states that, necessarily, God can cause significantly free essences to exemplify the property of *selective significant freedom*. If, necessarily, God can cause an essence to exemplify the property of restricted significant freedom, then, necessarily, God can weakly actualize what I call a *quasi-E-perfect world*. It follows that the thesis of universal transworld depravity is false.

According to the *Problem of Selective Freedom*, God does not decide once and for all whether his creatures are significantly free. God can make a creature that is free on some occasions and not free on others. Since God knows by foreknowledge or middle knowledge what a creature would do were he to freely act on a given occasion, God can grant freedom to a creature when and only when he knows that freedom will not be misused.[9]

---

[9] See David Lewis, "Evil for Freedom's Sake" in his *Papers in Ethics and Social Philosophy* (Cambridge: Cambridge University Press, 2000), pp. 119 ff. See also M. J. Almeida, "Transworld Enablers" unpublished manuscript.

I conclude that these three well-known objections to the free will defense seriously underestimate the argument. The free will defense is a consistency proof. It aims to show that the existence of God is broadly logically consistent with the existence of evil. The best known objections to the free will defense fail to appreciate the number of ways in which the consistency proof can succeed.[10]

In Chapter 4, I argue that, for all the resilience of the free will defense, the thesis of universal transworld depravity is necessarily false. And so are the weaker modal theses of multiworld depravity and intraworld depravity. It is a basic assumption in the free will defense that there are two senses in which God can bring it about that an instantiated essence $E_n$ performs an action A. God can *strongly actualize* the state of affairs of $E_n$ performing A. And God can *weakly actualize* the state of affairs of $E_n$ performing A.

But this basic assumption is false. There are at least two other senses in which God can bring it about that an instantiated essence $E_n$ performs an action A. It is true that, possibly, God can strongly actualize a maximal state of affairs T which includes, for instance, God *announcing* that $E_n$ performed A yesterday. And, necessarily, God announces that $E_n$ performed A yesterday only if $E_n$ performed A. If we add the supposition that God cannot announce that $E_n$ performed A yesterday in worlds where it is false that $E_n$ performed A, we call that *restricted actualization*.[11] Restricted

---

[10] It is surprising that the best objections to the free will defense fail to appreciate the variety of ways that the consistency proof can succeed, since Plantinga has been explicit about this. See *The Nature of Necessity*, op. cit. pp. 189–90.

Of course the conjunctions of (31) [every essence suffers from transworld depravity] with (32) [God actualizes a world containing moral good is not the only proposition that can play the role of R in the Free Will Defense. Perhaps, for example, it was within the power of God to actualize a world including much good but no moral evil, but not within his power to actualize one including no moral evil and including as much moral good as the actual world contains. So (33)—for any world W, if W contains no moral evil and W contains as much good as @ contains, then God could not have actualized W—(which is weaker than (31)) could be used in conjunction with (34)—God actualizes a world containing as much good as the actual world contains—to show that (1) [God exists] and (2) [there is evil] are consistent.

And there are many other possibilities including the thesis of intraworld depravity that are sufficient to prove the consistency.

[11] Ric Otte, "Transworld Depravity and Unobtainable Worlds" *Philosophy and Phenomenological Research* (2009), 165–77. I'm unpersuaded that God cannot utter that S performed A yesterday in worlds where S did not perform A. Of course, this would be a situation in which a backtracking counterfactual is true. But backtracking counterfactuals are sometimes true, though always under unusual conditions. But surely the case of an omniscient being

actualization ensures that, possibly, God can strongly actualize a state of affairs T such that, necessarily, T only if God actualizes a morally perfect world. But God cannot strongly actualize T in every world unrestrictedly.

It is also true that, necessarily, God can strongly actualize the state of affairs T that includes the state of affairs of God's having *predicted or prophesied* that $E_n$ will perform A. But if, necessarily, God can predict that $E_n$ performs A, then it is true in every world that God can bring it about that $E_n$ performs A *without causing* $E_n$ to perform A. Call that *unrestricted actualization.* Unrestricted actualization ensures that God can strongly actualize a maximal state of affairs T such that, necessarily, T only if God actualizes a morally perfect world. And God can actualize T in every possible world unrestrictedly, simply by making a suitable prediction. If God can unrestrictedly actualize a morally perfect world, then it's evident that the thesis of universal transworld depravity is necessarily false. And so are the weaker modal theses of multiworld depravity and intraworld depravity. There is no world in which any essence, or set of essences E, is such that God cannot actualize an E-perfect world.

I argue in this chapter that the thesis that God can unrestrictedly actualize a morally perfect world is consistent with the Molinist position on the prevolitional truth of counterfactuals of creaturely freedom. The thesis that God can unrestrictedly actualize a morally perfect world does not entail that God can *make* some counterfactuals of freedom true.[12] I also argue that the thesis that God can unrestrictedly actualize a morally perfect world is consistent with the significant freedom of creaturely essences. God's predicting that every instantiated essence will always go right does not entail that God causes anyone to go right and does not entail any troublesome form of theological fatalism.

In Chapter 5, I show how the unrestricted actualization of morally perfect worlds generates a logical problem of evil that no free will defense can resolve. Indeed the argument suggests that John Mackie's atheological argument from evil was entirely right. Necessarily it is within God's power to predict that every significantly free essence he instantiates will always go right. God's omnipotence and omniscience ensure that he can utter the

uttering "S performed A yesterday" seems like just the sort of case in which the backtracking counterfactual is true.

12 See, for instance, Jon Kvanvig, "On Behalf of Maverick Molinism" *Faith and Philosophy* (2002), 348–57. Maverick Molinism denies that, necessarily, every counterfactual of creaturely freedom is prevolitionally true.

prediction that every instantiated essence always goes right and that his predictions are necessarily accurate. So God predicts that every significantly free essence always goes right only if every significantly free essence always freely goes right. But then Mackie's conclusion follows: necessarily, God can actualize a morally perfect world. So the logical problem of evil re-emerges in a much more serious form. Indeed there are at least three serious versions of the logical problem of evil.

The solution to the *Logical Problem of Evil Redux* must be consistent with the thesis that God can unrestrictedly actualize a morally perfect world. God can unrestrictedly actualize a morally perfect world if and only if, necessarily, God can actualize a morally perfect world. So it is natural to suppose, as John Mackie and many others have supposed, that there can be no solution to the logical problem forthcoming.

But I show in Chapter 5 that the well-entrenched principles that serve as basic assumptions in logical problems of evil redux are nothing more than philosophical dogmas. A set of impossibility arguments is advanced that prove, among other things, that there is a world in which God *can* actualize a morally perfect world and God *does not* actualize a morally perfect world. The impossibility arguments in general show that (3.3)–(3.5) are all necessarily false. The logical problems of evil redux are therefore necessarily unsound. The main consequences of each impossibility arguments are in C1–C6:

C1. It is impossible that, necessarily, God actualizes a morally perfect world.

C2. It is a necessary truth that, possibly, God can actualize a morally perfect world and does not.

C3. It is impossible that, necessarily, God actualizes the best possible world.

C4. It is a necessary truth that, possibly, God can actualize the best possible world and does not.

C5. It is impossible that, necessarily, God actualizes a good enough world.

C6. It is a necessary truth that, possibly, God can actualize a good enough world and does not.

The moral we draw from impossibility arguments is that there are no extremely good worlds unless there are extremely bad worlds. God cannot actualize extremely good worlds unless he can also actualize extremely bad worlds. It is no more than a philosophical dogma that, necessarily, God actualizes a morally perfect world or that necessarily God actualizes the best possible world, or that necessarily God actualizes a good enough world. It is indeed impossible that, necessarily, God actualizes any of those worlds.

It is the aim of Chapters 6 and 7 to observe and note additional implications of the impossibility arguments. The arguments provide the resources to resolve several other atheological problems. I consider in turn the problem of Heller's worst world, the problem of God existing alone, the problem of gratuitous evil and the problem of horrendous evil. I show that four additional atheological arguments are unsound. The impossibility arguments prove unsound the problem of divine freedom, the problem of no best world, the evidential argument from evil, and the Darwinian problem of evil.

In the first seven chapters of the book, I proposed that we abandon traditional Anselmianism in favor of moderate Anselmianism. The traditional Anselmian enterprise is extremely unlikely to succeed since it cannot accommodate even the conceivability of states of affairs incompossible with the Anselmian God. I argue that Anselmians should embrace moderate Anselmianism according to which it is aposteriori necessary that God possesses the divine attributes.

Despite Plantinga's well-founded reservations, I show that there are three valid formulations of the logical problem of evil. The traditional response to the problem, the free will defense, is perhaps the most frequently misunderstood and misconstrued argument in the literature on the logical problem of evil. But I show that the argument is much more powerful and much more resilient than its best critics have appreciated.

For all the power of the free will defense, the thesis of universal transworld depravity is necessarily false. And so are the weaker modal theses available to the free will defense. I show how to generate a logical problem of evil that no free will defense can resolve. So it is natural to suppose, as John Mackie and many others have supposed, that there can be no solution to the logical problem forthcoming. But I show that the well-entrenched principles that serve as basic assumptions in, among other atheological arguments, the *Logical Problem of Evil Redux* are no more than philosophical dogmas.

The *Impossibility Arguments* show that several well-entrenched principles in philosophical theology are in fact necessary falsehoods. Since these principles function as assumption in the logical problem of evil redux, and several other troublesome atheological arguments, the impossibility arguments undermine the most serious atheological arguments against moderate Anselmianism.

In Chapter 8, "Redeeming Worlds," I argue that worlds in which God exists and there is gratuitous evil are nonetheless worlds containing *redeemable evil*. Gratuitous evil is not irredeemable evil. Indeed the free actions of God and other significantly free beings can render each gratuitous evil necessary to some greater good. There is no doubt gratuitous evil, but there is no irredeemable evil.

Plantinga has recently advanced the theodicy that the Christian incarnation and atonement are among the greatest goods. But the value incarnation and atonement depend on the existence of redeemable evils. I argue that the impossibility arguments make every defense and theodicy unnecessary. The incarnation and atonement are examples of how pointless evil might be redeemed. But significantly free finite beings can also redeem pointless evils. I conclude that the existence of gratuitous evils is largely the result of significantly free finite beings choosing not to redeem gratuitous evils. In Chapter 9, I offer some conclusions and some closing comments on the argument of the book.

# 1

# A Moderate Anselmian Plea

## 1.0 Introduction

Incompossibility arguments are apriori atheological arguments according to which the conceivability of certain statements or propositions constitutes good evidence against the Anselmian God. The conceivability of a world so bad that an Anselmian God could not actualize it, for instance, has been persuasively advanced against traditional forms of Anselmianism, and so has the conceivability of a single sentient being leading a pointless and pain-racked existence. There are of course countless other troublesome examples for traditional Anselmians including the conceivability of godless worlds and even the conceivability of there being nothing at all.[1]

In Section 1.2, I show that the traditional Anselmian project fails. Traditional Anselmianism as elaborated, for instance, in Anselm, Hartshorne, Malcolm, Plantinga, and Morris describes a God who possesses the divine attributes as a matter of apriori necessity.[2] On the traditional view, God is a being than which none greater can be *conceived*. It is part of the meaning of "God" that he is maximally excellent and maximal excellence entails essential omnipotence, essential omniscience, essential perfect goodness, and essential necessary existence.

---

[1] See David Chalmers, "Materialism and the Metaphysics of Modality" *Philosophy and Phenomenological Research* 1999, esp. sec. 3.3; and Stephen Yablo, "Textbook Kripkeanism and the Open Texture of Concepts" in *Thoughts: Philosophical Papers I* (Oxford: Oxford University Press, 2008) sec. 2.

[2] See S. N. Deane, *St Anselm: Basic Writings* (Peru, Ill.: Open Court Publishing Company, 1962); *Proslogium* III, Thomas Morris, *Anselmian Explorations* (Notre Dame: University of Notre Dame Press, 1987); Charles Hartshorne, *Man's Vision of God* (New York: Harper & Row Inc., 1941); Norman Malcolm, "Anselm's Ontological Arguments" *Philosophical Review* (1960) 41–62; and Alvin Plantinga, *The Nature of Necessity* (Oxford: Oxford University Press, 1974).

Most efforts to defend traditional Anselmianism have tried to show that states of affairs incompossible with the attributes of the Anselmian God are not metaphysically possible. But since it is taken as a conceptual truth that God is essentially omnipotent, essentially omniscient, essentially perfectly good, and essentially necessarily existent, traditional Anselmianism entails that no state of affairs incompossible with the divine attributes is so much as conceivable. So any adequate defense of traditional Anselmianism must also show that such states of affairs are not, in a broad sense, epistemically possible.

I show that the traditional Anselmian project does not have the re-sources to explain the persistence of modal intuitions evincing the broad epistemic possibility that, for instance, rabbits suffer pointlessly, people endure pointless abuse, fawns die painful and pointless deaths, and so on. The apriori necessity of divine attributes does afford the traditional Anselmian an unexpectedly straightforward and valid ontological argu-ment. But traditional Anselmianism cannot accommodate the broad conceivability of countless states of affairs incompatible with the view that God's attributes are apriori necessary.

In Section 1.3, I introduce *Moderate Anselmianism*. Moderate Anselmian-ism rejects the traditional position that, for the most important essential properties of God, it is apriori necessary that God has those properties.[3] It is not apriori necessary, for instance, that God instantiates the essential properties of omnipotence, omniscience, perfect goodness, or necessary existence.[4] Moderate Anselmianism can accommodate the broad conceiv-ability of states of affairs incompossible with the traditional Anselmian

[3] There is work in the literature that seems sympathetic to the moderate Anselmian view. See, for instance, William P. Alston, *Epistemic Justification: Essays in the Theory of Knowledge* (Ithaca: Cornell University Press, 1989); and Jordan Howard Sobel, *Logic and Theism: Argu-ments For and Against Beliefs in God* (Cambridge: Cambridge University Press, 2004). See Thomas Senor, "God, Supernatural Kinds, and the Incarnation" *Religious Studies* 27 (1991) 353–70; and his "Defending Divine Freedom" in Jon Kvanvig (ed.) *Oxford Studies in the Philosophy of Religion Volume I* (Oxford: Oxford University Press, 2008) 168–95. See also Meghan Sullivan, "Semantics for Blasphemy" in Jon Kvanvig (ed.) *Oxford Studies in the Philosophy of Religion Volume IV* (Oxford: Oxford University Press, 2012) 160–73.

[4] See footnote 1 on p. 3 of this volume.

God. Moderate Anselmians concede the epistemic possibility that rabbits suffer pointlessly and that people endure pointless abuse. These broad epistemic possibilities constitute either a genuinely possible state of affairs (ultimately) compossible with the Anselmian God or *Anselmian Illusions*.

A state of affairs is an Anselmian illusion only if it is not metaphysically compossible with the Anselmian God and it obtains in (at least) some apriori consistent maximal states of affairs that include an Anselmian God. Anselmian illusions are epistemically compossible with the Anselmian God though not metaphysically compossible with the Anselmian God. I argue in Section 1.3 that many apriori atheological arguments appeal to states of affairs that are nothing more than Anselmian illusions. In Section 1.4, I defend moderate Anselmianism against several incompossibility arguments. I conclude in Section 1.5 that moderate Anselmianism is the most promising Anselmian response to apriori atheological arguments.

## 1.1 The Failure of Traditional Anselmianism

Every incompossibility proof assumes that there are conceivable propositions that are inconsistent with the existence of an Anselmian God. Compare the proposition in (1).

1. There exist rabbits enduring pointless pain.[5]

The proposition in (1) seems broadly conceivable. The proposition is conceivable in the sense that there is no apriori true proposition that entails that (1) is false. Conceivability in this sense evinces a broad form of epistemic possibility.[6] Broadly epistemically possible propositions are just those that are true in broadly epistemically possible worlds.

---

[5] The example in (1) is due to Theodore Guleserian, "God and Possible Worlds: The Modal Problem of Evil" *Noûs* (1983) 221–38. The argument that the statement in (1) is incompossible with an Anselmian God assumes the standard view on evil. Among those who have defended the standard position on evil is William Rowe.

An omniscient, wholly good being would prevent the occurrence of any intense evil it could, unless it could not do so without thereby losing some greater good or permitting some evil equally bad or worse.

See William Rowe, "The Problem of Evil and Some Varieties of Atheism" collected in Daniel Howard-Snyder (ed.) *The Evidential Argument from Evil* (Indianapolis: Indiana University Press, 1996) 1–11.

[6] There are many concepts of epistemic possibility in the literature that are much less restrictive than the concept described here. The concept I have in mind satisfies the

Broadly epistemically possible worlds, just as metaphysically possible worlds, are maximal states of affairs. A state of affairs S is maximal just in case, for every state of affairs S', S includes S' or S includes ~S'. A maximal state of affairs S is consistent just in case the set of propositions describing S is simultaneously satisfiable.

Let the maximal set of propositions B describing a maximal state of affairs S be the *book* on S.[7] If B is the book on S, then S obtains only if B is true or S entails B. Let's say that a maximal state of affairs S is *apriori consistent* just in case it is apriori possible that B is simultaneously satisfiable.[8] If ~p is not a member of the set A of apriori truths at W, then p is apriori possible at W. If B is the book on S, then S is apriori consistent just in case ~B is not apriori true at W. So, a maximal state of affairs S is apriori consistent at world W just in case it is not among the apriori truths at W that S is not simultaneously satisfiable. The set of broadly epistemically possible worlds at W is just the set of apriori consistent maximal states of affairs at W.

Every apriori consistent maximal state of affairs exists at every metaphysically possible world. But some apriori consistent maximal states of affairs obtain at no metaphysically possible worlds. Some epistemically possible worlds are metaphysically *impossible worlds*. In general, an apriori consistent maximal state of affairs is (aposteriori) inconsistent if and only if it includes an aposteriori impossible state of affairs.[9] But since any maximal state of affairs that includes the states of affairs p and ~p is *apriori inconsistent*, no impossible worlds include every state of affairs.

No impossible world is closed under logical consequence, since no impossible world includes every state of affairs. But every impossible world is apriori consistent and maximal. So every impossible world W is such that the book on W is *apriori closed* under logical consequence.

Consider the concept of epistemic possibility described in E1.

E1. q is epistemically possible at W if and only if q is true in some apriori consistent maximal state of affairs.

biconditional that the state of affairs p is epistemically possible if and only if p obtains in some apriori consistent maximal state of affairs.

[7] The notion of the book on a possible world is introduced in Alvin Plantinga, *The Nature of Necessity*, op. cit. p. 44 ff.

[8] Strictly speaking the set of epistemically possible worlds will vary from world to world, since the set of apriori consistent maximal states of affairs varies from world to world.

[9] Apriori consistent maximal states of affairs need not be consistent maximal states of affairs.

We will say the set containing q and all apriori true propositions p at W is apriori consistent if and only if p & ~q is not a member of A at W. q is apriori necessary just in case ~q is not epistemically possible. Let's stipulate that the proposition in (1) is conceivable if and only if the proposition is epistemically possible in the sense of E1.[10]

Note that q is conceivable just in case there *exists* an apriori consistent maximal state of affairs W in which q is true. q is conceivable because W is conceivable. And there may exist such an apriori consistent maximal state of affairs even if you know that q is aposteriori impossible.

It is not in general true that apriori consistent maximal states of affairs could "turn out" to obtain, even in an extended two dimensionalist sense of turning out to obtain. It is apriori possible that water is not $H_2O$, on the account I am proposing, since the proposition that sentence expresses is *true in* some epistemically possible world. But all that means is that were such a world actual, that proposition would be true. On some two dimensionalist accounts "water is not $H_2O$" expresses two propositions, one of which is true just in case the actual world turns out to have watery stuff that is XYZ rather than $H_2O$. At least some two dimensionalists maintain that there is a metaphysically possible world at which water is not $H_2O$. I'm proposing that there is no interesting sense in which it could turn out that water is not $H_2O$; "water is H2O" might have, but does not, express a (different) proposition that is true in some metaphysically possible worlds. And even if the sentence expresses two propositions, the de re modal proposition is false that dthat (the body of water in the Gulf) might not have been $H_2O$. But there do exist apriori consistent worlds at which it is true that the body of water in the Gulf is not $H_2O$ and these worlds provide the illusion that it's genuinely possible that dthat (the body of water in the Gulf) is not $H_2O$.

Let q be the proposition that there are rabbits enduring pointless pain. If q is epistemically possible, there is an apriori consistent world in which q is true. So, were W to obtain then it would be true that q. But that conditional might be a counterpossible since the maximal states of affairs W might not be consistent. So q is epistemically possible just in case the state of affairs that q describes is included in some apriori consistent

---

[10] Throughout I use "conceivable" for "ideally conceivable" in cases of both primary conceivability and secondary conceivability. These are serious issues, of course, but too large to address in the scope of this chapter.

maximal state of affairs, even if q is not included in any maximal meta-physical state of affairs.

Some incompossibility arguments urge that (1) is also true as an assertion of metaphysical possibility. Let's understand metaphysical possibility as consistency with all necessary truth at a world.

E2.  q is metaphysically possible at W if and only if q is consistent with all necessary truth at W.

A proposition q is metaphysically possible if and only if it genuinely might have been the case that q.[11]

According to traditional Anselmianism we can know apriori the most important essential properties of God.[12] It is apriori impossible, for instance, that God should not have the essential property of moral perfection or the essential property of necessary existence. It is a conceptual impossibility on the traditional view that God should not have these essential properties, since it is part of what it means to be God that such a being has these essential properties. In *Proslogium* III Anselm expresses the position characteristic of traditional Anselmianism that it is apriori necessary that God has, among other essential properties, the property of necessary existence.

> And it so truly exists that it cannot be conceived not to exist. For it is possible to conceive of a being which cannot be conceived not to exist; and this is greater than one which can be conceived not to exist. Hence, if that, than which nothing greater can be conceived, can be conceived not to exist, it is not that than which nothing greater can be conceived. But this is a contradiction. So truly, therefore, is there something than which nothing greater can be conceived, that it cannot even be conceived not to exist; and this being thou art, O Lord, our God.[13]

Charles Hartshorne also defends the traditional Anselmian view on the concept of God.

> If . . . there exists no God, then there also can be no possibility of the existence of a God, and the concept is nonsense, like that of "round square". If further it can be

---

[11] In (E2) I have in mind consistency with all broadly logically necessary truth. I assume throughout that metaphysical possibility and metaphysical necessity are governed by a version of S5 that does not validate the Barcan Formula.

[12] If there are world-indexed properties that are essential to God, then of course most essential properties are not knowable apriori. But, most importantly, the traditional divine attributes are known apriori.

[13] See S. N. Deane, *St Anselm: Basic Writings* (Peru, Ill.: Open Court Publishing Company, 1962); *Proslogion* III 54–5.

shown that the idea of God is not nonsensical, that it must have an at least possible object, then it follows that it has an actual object, since a "merely possible" God is, if the argument is sound, inconceivable.[14]

We find another defense of what I am calling the traditional Anselmian conception of God in Norman Malcolm.

It may be helpful to express ourselves in the following way: to say, not that omnipotence is a property of God, but rather that necessary omnipotence is; and to say, not that omniscience is a property of God, but rather that necessary omniscience is....Necessary existence is a property of God in the same sense that necessary omnipotence and necessary omniscience are His properties....The apriori proposition "God necessarily exists" entails the proposition "God exists," if and only if the latter also is understood as an apriori proposition....In this sense Anselm's proof is a proof of God's existence.[15]

On the traditional Anselmian conception of God, then, anything identical to God satisfies the conditions in TA.

TA.  A being x = God only if (i) for most essential properties P of x, it is apriori necessary that x has P, and (ii) the essential properties of x include omnipotence, omniscience, perfect goodness, and necessary existence.[16]

According to TA, it is apriori necessary that God is, at least, essentially perfectly good, essentially omnipotent, essentially omniscient, and necessarily existent. But if it is apriori necessary that God is essentially perfectly good, essentially omnipotent, essentially omniscient, and necessarily existent, then God has those properties in every *epistemically possible* world.

---

[14] See Charles Hartshorne, "The Necessarily Existent" in Alvin Plantinga (ed.) *The Ontological Argument* (New York: Anchor Books, 1965).

[15] See Norman Malcolm, "Anselm's Ontological Arguments," op. cit. pp. 50–1. Malcolm adds,

...[W]hen the concept of God is correctly understood one sees that one cannot "reject the subject." "There is no God" is seen to be a necessarily false statement. Anselm's demonstration proves that the proposition "God exists" has the same a priori footing as the proposition "God is omnipotent."

Alvin Plantinga also defends a traditional Anselmian conception of God. See *The Nature of Necessity*, op. cit. esp. chapter X, sect. 7. For another defense, see also Thomas Morris, *Anselmian Explorations*, op. cit.

[16] If we assume there are world-indexed properties, then clause (i) in TA would have to be changed to "for most non-world-indexed essential properties P of x, it is primarily necessary that x has P."

There is no apriori consistent maximal state of affairs that does not include the traditional Anselmian God.

According to traditional Anselmianism, we could not discover that God's nature was different with respect to these attributes any more than we could discover that triangles are not three-sided or discover that red is not a color. We could not discover that the being Anselmians have been worshiping all along was importantly different with respect to these, or any other, essential properties of God. Were we to discover that the best possible being is a contingently existing, less-than-omnipotent, less-than-morally perfect being, then we would discover that "God" refers to nothing at all. God would not exist. Were the being that called Abraham and spoke to Moses to inform us directly that he is not omnipotent or even close, then traditional Anselmians would have to conclude that, as a matter of conceptual truth, the being that called Abraham is not God. It is apriori impossible that God should fail to be omnipotent.

Traditional Anselmians exploit the conditions in TA and some intuitive logical relations between epistemic possibility and metaphysical possibility to generate an apriori demonstration that God exists. Let M be restricted to essential properties understood as properties objects have in every world in which they exist.[17] Let $\Box_1$ and $\Box_2$ represent apriori necessity and metaphysical necessity respectively. TA provides the basis for a concise ontological argument.

P1.  $\Box_1 \forall x(\Box_1 Mx \supset \Box_2 Mx)$

According to the principle in P1, it is apriori necessary that, for all x, it is apriori necessary that x has essential property M only if it is metaphysically necessary that x has essential property M. That is, it is true in every epistemically possible world in which x exists that x has M only if it is true in every metaphysically possible world in which x exists that x has M. So, for instance, it is true apriori that two is essentially the smallest prime number only if it is metaphysically necessary that two is essentially the smallest prime number and it is true apriori that the empty set is essentially non-membered only if it is metaphysically necessary that the empty set is essentially non-membered.

---

[17]   The forthcoming argument owes much to discussion with Stephen Yablo. I can safely say that he does not believe the argument is sound. Neither do I. P3 is false, but the argument is valid, and P1 is true under the assumption that M is restricted to essential properties.

One might object that P1 allows as a substitution instance that round-squares are essentially round and square or that $\square_1 Ra$. But it is false that round-squares have, as a matter of apriori necessity, the essential property of being round and square. Indeed we know apriori that impossible objects have no de re modal properties. Otherwise we could infer that there exists something that the de re property of being round and square or that $(\exists x)\square_1 Rx$. But of course it is false that there is some something such that it is round and square as a matter of apriori necessity. Premise P2 in the argument just instantiates the principle in P1.

P2.  $\square_1(\square_1 M_G \supset \square_2 M_G)$

According to P2 it is apriori necessary that God has essential property M only if it is metaphysically necessary that God has essential property M.[18] But according to traditional Anselmianism it is apriori necessary that God has the essential properties of omnipotence, omniscience, perfect goodness, and necessary existence. So, TA entails P3.

P3.  $\square_1 M_G$

According to P3 it is apriori necessary that God has the essential properties of omnipotence, omniscience, perfect goodness, and necessary existence. The conditions on the traditional Anselmian God entail P3. And we easily derive P4.

P4.  $\therefore \square_2 M_G$

According to P4 it is metaphysically necessary that God has the essential properties of omnipotence, omniscience, perfect goodness, and necessary existence. But then of course the traditional Anselmian God exists.[19]

P3 and P4 display the traditional Anselmian commitment to the thesis in E3.

E3.  $\square_1 M_G \ \& \ \square_2 M_C$

---

[18]  The principle does not hold for non-essential properties, since there are true, contingent apriori propositions, for instance, fire is the stuff that's hot.

[19]  Simpler versions of the argument suggest themselves. (1) can be replaced with (1′) $\square_1 \forall x$ ($\square_1 Mx \supset Mx$). If it is apriori true that x instantiates the essential property M, then it is true that x instantiates the essential property M. We could derive from (1′) that two is essentially the smallest prime and that God necessarily exists.

Traditional Anselmianism entails that, for the most important essential properties P of God, it is apriori necessary that God has P and it is metaphysically necessary that God has P.[20]

There is another simple argument from E3 to the conclusion that (1), and relevantly similar statements, are both apriori and metaphysically impossible. Let $\Diamond_1$ and $\Diamond_2$ represent apriori and metaphysical possibility respectively, and let P be the statement in (1) that there exists a rabbit suffering pointless pain. The argument that traditional Anselmianism entails that (1) is both apriori and metaphysically impossible appeals to the complex thesis in E4.[21]

E4.  $(\Box_1(\Box_1 M_G \supset \sim\Diamond_1 P) \;\&\; \Box_1 M_G) \supset \sim\Diamond_1 P$

According to E4 we know apriori that the traditional Anselmian God exists only if it is apriori impossible that rabbits suffer pointless pain. Semantically this amounts to the claim that God is omnipotent, omniscient, and perfectly good in every epistemically possible world only if there is no epistemically possible world in which rabbits suffer pointlessly. Since traditional Anselmianism entails that it is apriori necessary that God is omnipotent, omniscient, perfectly good, and necessarily existing, it follows that it is apriori impossible that rabbits suffer pointlessly.

The argument assumes, of course, the standard view on evil that it's apriori necessary that God prevents all pointless pain. From E3 and E4 it follows that (1) is apriori impossible. And apriori impossibility entails

<hr/>

[20] It is not always clear that traditional Anselmians recognize that the view entails that (1) is apriori impossible. Plantinga defends a traditional Anselmian position. See Alvin Plantinga, *The Nature of Necessity*, op. cit. esp. p. 214 ff. If it is a conceptual truth that God has property P in every possible world, then it is apriori necessary that God has the property P essentially. But then we could not discover that God fails to have P essentially. If we could not discover that God fails to have the traditional Anselmian properties essentially—omnipotence, omniscience, and perfect goodness—then we could not discover that there is a single rabbit leading a pointless, pain-racked existence. The proposition in (1) is apriori impossible.

[21] Principles such as (E4) are used regularly and persuasively in incompossibility arguments. Theodore Guleserian implicitly assumes something like (E4) in "God and Possible Worlds: The Modal Problem of Evil" *Noûs* (1983) 221–38; and John Mackie makes a similar assumption in "Evil and Omnipotence" in Louis P. Pojman and Michael Rea (eds.) *Philosophy of Religion* (Belmont: Wadsworth, 2008) 173–81. It is perhaps worth noting that not everyone finds the genuine possibility of (1) problematic for the Anselmian God. See Peter van Inwagen, "The Magnitude, Duration, and Distribution of Evil: A Theodicy" and "The Problem of Evil, the Problem of Air, and the Problem of Silence" in his *God, Knowledge and Mystery: Essays in Philosophical Theology* (Ithaca: Cornell University Press, 1995).

metaphysical impossibility. So, traditional Anselmians are committed to E5 as well.

E5.  $\sim\Diamond_1 P \ \& \ \sim\Diamond_2 P$

And this presents a serious problem for traditional Anselmianism. It seems at least epistemically possible that rabbits endure pointless pain. The epistemic possibility that rabbits suffer pointless pain is, in any case, at least as likely as the epistemic necessity that $M_G$. The epistemic necessity that $M_G$ is definitive of traditional Anselmianism, but it is not especially credible in light of propositions like (1). But matters are worse for traditional Anselmianism. The traditional view does not have the resources to defend even the weaker thesis that God has the divine attributes as a matter of metaphysical necessity in $\Box_2 M_G$.

Traditional Anselmians sometimes assert that we have good Anselmian grounds to reject the metaphysical possibility of any state of affairs incompossible with $\Box_2 M_G$. Thomas Morris, for instance, asserts that modal intuitions that normally evince metaphysical possibility are not in general reliable for traditional Anselmians. In cases of conflicting modal intuitions Morris defends the reliability of specifically Anselmian intuitions.

Against this backdrop of general doubt about the status of many metaphysical intuitions . . . I believe the Anselmian theist to be justified in marking out some few intuitions about metaphysical matters as trustworthy. . . . For if an Anselmian God exists, and creates rational beings whose end is to know him, it makes good sense that they should be able to know something of his existence and attributes without the need of highly technical arguments accessible to only a few.[22]

Alvin Plantinga urges that Anselmians may rationally ignore credible intuitions concerning states of affairs incompossible with the traditional Anselmian God.

. . . [But] a sane and rational man who thought it through and understood [the premise that maximal greatness is possibly exemplified] might nonetheless reject it, remaining agnostic or even accepting instead the possibility of no-maximality.

Well, then, why accept this premise? Is there not something improper, unreasonable, irrational about doing so? I cannot see why.[23]

[22] Thomas Morris, *Anselmian Explorations*, op. cit. pp. 67–8.
[23] See Alvin Plantinga, *The Nature of Necessity*, op. cit. pp. 219–20.

But neither Morris nor Plantinga advance any explanation for how we can reasonably remain unmoved by intuitions supporting states of affairs incompossible with the traditional Anselmian God. There is no explanation why a rational or reasonable person might treat the particular recalcitrant intuition that rabbits might suffer pointless pain or, for that matter, that fawns might die painful deaths, and so on, as unreliable.[24] There is no credible explanation for why the Anselmian theist is justified in marking out intuitions about God's nature as trustworthy and intuitions about the possibility of pointless suffering as untrustworthy.

If there are exceptions to the general reliability of modal intuition, we should expect that they constitute a special class of intuitions: modal illusions of some sort. The conceivability of rabbits suffering pointless pain, for instance, might describe the possibility of some state of affairs that we mistake for the genuine possibility of rabbits suffering pointless

---

[24] Plantinga observes that there seem to be properties whose instantiation in any world is incompossible with the instantiation of maximal greatness in any world. We don't know that the incompossible property of there being no maximal being is not possibly instantiated. But Plantinga maintains that there's nonetheless no epistemological need to abandon the position that maximal greatness is possibly exemplified. We are offered no explanation from Plantinga as to why we have the intuition that such a property is possibly instantiated.

And (36) [that maximal greatness is possibly exemplified] . . . is not of this sort. A sane and rational man who thought it through and understood it might nonetheless reject it, remaining agnostic or even accepting instead the possibility of no-maximality.... Well, then, why accept this premise? Is there not something improper, unreasonable, irrational about doing so? I cannot see why.

See *The Nature of Necessity*, op. cit. p. 220. Thomas Morris, on the other hand, says that Anselmians might not share the intuitions of non-Anselmians. In defense of the reliability of Anselmian intuitions Morris offers the following.

Against this backdrop of general doubt about the status of many metaphysical intuitions . . . I believe the *Anselmian theist to be justified in marking out some few intuitions about metaphysical matters as trustworthy* . . . . The Anselmian intuitions about God, or more broadly, all those intuitions which together yield the Anselmian conception of God, generate without intentional contrivance an overall belief-set in which it makes sense that there should be such intuitions and that they should be, at least a core of them, reliable. For if an Anselmian God exists, and creates rational beings whose end is to know him, it makes good sense that they should be able to know something of his existence and attributes without the need of highly technical arguments accessible to only a few.

See Thomas Morris, *Anselmian Explorations*, op. cit. pp. 67–8 (emphasis added). Certainly if you justifiably believe that the traditional Anselmian God exists, then you should regard your Anselmian intuitions as reliable. But obviously the very point in question is whether the traditional Anselmian conception of God is correct.

pain. The problem for Morris and Plantinga is that there is no suitable source of modal illusion.

The illusion cannot result from mistakenly conflating the epistemic possibility of rabbits suffering pointlessly with the metaphysical possibility of them doing so since, on the traditional view, it is also epistemically impossible that rabbits suffer pointlessly. The illusion cannot result from conflating the epistemic possibility that God permits suffering that he ought to prevent with the metaphysical possibility that God does so since traditional Anselmianism entails that it is epistemically impossible that God permits any suffering he ought to prevent. The illusion cannot result from the absence of proof that it's apriori impossible that rabbits suffer pointlessly. We have given a proof that it's apriori impossible on the basis of principles traditional Anselmians cannot abandon.[25] But the modal intuitions that rabbits might suffer pointless pain and that fawns might die a pointless death persist.

Traditional Anselmians might sharply distinguish between the metaphysical status of what's conceivable and the metaphysical status of what's genuinely possible. Compare Soames.

. . . this route . . . contains a sharp distinction between epistemic and metaphysical possibility—between ways that the universe could *conceivably* be . . . , and ways that the universe could *really* be. . . . On this picture, some things that are coherently conceivable are not genuinely possible.[26]

On this picture many conceivable things are not genuinely possible. But this approach too is unhelpful to the traditional Anselmian project. Traditional Anselmianism entails not only that it's metaphysically impossible that something should suffer pointless pain, but that it's inconceivable that anything should do so. So we cannot explain the modal intuition that rabbits might suffer pointless pain by appealing to Soames' broad set of non genuine, epistemic possibilities. Traditional Anselmianism is committed to the position that a rabbit suffering pointless pain is not included even among the expansive epistemic, non-metaphysical possibilities.

---

[25] We might explain why a particular theorem looks apriori possible, even if it isn't, by appeal to the absence of a proof that it is apriori possible. That line of argument is not available to traditional Anselmianism.

[26] See Scott Soames, "The Philosophical Significance of the Kripkean Necessary Aposteriori" in E. Sosa and E. Villanueva (eds.) *Philosophical Issues* Vol. 16 (Malden, Mass.: Blackwell Publishing Co., 2006) 287–309.

Traditional Anselmianism offers no good reason to believe that the intuition that rabbits might suffer pointless pain or that fawns might suffer painful and pointless deaths constitute modal illusions. So they offer no reason to believe that these intuitions are unreliable or rationally rejectable.

## 1.2  A Dilemma for Traditional Anselmianism

According to traditional Anselmianism it is inconceivable that God should fail to be essentially perfectly good, essentially omnipotent, essentially omniscient, and essentially necessarily existent. It is not central to traditional Anselmianism that conceivability be especially good evidence for metaphysical possibility. It is central to traditional Anselmianism that conceivability be good evidence for apriori or epistemic possibility. But whether or not conceivability is good evidence for epistemic possibility we are not justified in believing traditional Anselmianism.

There are many propositions—mathematical propositions, for instance—that seem to be conceivable but are not apriori possible. Goldbach's conjecture, to take a well-known example, seems conceivable and its negation seems no less conceivable. But we know that either Goldbach's conjecture or its negation is epistemically impossible. It is certain that the evidence from conceivability does not justify us in believing that Goldbach's conjecture is epistemically possible.

But the supposition that conceivability is not good evidence that philosophical theses are epistemically possible is particularly bad news for traditional Anselmianism. The main thesis of traditional Anselmianism states that it is *inconceivable* that God should fail to be essentially perfectly good, essentially omnipotent, essentially omniscient, and essentially necessarily existent. Contrary to the position of traditional Anselmians, the conceivability evidence gives us no reason to believe it is epistemically impossible that God should fail to be essentially perfectly good, essentially omnipotent, essentially omniscient, and essentially necessarily existent.

But it might be true, as it is widely believed, that conceivability is good evidence for epistemic possibility. For instance, it is conceivable that I was born three seconds earlier than I in fact was born. And that seems to be very good evidence that there is some epistemically possible world in which I was born three seconds earlier. I do not of course have adequate knowledge of my essential properties, so it might be true that I instantiate the essential property of not being born three seconds earlier than I was in fact born. But such adequate knowledge would not defeat the evidence from conceivability, since I certainly do not instantiate that essential property as a matter of apriori necessity. So, it is reasonable to conclude that there is some epistemically possible world in which I am born three seconds earlier and do not possess that essential property.

We reach similar conclusions for various propositions conceivable de dicto. Let's say a property P entails a property Q only if necessarily, x is P only if x is Q.[27]

E6.  $\Box_2 \forall x (Px \supset Qx)$

And let's say that a property P *apriori entails* a property Q only if it's apriori necessary that x is P only if x is Q.

E7.  $\Box_1 \forall x (Px \supset Qx)$

Some essential properties of a property P are also entailed by P, but certainly not all of them are. P has the essential property of being a property, for instance, but not everything that instantiates P has the property of being a property. On the other hand, the property of being round has the essential property of not being square and it also entails that property.

Consider the more interesting set of properties composing the divine attributes. According to both traditional Anselmianism and moderate Anselmianism there are properties Q such that the divine attributes M entail Q, the divine attributes M *apriori entail* Q. These are properties P and Q that are such that it is inconceivable that anything instantiates M and does not instantiate Q. For instance, it is inconceivable that anything instantiates the property of being perfectly good and does not instantiate the property of not permitting suffering for no good reason. So it is epistemically impossible that anything instantiates the property of being perfectly good and does not instantiate the property of not permitting suffering for no good reason. It is inconceivable, for instance, that anything instantiates the property of being omnipotent and does not also instantiate the property of having at least no non-logical limit to what one

[27] See Alvin Plantinga, *The Nature of Necessity*, op. cit. p. 65 ff.

can do. So there is no epistemically possible world in which something is omnipotent and cannot perform a metaphysically possible action.

But it is again bad news for traditional Anselmianism if conceivability is good evidence for epistemic possibility. If conceivability is good evidence for epistemic possibility, then we have good reason to believe that it's epistemically possible that rabbits suffer for no good reason. The claim here is not that conceivability is good evidence for metaphysical possibility. It might be metaphysically impossible that rabbits suffer for no good reason. Nonetheless it is not merely conceivable that rabbits suffer for no good reason, it is a state of affairs that many people believe obtains. If conceivability is good evidence for epistemic possibility, then we have good reason to believe that some epistemically possible worlds are so bad that God could not actualize them. There may be no genuinely possible worlds which are so bad that God could not actualize them, but it is difficult to deny that such worlds are conceivable.

If conceivability is good evidence for epistemic possibility, then we have good reason to believe that there are epistemically possible worlds in which the traditional Anselmian God does not exist. But if we have good reason to believe there are epistemically possible worlds in which the traditional Anselmian God does not exist, then we have good reason to believe that the traditional Anselmian God does not exist.

Traditional Anselmianism faces a difficult dilemma. If conceivability is not good evidence for epistemic possibility, then we do not have good evidence that the traditional Anselmian God exists. It is inconceivable that God should fail to have any of the traditional divine attributes, but that constitutes no evidence that God has those attributes. If conceivability is good evidence for epistemic possibility, then we again do not have good evidence that the traditional Anselmian God exists. There are conceivable worlds in which the traditional Anselmian God does not exist. The conceivability of such worlds is good evidence that the traditional Anselmian God does not exist.

## 1.3 Moderate Anselmianism

Moderate Anselmianism rejects the thesis that the essential properties of God are apriori necessary. If the essential properties of God are apriori necessary then no being other than one that instantiates just those properties could have been the referent of "God." It is apriori necessary that God is just that being in each world that satisfies the attributes that traditional Anselmianism describes. But moderate Anselmians reject the initial clause in TA above. According to moderate Anselmianism anything identical to God satisfies the description in MA.

> MA. A being x = God only if (i) for every essential property P of x, it is metaphysically necessary that x has P, (ii) for most essential properties P of x, it is not apriori necessary that x has P, and (iii) the essential properties of x include omnipotence, omniscience, perfect goodness, and necessary existence.

Clause (i) in MA is unsurprising. It entails that, for every essential property P of God, it is metaphysically necessary that God has P. It is clause (ii) that is most distinctive about moderate Anselmianism. (ii) entails that, for most essential properties P of God, it is not apriori necessary that God has P. Moderate Anselmians allow that we do know apriori the trivial essential properties of God such as being identical to God, not being a prime number, and so on. But we do not know apriori any non-trivial essential properties of God.

Supposing again that M includes all of the essential properties of the Anselmian God, moderate Anselmianism endorses E6.

> E6. $\Box_2 M_G \ \& \ \sim\Box_1 M_G$

The thesis in E6 allows moderate Anselmians to resist the conclusion that it's inconceivable that rabbits suffer pointless pain. Moderate Anselmians agree that it is epistemically possible that rabbits and fawns suffer pointless pain. It is epistemically possible that people endure pointless abuse and so on. There seems no question that these states of affairs are conceivable. And, in any case, certainly it is more credible than not that these states of affairs are not apriori impossible.

It is epistemically possible that rabbits and fawns suffer pointless pain, according to moderate Anselmians, since there are epistemically possible worlds in which God lacks one or more of his essential properties. There are apriori consistent maximal states of affairs, for instance, in which God does not have the power to eliminate every instance of pointless evil. And there are apriori consistent maximal states of affairs in which God lacks the power to eliminate every instance of pointless evil and rabbits suffer pointless pain.

The conceivability that rabbits suffer pointless pain is good evidence that it is not apriori necessary that God is essentially perfectly good, essentially omnipotent, essentially omniscient, and necessarily existing. But it is not good evidence that it is not metaphysically necessary that God is essentially perfectly good, essentially omnipotent, essentially omniscient, and necessarily existing. The conceivability that rabbits suffer pointless pain shows that it's apriori possible that God is essentially different from what moderate Anselmians claim. It does not show that God is, in fact, essentially different from what the moderate Anselmians claim.

Of course, there are strong modal intuitions evincing the metaphysical possibility of many other states of affairs that are incompossible with the moderate Anselmian God. Moderate Anselmianism must provide some independent argument that these modal intuitions describe states of affairs that are illusory epistemic possibilities. There is, for instance, the modal intuition that an omnipotent being might command a morally wrong action, that there are worlds in which God does not exist, that there are evils that God does not or cannot prevent, and so on. Moderate Anselmianism provides an explanation for all of these intuitions. In addition moderate Anselmianism offers an explanation for the persistent apriori disagreement on the nature of God.

## 1.4  Defending Moderate Anselmianism

John Mackie and many others have argued that it is apriori impossible that the Anselmian God have the essential property of omnipotence. It is apriori true that omnipotent beings can perform any logically possible action. Among the possible actions, of course, are morally wrong actions.[28] But, according to Mackie, it is apriori impossible that an Anselmian God might perform a morally wrong action. So it is apriori impossible that an Anselmian God is omnipotent.

But the traditional objection presents no problem for moderate Anselmians. It is metaphysically necessary that the moderate Anselmian God is essentially perfectly good and essentially omnipotent. But it's not apriori impossible that the moderate Anselmian God perform a morally wrong

[28] See Nelson Pike, "Omnipotence and God's Ability to Sin" in Louis Pojman (ed.) *Philosophy of Religion: An Anthology* (Boston: Wadsworth Publishing Co., 1998) 283–93.

action. God does not have the essential properties of omnipotence and perfect goodness as a matter of apriori necessity. Since it is epistemically possible that God is less than perfectly good, it is also epistemically possible that God perform morally wrong actions.

It has been persuasively argued that it is apriori impossible that the Anselmian God actualize possible worlds with widespread gratuitous evil.[29] The apriori atheological argument urges that there are worlds so bad that it is apriori impossible that the Anselmian God actualizes them. According to traditional Anselmians, the space of metaphysical possibility cannot include such worlds. But traditional Anselmians offer no explanation at all for the persistence of the modal intuition that there are such worlds.

According to moderate Anselmians, it's not apriori impossible for the Anselmian God to actualize a world with widespread gratuitous evil. It is not apriori necessary that the Anselmian God is essentially perfectly good, omniscient, or omnipotent. In many epistemically possible worlds God does not know there is gratuitous evil and in other epistemically possible worlds God knows about the widespread gratuitous evil but lacks the desire to prevent it. The apriori possibility that the Anselmian God actualizes a world with widespread gratuitous evil is consistent with the fact that it is metaphysically impossible that the Anselmian God actualize such worlds.

Traditional Anselmianism entails that it is apriori impossible that God fail to exist. It's central to the ontological argument, for instance, that it is apriori impossible that God fail to exist. But it seems certain that atheists and agnostics are not maintaining positions that are apriori impossible. According to moderate Anselmians, God has the essential property of necessarily existing as a matter of metaphysical necessity. But God does not necessarily exist as a matter of apriori necessity. There are epistemically possible worlds in which God fails to exist, so atheists and agnostics are definitely not maintaining positions that are apriori impossible.

Indeed, moderate Anselmianism provides an explanation for persistent and widespread disagreement on the nature of God. There are well-known apriori disagreements concerning whether God created everything. Moderate Anselmians observe that it is not apriori necessary that

---

[29] See in particular Theodore Guleserian, "God and Possible Worlds," op. cit. pp. 221–38.

God created everything and it is not apriori impossible that God created everything. There are epistemically possible worlds in which God created everything and worlds in which God did not create everything. Apriori disagreement persists because the question simply cannot be settled apriori. The moderate Anselmian position is that it is aposteriori necessary that God created everything, but that we might have discovered otherwise.

There is widespread and persistent disagreement concerning whether God is an eternal being or a being in time. Moderate Anselmians observe that it is not apriori necessary that God is an eternal being and it is not apriori necessary that God is in time. There are epistemically possible worlds in which God is eternal and there are worlds in which God's role is in time. So the question cannot be settled apriori.

In general apriori atheological arguments and disagreements present no serious problem for moderate Anselmians. Moderate Anselmians maintain that there are aposteriori facts about God that might have turned out differently. Disputes about the nature of God, and states of affairs compossible with God, persist because they simply cannot be settled apriori. These are metaphysical issues that can be settled only by aposteriori discovery.

## 1.5  Concluding Remarks

Among the advantageous implications of an aposteriori necessary Anselmian God is that apriori atheological arguments in general lack cogency. Moderate Anselmians concede that, conceivably, rabbits lead pointless, pain-racked lives in the same way that, conceivably, the table in my office is made of ice. There are epistemically possible worlds at which each of these is true. But, as a matter of fact, it is genuinely impossible that rabbits lead pointless, pain-racked lives and genuinely impossible that this table is made of ice.

Among the disadvantages of an aposteriori necessary Anselmian God is an extensive modal defeasibility. The essential properties of God determine the shape of metaphysical possibility. But there is almost no limit to what we might discover concerning the essential properties of the Anselmian God. So, there are almost no limits to what we might discover concerning the shape of metaphysical possibility. It is among the surprising facts about the shape of metaphysical possibility—if it is such a fact—that it is not metaphysically possible that rabbits suffer pointlessly. Equally surprising is the discovery—if it is such a discovery—that it's genuinely impossible for some omnipotent beings to perform wrong actions and the discovery that there are no worlds bad enough that an Anselmian God could not actualize it. Perhaps none of these is metaphysically possible, though each of them is apriori possible, and we retain at least an illusion that they are metaphysically possible. The extensive modal defeasibility of moderate Anselmianism entails that the exact shape of metaphysical possibility is an open question.

# 2

# Metaphysical Atheological Arguments and the Free Will Defense

## 2.0 Introduction

Traditional Anselmianism is incompatible with even the apriori possibility of certain evil states of affairs. The mere conceivability that there is a fawn suffering for no God-given purpose entails that traditional Anselmianism is false. And according to traditional Anselmianism it is inconceivable that anything other than an Anselmian God in essential possession of the traditional divine attributes should play the role of God.

Moderate Anselmians urge that, surely, we might have discovered that the traditional attributes were mistaken in various ways. The nature of God is not a semantic question settled if and only if competent language users get sufficiently clear about the meaning of "God." The nature of God is a metaphysical question settled if and only if we discover the essential properties of God. And semantic investigation does not tell us much about any interesting essential properties of God.

Metaphysical atheological arguments do not aim to show that it's inconceivable that God co-exists with certain states of affairs. It is not a conceptual truth that God has any traditional attribute that might be incompatible with some worrisome state of affairs. Metaphysical atheological arguments aim to show that it is *metaphysically impossible* that the Anselmian God co-exists with certain states of affairs.[1]

---

[1] Note that it is not inconceivable that water $\neq$ H$_2$O, despite the fact that, necessarily, water = H$_2$O. It is conceivable that water $\neq$ H$_2$O since it is not a conceptual truth that water = H$_2$O. Slightly more technically, $\Diamond_1$ (water $\neq$ H$_2$O) and $\Box_2$ (water = H$_2$O). Similarly,

*The Logical Problem of Evil* is the best known metaphysical argument against Anselmian theism. Defenders of the logical problem of evil advance the position that, necessarily, an omnipotent and wholly good being does not actualize a world that contains evil. The argument aims to establish that it is metaphysically impossible that the Anselmian God exists and that there exists a single instance of evil. Alvin Plantinga famously urged that there is no cogent formulation of the logical problem of evil.[2] In *God and Other Minds* he concludes exactly that.

. . . we have not been able to find a proposition, necessarily true or an essential part of theism or a consequence of such propositions, which in conjunction with [(1) God is omnipotent, omniscient and wholly good and (2) evil exists] entails a contradiction. Indeed we have not so much as produced a plausible candidate. If this does not show that there is *no* such proposition, it suggests that finding one is much more difficult than most atheologians seem to suppose.[3]

And in *God, Freedom, and Evil* he arrives at a similar conclusion.

To summarize our conclusions so far: although many atheologians claim that the theist is involved in a contradiction when he asserts the members of set A [which includes the existence of an omnipotent, omniscient, and wholly good being and the existence of evil], this set, obviously, is neither explicitly nor formally contradictory; the claim, presumably, must be that it is implicitly contradictory. To make good this claim the atheologian must find some necessarily true proposition p . . . such that the addition of p to set A yields a set that is formally contradictory. No atheologian has produced even a plausible candidate for this role, and it is certainly not easy to see what such a proposition might be.[4]

Plantinga's critical conclusions on formulating the logical problem of evil have been very well-received. But I will argue that there are (at least) three cogent reconstructions of the logical problem of evil that appeal to principles many believe are metaphysically necessary. The principles vary in strength and differ in implications but each is sufficient to generate a valid logical problem of evil

---

$\Diamond_1$(God exists and certain evil states of affairs obtain) and $\Box_2$ (God exists only if it is not the case that certain evil states of affairs obtain).

[2] See Alvin Plantinga, *God and Other Minds* (Ithaca: Cornell University Press, 1972); *God, Freedom, and Evil* (Grand Rapids: Eerdmans Publishing, 1974); and *The Nature of Necessity* (Oxford: Oxford University Press, 1976).

[3] See *God and Other Minds*, op. cit. p. 128 ff. The modifications to this passage include an inserted abbreviation in (1) and (2). There are no substantial modifications.

[4] See *God, Freedom, and Evil*, op. cit. p. 24. The set A = {God is omnipotent, God is wholly good, Evil exists}.

The best known response to the logical problem of evil is surely Alvin Plantinga's free will defense. But the free will defense is also the most frequently misunderstood and misconstrued argument in the literature on the logical problem of evil.[5] The misunderstandings are due in part to less-than-cautious assessments of the structure and aim of the argument. But they are also due to the less than perspicuous presentation of the argument.[6] Given the prominence of the free will defense in the literature on the logical problem of evil, I take special care in Sections 2.3–2.6 to present the argument as clearly as possible. The thesis of universal transworld depravity is generally taken to be the cornerstone of Plantinga's solution to the logical problem of evil, but I show in Section 2.7 that it cannot resolve the logical problem of evil without additional assumptions. On the other hand, I take time to emphasize that nothing as strong as universal transworld depravity is necessary to resolve the logical problem of evil. So, universal transworld depravity resolve the problem of evil might, but nothing as strong as universal transworld depravity is necessary to resolve the problem.

## 2.1  Plantinga's Reconstruction of the Logical Problem of Evil

The logical argument of evil is among the most serious challenges to Anselmian theists. The problem famously maintains that the propositions in (1) and (2) are broadly logically inconsistent.

---

[5] For discussion of these common errors, see Michael Bergmann, "Review of R. Douglas Geivett's *Evil and the Evidence for God: The Challenge of John Hick's Theodicy*" *Faith and Philosophy* (1996) 436–41; and his "Might-Counterfactuals, Transworld Untrustworthiness and Plantinga's Free Will Defense" *Faith and Philosophy* 16 (1999) 336–51. The misunderstandings occur consistently. Some prominent places where these errors are found include Douglas Geivett, *Evil and the Evidence for God: The Challenge of John Hick's Theodicy* (Philadelphia: Temple University Press, 1993); John Hick, *Evil and the God of Love* (revised edition) (San Francisco: Harper and Row, 1978); J. L. Mackie, *The Miracle of Theism* (Oxford: Clarendon Press, 1982).

[6] Plantinga acknowledges that the most frequently cited version of the argument in *The Nature of Necessity*, op. cit., does not contain an especially perspicuous presentation. The argument there is truncated in ways that make it more difficult to follow. But he offers versions of the argument in several places. See especially *God, Freedom, and Evil*, op. cit. For a particularly powerful version, see H. Tomberlin and Peter van Inwagen (eds.) *Profiles: Alvin Plantinga* (Dordrecht-Holland: D. Reidel Publishing Co., 1985).

1. God is omnipotent, omniscient, and wholly good.
2. Evil exists.

Making the inconsistency explicit has proven to be surprisingly difficult. Propositions (1) and (2) are inconsistent just in case there are some substantive necessary truths—necessary truths in philosophical theology one would expect—which, together with (1) and (2), form an inconsistent set. Plantinga proposes for inclusion in the set a thesis about the kinds of evils a wholly good being would eliminate.

3. Necessarily, an omnipotent, omniscient, wholly good being eliminates every evil that it can properly eliminate.

According to (3), there is an omnipotent, omniscient, wholly good being only if there are no worlds with properly eliminable evil states of affairs. An evil state of affairs E is *properly eliminable* in world W if E obtains in W and there is no good state of affairs G such that G obtains in W, G entails E, and the conjunctive state of affairs (G & E) is better than the state of affairs (∼G & ∼E).[7] So an evil state of affairs E is properly eliminable in W if E is unnecessary to some greater good G in W. Otherwise E is at best improperly eliminable.

An omnipotent, omniscient, wholly good being eliminates every evil that it can properly eliminate but, Plantinga argues, such a being would not be required to *improperly* eliminate any evil states of affairs.

A really impressive good state of affairs G will outweigh a trivial evil E—that is, the conjunctive state of affairs G and E is itself a good state of affairs. And surely a good person would not be obligated to eliminate a given evil if he could do so only by eliminating a good that outweighed it.[8]

A wholly good being is not obligated to improperly eliminate evil since improperly eliminable evils are necessary to some greater good. Enduring the pain in your knee, for instance, might be necessary to the greater good of bearing up magnificently to that specific pain. The good state of affairs of Smith bearing up magnificently to that particular pain is impossible without Smith enduring that particular pain.

[7] Strictly, states of affairs do not stand in entailment relations to one another. A more rigorous formulation of the claim would have the propositions G′ and E′ that the state of affairs G and E obtain be such that G′ entails E′.
[8] Tomberlin and van Inwagen *Profiles: Alvin Plantinga*, op. cit. pp. 20–1.

But even if an evil state of affairs E is necessary to some greater good G, E might be *unnecessary* to an even greater good G'. The world in which Smith endures the pain and bears up well is a good world. But there might be an even better actualizable world in which Smith does not exist and therefore endures no pain at all. Suppose W is a possible world that includes an evil state of affairs E that cannot be properly eliminated. A wholly good being might have to improperly eliminate E in order to actualize a better world W'. The improper elimination of E—the elimination of the on balance good conjunctive state of affairs (G & E)—in W is necessary to the actualization of a better world W'. An evil state of affairs E might be improperly eliminable in W since there is a good G in W such that G entails E and the conjunctive state of affairs (G & E) is better than ($\sim$G & $\sim$E). But there might also be a good state of affairs W' such that W' entails $\sim$E, and the conjunctive state of affairs (W' & $\sim$E) is better than (W & E).

In general, an improperly eliminable evil E in W is necessary to a greater actualizable good G (= W') if E fails to obtain in a better actualizable world W'. Suppose W' is a better actualizable world than W and the evil state of affairs E does not obtain in W'. Let E be improperly eliminable in W. Since E is improperly eliminable in W we know there's some greater good G in W such that E is necessary for G. But since $\sim$E is necessary to bringing about the better actualizable world W', $\sim$E is necessary to a greater actualizable good, namely, the better state of affairs W'.[9] So E is improperly eliminable in W and $\sim$E is improperly eliminable in W', and W' is better than W. According to the thesis in (3), an omnipotent, omniscient, wholly good being would not eliminate the evil E in W despite the fact that $\sim$E is necessary to a greater actualizable good. But there is as good a reason to improperly eliminate E in W as there is to properly eliminate an evil E' in W if improperly eliminating E is necessary to a moral improvement at least as great as the moral improvement for which properly eliminating E' is necessary. So, there are good grounds to object that thesis (3) is too weak.[10]

---

[9]  By hypothesis (E & G) is a good state of affairs, E is necessary to G, and E does not obtain in the best world. I'm assuming that there are good states of affairs that do not obtain in the better possible worlds. I take this to be non-controversial. Smith might bear up well to the pain he endures in W, but there are no doubt even better worlds in which Smith does not exist.

[10]  See Plantinga, *God and Other Minds*, op. cit. p. 121. Plantinga makes a similar point with regard to a thesis analogous to (3).

It is not necessary that every evil state of affairs E that God ought to eliminate is such that God properly eliminates E.

Plantinga's set also includes an improbable thesis about the evil states of affairs that an omnipotent, omniscient, wholly good being can properly eliminate.[11]

> 4. Necessarily, an omnipotent, omniscient, wholly good being *can* properly eliminate every evil state of affairs.

It is very likely that there is some evil state of affairs E in some world W that an omnipotent, omniscient, wholly good being *cannot* properly eliminate. The evil E in W is necessary to some greater good G in W. So it is difficult to see how (4) could be true. But, of course, there are almost certainly better actualizable worlds in which the state of affairs E has been improperly eliminated. Consider a world W′ in which God miraculously prevents Jones kidnapping in world W. Jones, we can imagine, lives a morally perfect life in W′ and things otherwise go morally much better in W′ than they do in W. The state of affairs of Jones' kidnapping does not obtain in W′ and neither does the state of affairs of Smith's dramatic rescue of Jones. But not even an omnipotent being could eliminate Jones' kidnapping and not eliminate Smith's dramatic rescue of Jones. So there is good reason to believe that Jones' kidnapping is an improperly eliminable evil and that an omnipotent, omniscient, wholly good being should have improperly eliminated Jones' kidnapping.

We can agree that there are good grounds to object that thesis (4) is too strong. It is false that God can properly eliminate every evil state of affairs. But it does not follow that there are evils in some worlds that God should not eliminate. It is not necessary that every evil state of affairs E that God should eliminate is such that God can properly eliminate E. There are also improperly eliminable evils that God should eliminate.

On Plantinga's reconstruction the problematic atheological conclusion is in (5) which entails that there are no actual (or possible) evil states of affairs.

> 5. Necessarily, an omnipotent, omniscient, wholly good being eliminates all evil states of affairs.

---

[11] See Plantinga, *God, Freedom, and Evil*, op. cit. pp. 22–3. Plantinga agrees that (4) is likely false.

The conclusion in (5) is inconsistent with the observation in (2). But theses (1)–(4) provide no credible evidence for (5). The thesis in (3) is unnecessarily weak. An omnipotent, omniscient, wholly good being is required to eliminate more than merely properly eliminable evil states of affairs. There is good reason to believe that an omnipotent, omniscient, wholly good being is obligated to eliminate at least some improperly eliminable evil states of affairs. The thesis in (4) is unnecessarily strong. An omnipotent, omniscient, wholly good being cannot reasonably be expected to properly eliminate every evil state of affairs. There is good reason to believe that some evil states of affairs are not properly eliminable.

Plantinga has considered alternative theses to substitute for (3), (4), and (5). Consider, for instance, (3.1).

> 3.1. Necessarily, any good G that entails an evil E is or is equivalent to a conjunctive state of affairs one conjunct of which is E and the other a good that (i) outweighs and is logically independent of E, and (ii) is better than G.[12]

The thesis in (3.1) might be proposed in defense of the proposition that, necessarily, there are evil states of affairs only if there are properly eliminable states of affairs.

We might trace some of the implications of (3.1) more formally. Let $\square$ represent metaphysical necessity, $\supset$ material implication, $>$ the better than relation and $\equiv$ the biconditional. According to (3.1), for any G and E such that (1) $\square(G \supset E)$ and (2) $(G \& E) > (\sim G \& \sim E)$ there is a $G' \&$ E such that (3) $\square((G \& E) \equiv (G' \& E))$ and (4) $\sim\square(G' \supset E)$ and $G' > G$. The idea is that every good state of affairs G that entails an evil state of affairs E is (or is equivalent to) a conjunctive state of affairs of the form $G\star \& E$. If that's necessarily true, then for every such on balance good state of affairs $G = (G\star \& E)$ in any world W there is a better state of affairs $G' = G\star$ in W such that $G'$ does not entail E. But then it is a necessary truth that every evil state of affairs is properly eliminable. (3.1) entails (3.2).

> 3.2. Necessarily, every evil state of affairs E is such that for every good G that entails E, there is some greater good $G'$ that does not entail E.

---

[12] See *God and Other Minds*, op. cit. p. 125 ff.

Suppose Plantinga is right that (3.2) entails that every evil state of affairs is unjustified. We might then arrive at the conclusion that, necessarily, an omnipotent, omniscient, wholly good being eliminates all evil states of affairs.

But certainly (3.1) is false. There are some good states of affairs G that entail an evil state of affairs E, but that are not equivalent to the sort of conjunctive state of affairs described in (3.1). The state of affairs of Smith enduring a punishment of twenty years imprisonment for homicide, for instance, is a just punishment for committing a serious moral evil. But if we eliminate the state of affairs of Smith committing the moral evil, then we are left with the obviously bad state of affairs of Smith enduring punishment for committing no moral wrong at all. There are alternatively intentional actions whose objects are particular evil states of affairs. Jones's action of compensating Smith for having stolen Smith's brown, 1982 Triumph TR 6 on June 8th, 1988, cannot be analyzed as a conjunction. Certainly there are act tokens similar to Jones's act of compensating Smith that might be featured as a conjunct in such an analysis, but which do not share the intentional object of Jones's act. But Jones's action takes its intentional object essentially: Jones cannot perform the act of compensating Smith *for having* stolen Smith's brown, 1982 Triumph TR 6 on June 8th, 1988, unless Jones stole that particular car on that particular date.

There are alternatives to (3.1)–(3.2) that do not commit the atheologian to showing that every evil is properly eliminable. Every evil is either properly eliminable or improperly eliminable and we alluded above to the possibility that every evil should be either properly eliminated or improperly eliminated. Suppose we simply grant that there are evil states of affairs that are not properly eliminable. The thesis that there are evil states of affairs that are not properly eliminable is consistent with the position that God actualizes a world that contains no evil states of affairs. It might be true, for instance, that for every improperly eliminable evil state of affairs E such that G entails E in world W that includes G and E, there is another world W' that is better than W and that does not include E or G. If so, then we have good reason to believe that God would eliminate every evil state of affairs.

Let's consider some less controversial reconstructions of the logical problem of evil. Each of the reconstructions entails that every evil state of affairs would be properly or improperly eliminated. In addition to (1) and (2) many theists are committed to one of (3.3)–(3.5) below. Indeed,

J. L. Mackie attributes (3.3) to anyone who believes that an omnipotent, omniscient, wholly good being exists.[13]

If God has made men such that in their free choices they sometimes prefer what is good and sometimes what is evil, why could he not have made men such that they always freely choose the good? If there is no logical impossibility in a man's freely choosing the good on one, or on several, occasions, there cannot be a logical impossibility in his freely choosing the good on every occasion. God was not, then, faced with a choice between making innocent automata and making beings who, in acting freely, would sometimes go wrong: there was open to him the obviously better possibility of making beings who would act freely but always go right. Clearly, his failure to avail himself of this possibility is inconsistent with his being both omnipotent and wholly good.[14]

But (3.3)–(3.5) each entails that, necessarily, an omnipotent, omniscient, wholly good being eliminates all evil states of affairs.

3.3. Necessarily, an omnipotent, omniscient, wholly good being brings about *the best possible world* and the best possible world includes no evil states of affairs at all.

3.4. Necessarily, an omnipotent, omniscient, wholly good being brings about *the best actualizable world* and the best actualizable world includes no evil states of affairs.

3.5. Necessarily, an omnipotent, omniscient, wholly good being brings about *a good enough world* and a good enough actualizable world includes no evil states of affairs.

Propositions (3.3)–(3.5) do not entail that, necessarily, an omnipotent, omniscient, wholly good being is not obligated to improperly eliminate evil states of affairs. As we have seen, it's false that, necessarily, an omnipotent, omniscient, wholly good being is not obligated to improperly

---

[13]  See Plantinga, *The Nature of Necessity*, op. cit. p. 168 ff. Plantinga observes,

Leibniz . . . insisted that this world, the actual world, must be the best of all possible worlds. His reasoning is as follows. Before God created anything at all, he was confronted with an enormous range of choices; he could have created or actualized any of the myriads of different possible worlds. Being perfectly good, he must have chosen to create the best world he could; being omnipotent, he was able to create just any possible world he pleased. He must therefore have chosen the best of all possible worlds. . . . Now Mackie agrees with Leibniz that God, if omnipotent, could have created just any world he pleased and would have created the best world he could. But . . . Mackie concludes . . . there is no omnipotent, wholly good God.

[14]  See J. L. Mackie, "Evil and Omnipotence" *Mind* (1955) 200–12.

eliminate some evil states of affairs. Propositions (3.3)–(3.5) do not entail that every evil state of affairs is properly eliminable. It's false that, necessarily, every evil state of affairs is properly eliminable. Propositions (3.3)–(3.5) do not entail that every evil state of affairs E is such that for every good G that entails E, there is some greater good G′ that does not entail E. It is false that every good state of affairs that entails an evil state of affairs is equivalent to some conjunctive states of affairs (G & E) such that G is better than (G & E).

So, of course, (3.3)–(3.5) do not entail that, necessarily, an omnipotent, omniscient, wholly good being properly eliminates all evil states of affairs. But the atheologian requires only the weaker conclusion that, necessarily, all evil states of affairs are eliminated. The weaker conclusion is inconsistent with the existence of any evil states of affairs and (3.3)–(3.5) entail that, necessarily, an omnipotent, omniscient, wholly good being eliminates all evil states of affairs.

In the reconstructed argument from evil the theses in (3.3)–(3.5) together with (1) God is omnipotent, omniscient, and wholly good, and (2) evil exists, form three distinct and valid versions of the logical problem of evil.

## 2.2  Epistemic Matters

Plantinga's free will defense aims to show that it is broadly logically possible that an omniscient, omnipotent, wholly good being exists and an evil state of affairs obtains. "Broad, logical possibility" is just another name for metaphysical possibility.[15] So, the aim is to show that it is *not* metaphysically impossible that an omniscient, omnipotent, wholly good being should exist in a world in which an evil state of affairs obtains.

In general it is agreed that a good theistic defense against the logical problem of evil might—though does not in general—include assumptions that are highly improbable. But it is also true that a good theistic defense might include assumptions whose epistemic probability is zero.[16] There are possible worlds where the past is vastly different from ours, possible worlds where pigs fly, possible worlds where there are no laws of nature, and

---

[15] See Plantinga, *The Nature of Necessity*, op. cit. pp. 1–9; and *God, Freedom, and Evil*, op. cit. pp. 12–16.

[16] Epistemic probability should be distinguished from chance. Epistemic probability is the credence an agent places in a proposition or the subjective probability of a proposition. Chance is the objective probability of a proposition.

so on. The probability of these worlds *obtaining* is reasonably placed at zero. There is zero probability that we inhabit such a world. But a good theistic defense could show that a world whose epistemic probability of obtaining is zero includes an omniscient, omnipotent, wholly good being and an evil state of affairs.

### 2.2.1 Theistic Defense and its Alternatives

David Lewis has argued that a proper free will response to the logical problem of evil requires a free will theodicy. Lewis complains that providing a free will defense is just too easy.

> "Defense"... means just any hypothesis about why [an] omniscient, omnipotent, benevolent God permits evil. Its sole purpose is to rebut the contention that there is no possible way that such a thing could happen. To serve that purpose, the hypothesis need not be put forward as true. It need not be at all plausible. Mere possibility is enough.[17]

Discovering a broadly logically possible world in which it is true that (1) God is omnipotent, omniscient, and wholly good and (2) evil exists is too easy, according to Lewis, since he includes among the modal hypotheses suitable for a free will defense the full range of highly controversial modal hypotheses. He proposes the following defense, for instance.

> We are partly right, partly wrong in our catalog of values. The best things in life include love, joy, knowledge, vigor, despair, malice, betrayal, torture,... God in His infinite love provides all His children with an abundance of good things. Different ones of us get different gifts, all of them very good. So some are blessed with joy and knowledge, some with vigor and malice, some with torture and despair. God permits evil-doing as a means for delivering some of the goods, just as He permits beneficence as a means for delivering others.[18]

Lewis considers any false value judgments, however preposterous, to be possibly true. The judgment that torture is valuable isn't true and certainly qualifies as preposterous but, Lewis urges, it's nonetheless possibly true. But why believe that such a modal hypothesis is suitable in a free will defense?

---

[17] See David Lewis, "Evil for Freedom's Sake" in his *Papers in Ethics and Social Philosophy* (Cambridge: Cambridge University Press, 2000) 104 ff.
[18] Ibid. p. 105.

But suppose you disagree and deny that value judgments are contingent. No matter. What you deny is a disputed metaphysical thesis. Plantinga incorporates a disputed metaphysical thesis into his own free-will defense—the thesis that there are truths about how unactualized free choices would have come out. . . . Evidently he takes for granted that whether or not it's true, still it is possible in the relevant sense. So why may I not follow his precedent?[19]

The observations here are doubly mistaken. In the free will defense the thesis that counterfactuals of creaturely freedom take truth values is not proposed as a contingent truth. It is necessarily true, if true at all. So Plantinga takes the thesis to be true, if possibly so. Of course, there is some dispute about whether it is true at all.

It is no doubt true that every metaphysical thesis is a more or less disputed thesis, so any credible modal thesis in a free will defense will be more or less disputed. But the converse is false. Not just any disputed modal thesis suitable for a free will defense will be credible. Some metaphysical theses that are suitable for a free will defense are not credible at all. Some disputed metaphysical theses are much more highly disputed than others, so not just anything goes. Lewis offers a perfect example. The thesis that, possibly, torture is good might be the inevitable consequence of a dispositional theory of value that takes the dispositional account as an (more or less informative) analytic truth, but it is not even approximately credible as a modal hypothesis. It is not credible that there is a world in which torture is something good or valuable since, *inter alia*, it is not credible that the dispositional account of value is an analytic truth. The free will defense, at least as Plantinga elaborates it, certainly includes some disputed modal theses. But the defense includes no modal thesis that shares the deep epistemic liabilities of Lewis's modal hypothesis.

Lewis takes the primary aim of a free will response to the logical problem of evil to show that the existence of an omnipotent, omniscient, wholly good being is consistent with the quality, quantity, and distribution of *actual evil* that we observe.[20] That aim is not easy to achieve, according to Lewis, and the free will defense fails to achieve it.

But these observations on the free will defense are also mistaken. The primary aim of the free will defense is not to show that the existence of an omnipotent, omniscient, wholly good being is consistent with the quality,

---

[19]  Ibid. p. 105.
[20]  Ibid. p. 106 ff.

quantity, and distribution of actual evil. The primary aim of the free will defense is to show that the existence of an omnipotent, omniscient, wholly good being is consistent with the existence of evil simpliciter. But further it is certainly not obvious that the free will defense fails to achieve the *secondary aim* to show that the existence of an omnipotent, omniscient, wholly good being is consistent with actual evil. Among the many other theses, the quantity, quality, and distribution of actual evil fail to disconfirm Plantinga's thesis (42).

God is the omnipotent, omniscient, and morally perfect creator of the world; and every world that God could have actualized and that contains less than $10^{32}$ turps of evil, contains less broadly moral good and a less favorable overall balance of good and evil than the actual world contains.[21]

It is difficult to know what evidence there is that this thesis is not credible. Perhaps the argument from actual evil, supplemented with additional atheological arguments, would give us good reason to conclude that the thesis is not credible. But it is certainly not obvious that it would. And so it is certainly not obvious that the free will defense fails to achieve the secondary aim to show that the existence of an omnipotent, omniscient, wholly good being is consistent with actual evil.

### 2.2.2 Modal Epistemic Matters

It's agreed that a good theistic defense must show that the epistemic probability is not zero that *there is a possible world* that includes an omniscient, omnipotent, wholly good being and an evil state of affairs. But the exact epistemic standards appropriate here seem to depend on the epistemic probability and significance of alternative hypotheses about the sorts of worlds that exist. Consider the epistemic standard for a good theistic defense in (S0).[22]

S0. It is not reasonable to believe that there is no possible world that includes an omniscient, omnipotent, wholly good being and an evil state of affairs.

[21] Plantinga, *The Nature of Necessity*, op. cit. p. 194.
[22] Compare John O'Leary-Hawthorne and Daniel Howard-Snyder, "Transworld Sanctity and Plantinga's Free Will Defense" *International Journal for Philosophy of Religion* (1998) 1–21. Plantinga's free will defense is assessed against the strong epistemic condition that one shows that God is compatible with evil only if it is not reasonable to refrain from believing those claims that constitute it. This is condition EC1.

The hypothesis that there is some world that includes an omniscient, omnipotent, wholly good being and an evil state of affairs might meet the epistemic condition in (EC0) and still not satisfy the standard in (S0). It depends on the epistemic probability and significance given to alternative hypotheses.

EC0. It epistemically much more probable than not that there is some possible world that includes an omniscient, omnipotent, wholly good being and an evil state of affairs.

Improbable modal hypotheses are not difficult to imagine. Imagine a possible world that includes an *antitheos*. Let an antitheos exist in any world in which there is an evil state of affairs and in no world where there exists an omniscient, omnipotent, and wholly good being. It seems likely that an antitheos is not possible but I do not *know* that an antitheos is not possible. And since I do not know that an antitheos is not possible, I can reasonably refrain from believing that some possible world includes an omniscient, omnipotent, wholly good being, and an evil state of affairs. I can reasonably refrain from believing that some possible world includes an omniscient, omnipotent, wholly good being, and an evil state of affairs despite the fact that EC0 is satisfied: it is much more likely than not that there is such a world.

The antitheos hypothesis functions like a skeptical hypothesis. The global skeptic argues that we have no knowledge of the world because we don't know that we are not being massively deceived. It seems extremely unlikely that we are being massively deceived but, on philosophical reflection, we do not know that we are not being so deceived. But then we can reasonably refrain from believing propositions that seem highly probable. Compare the possibility that someone has stolen your car.

Suppose you own a car which you parked a few hours ago on a side street in a major metropolitan area. You remember clearly where you left it. Do you know where your car is? We are inclined to say that you do. Now it is true that every day hundreds of cars are stolen in the major cities of the United States. Do you know that your car has not been stolen? Many people have the intuition that you would not know that.[23]

---

[23] See Jonathan Vogel, "Are There Counterexamples to the Closure Principle?" in M. Ross and G. Ross (eds.) *Doubting: Contemporary Perspectives on Skepticism* (Dordrecht-Holland: Kluwer, 1990). Vogel does not take the example as properly understood as a counterexample to closure.

You seem to know where your car is parked. But when you consider the rate of car theft, the probability of your car's having been stolen is given more epistemic weight. And we are inclined to say that you don't know where your car is after all.[24] It is not unreasonable to refrain from believing that your car is parked on a side street, despite the fact that it is quite probable that it is parked on a side street.

If we take seriously the skeptical hypotheses then only the highest epistemic probability will ensure that it is unreasonable not to believe that some world includes an omniscient, omnipotent, wholly good being, and an evil state of affairs. There are always imaginable modal hypotheses that function as skeptical hypotheses and make it not unreasonable not to believe there is such a world.

In contexts where skeptical modal hypotheses are introduced, the epistemic standard in (S0) is too high. No theistic defense could establish with certainty that some world includes an omniscient, omnipotent, wholly good being, and an evil state of affairs. Consider the epistemic standard in (S1).

S1.  It is reasonable to believe that there is a possible world that includes an omniscient, omnipotent, wholly good being, and an evil state of affairs.

Certainly, if it is more probable than not that some possible world includes an omniscient, omnipotent, wholly good being, and an evil state of affairs then it is reasonable to believe that there is such a world.[25] But there are weaker epistemic conditions that meet the standard in (S1).

EC1.  The epistemically probability that there is some possible world that includes an omniscient, omnipotent, wholly good being, and an evil state of affairs is greater than any other incompatible hypothesis.

Suppose the probability that there is some possible world that includes an omniscient, omnipotent, wholly good being, and an evil state of affairs is greater than any other incompatible hypothesis. It is reasonable to believe there is such a world but it might not be unreasonable not to believe that there is such a world. The probability that my lottery ticket wins might be slightly greater than the hypothesis that any other ticket wins. But my

---

[24]  Ibid. p. 19. See also John Hawthorne, *Knowledge and Lotteries* (Oxford: Oxford University Press, 2004).

[25]  Some would deny belief simpliciter, rather than a degree of credibility, is reasonable for some propositions whose epistemic probability is greater than 0.5. The probability might be slightly greater than 0.5 that you survive a serious heart operation, but it might be too much to suggest that you flatly believe you will.

epistemic position regarding the hypothesis that my ticket wins might not be significantly better. It certainly seems reasonable to believe that my ticket will win, but it is not unreasonable not to believe it.

But even the epistemic standard in (S1) might be too high. It might be that none of the incompatible hypotheses concerning which possible worlds exist is reasonable to believe. Consider the epistemic standard in (S2).

S2. It is not unreasonable to believe that there is a possible world that includes an omniscient, omnipotent, wholly good being and an evil state of affairs.

Certainly, if the probability that there is some world that includes an omniscient, omnipotent, wholly good being, and an evil state of affairs is greater than any other incompatible hypothesis, then it is not unreasonable to believe that there is such a world. But there are weaker epistemic conditions that meet the standard in (S2).

EC2. The epistemic probability that there is some possible world that includes an omniscient, omnipotent, wholly good being, and an evil state of affairs is as great as any other incompatible hypothesis.

If the probability is very low that there's a world that includes an omniscient, omnipotent, wholly good being, and an evil state of affairs, it might not be reasonable to believe there is such a world. But the probability might be equally low for any incompatible hypothesis about the sorts of worlds that exist. Modal hypotheses that function as skeptical hypotheses relative to the belief that there is a world that includes an omniscient, omnipotent, wholly good being, and an evil state of affairs might themselves be highly improbable. So it might not be unreasonable to believe that there is a possible world that includes an omniscient, omnipotent, wholly good being, and an evil state of affairs. And that might be the best that we could hope for epistemically.

The epistemic standards relevant to assessing a theistic defense against the logical problem of evil depend on the facts concerning the epistemic probability and significance of incompatible hypotheses. In contexts where imaginable modal hypotheses are deployed as skeptical hypotheses the epistemic standard in (S0) is too high. Only the highest epistemic probability will ensure that it is unreasonable not to believe that some world includes an omniscient, omnipotent, wholly good being, and an evil state of affairs.

The probability might be very low that there's a world that includes an omniscient, omnipotent, wholly good being, and an evil state of affairs.

But then the standard in (S1) might be too high. The probability might be equally low for every incompatible hypothesis about the sorts of worlds that exist. The belief that there is a world that includes an omniscient, omnipotent, wholly good being, and an evil state of affairs is then not unreasonable to believe. And no incompatible hypothesis about the sorts of worlds that exist has a better epistemic status.

## 2.3  The Free Will Defense

### 2.3.1  Preliminaries

The free will defense aims to prove that (1) and (2) are broadly, logically consistent.

1. God is omnipotent, omniscient, and wholly good.
2. Evil exists.

As noted in section (2) each of the conjunctions in (3.3)–(3.5) together with (1) entail that (2) is false. There are three inconsistent sets of propositions and (at least) three ways that the logical problem of evil might succeed. J. L. Mackie urged that anyone committed to (1) is committed to (3.3). But (1) might entail the weaker theses in (3.4)–(3.5).

3.3.  Necessarily, an omnipotent, omniscient, wholly good being brings about *the best possible world* and the best possible world includes no evil states of affairs at all.

3.4.  Necessarily, an omnipotent, omniscient, wholly good being brings about *the best actualizable world* and the best actualizable world includes no evil states of affairs.

3.5.  Necessarily, an omnipotent, omniscient, wholly good being brings about *a good enough world* and a good enough world includes no evil states of affairs.

Propositions (3.3)–(3.5) entail that an omniscient, omnipotent, wholly good being exists in every possible world.[26] (3.3)–(3.5) therefore entail

---

[26] Compare Plantinga, *God, Freedom, and Evil*, op. cit. p. 21 ff. In an effort to generate an inconsistent set Plantinga adds (19c): necessarily, an omnipotent, omniscient, good being eliminates every evil it can properly eliminate; (19c) also entails that an omniscient, omnipotent, wholly good being exists in every possible world.

that omniscient, omnipotent, perfect goodness, and necessary existence are essential properties of God. But the theses in (3.3)–(3.5) are not equivalent.

Proposition (3.3) entails that, necessarily, an omniscient, omnipotent, wholly good being brings about the best possible world and the best possible world includes no evil states of affairs. If (1) and (3.3) are true, there are no possible worlds that include evil states of affairs. If (1) is true and (3.3) is true, then (2) is necessarily false.

Proposition (3.4) entails that, necessarily, an omnipotent, omniscient, wholly good being brings about the best actualizable world and the best actualizable world includes no evil states of affairs. It follows from (3.4) that every possible world is a best actualizable world at itself. So no possible world includes an evil state of affairs. If (1) is true and (3.4) is true, then (2) is necessarily false.

The thesis in (3.4) is weaker than the thesis in (3.3). (3.3) entails that there is a best possible world and that necessarily an omnipotent, omniscient, wholly good being actualizes the best world. (3.4) does not entail either that there is a best possible world or that an omnipotent, omniscient, wholly good being brings about the best world. (3.4) is consistent with there being no world that is not bettered by another world. So, it is consistent with (3.4) that necessarily an omnipotent, omniscient, wholly good being fails to bring about the best possible world. Proposition (3.4) entails that an omnipotent, omniscient, wholly good being bring about the best world he can and the best world he can bring about, or he is able to bring about, might not be the best possible world.

Proposition (3.5) entails that, necessarily, an omnipotent, omniscient, wholly good being brings about a good enough world and a good enough world includes no evil states of affairs. It follows from (3.5) that every possible world is a good enough world. So no possible world includes an evil state of affairs. If (1) is true and (3.5) is true, then (2) is necessarily false.

The thesis in (3.5) is weaker than the thesis in (3.4). (3.4) entails that there is a best actualizable world and that necessarily an omnipotent, omniscient, wholly good being brings about the best actualizable world. (3.5) does not entail that either that there is a best actualizable world or that an omnipotent, omniscient, wholly good being brings about the best actualizable world. It is consistent with (3.5) that possibly an omnipotent, omniscient, wholly good being fails to bring about a best actualizable world. Proposition (3.5) requires only that an omnipotent, omniscient, wholly good being bring about a good enough world and it might be that some good enough worlds are not best actualizable worlds. Even if every world is a good enough world, it might be that some good enough worlds are better than others.

## 2.4 Proving Consistency

A set of propositions is consistent if and only if there is some possible world in which all of the propositions are true together. A typical way to prove consistency is to produce a model that simultaneously satisfies the propositions in the set. Suppose we wanted to prove that the proposition, < it is not the case that Smith is tall >, is consistent with the proposition, < it is not the case that Smith is not tall >.[27] We would need to produce a non-classical model for those propositions that does not validate bivalence. We could provide such a model in supervaluation semantics, for instance. Plantinga's approach to proving the consistency of the set including (1) and (2) is to provide another proposition R such that R is obviously, or intuitively, consistent with (1) and R & (1) together entail (2). If there is a possible world in which R and (1) are both true, then given standard closure principles and the fact that R & (1) entail (2), there is a possible world in which (1) and (2) are both true. It is perhaps a drawback of this approach to proving consistency that it must appeal to the intuition that R is consistent with (1), but the fact is that all consistency proofs appeal to intuition at one point or another.

There is any number of candidates for proposition R that have the formal property of entailing (2) when conjoined to (1). There is an initial, albeit improbable, candidate in R0.

R0. God actualizes a world containing moral good and moral evil.

The proposition in R0 together with (1) entails that there is evil and it would show the consistency of (1) and (2). Our worry, of course, is that we have no reason to believe that R0 is consistent with God being omniscient, omnipotent, and wholly good. R0 simply asserts that it is possible for God to actualize a world that contains evil. Plantinga suggests another place to locate a candidate for R.

---

[27] The bracketing convention indicates that we are referring to the proposition, not the sentence expressing the proposition. See David Armstrong, *Truth and Truthmakers* (Cambridge: Cambridge University Press, 2004).

A world containing creatures who are sometimes significantly free (and freely perform more good than evil actions) is more valuable, all else equal, than a world containing no free creatures at all. Now God can create free creatures, but he cannot cause or determine them to do only what is right. For if he does so, then they are not significantly free after all; they do not do what is right freely. To create creatures capable of moral good, therefore, he must create creatures capable of moral evil; and he cannot leave these creatures free to perform moral evil and at the same time prevent them from doing so. God did in fact create significantly free creatures; but some of them went wrong in the exercise of their freedom: this is the source of moral evil. The fact that these free creatures sometimes go wrong, however, counts neither against God's omnipotence nor against his goodness; for he could have forestalled the occurrence of moral evil only by excising the possibility of moral good.

... [T]he Free Will Defender tries to find a proposition that is consistent with (1) God is omniscient, omnipotent and wholly good and together with (1) entails there is evil. ... [W]e must find this proposition somewhere in the above story. The heart of the Free Will Defense is the claim that it is possible that God could not have created a universe containing moral good (or as much moral good as this world contains) without creating one that also contained moral evil.[28]

We do find a proposition in the above story that is consistent with (1). Plantinga offers R1 as a worthy candidate for R.

R1.  God is omnipotent and it is not within God's power to actualize a world containing moral good but no moral evil.[29]

Propositions R1 and (1) are consistent. So there is a world W at which God exists and it is not within God's power to create a world containing moral good and no moral evil. The problem is that we don't know that there is any moral evil in W. For all we know there are no free and rational agents in W apart from God, and so there is neither moral good nor moral evil.[30] That is, it might be true that any actualizable world in which there is moral good and moral evil is a world which is on balance bad. That is consistent with the truth of R1 and God deciding that it's better to actualize a world that is neutral on moral value. So R1 and (1) do not entail (2).

---

[28] See Plantinga, *The Nature of Necessity*, op. cit. p. 167.

[29] See ibid. p. 184; and his *God, Freedom, and Evil*, op. cit. p. 45.

[30] There is another worry for R1 that's worth mentioning. If God creates no moral agents at all, then there is no moral good forthcoming from finite agents, but it might be reasonable to believe that there is moral good forthcoming from God.

But there are other propositions suggested in the story. The proposition in R2 and (1), for instance, do entail (2).

> R2.  God actualizes a world with moral good and it is not within God's power to actualize a world containing moral good but no moral evil.

Propositions R2 and (1) are consistent just in case there is some world at which God creates free agents who bring about both moral good and moral evil and it is true there that God cannot actualize a world with moral good and no moral evil.

Propositions R2 and (1) are consistent only if a perfectly good being might be permitted to actualize a world that includes moral good and moral evil and it is not obvious that a perfect being might be permitted to do so. Certainly, God cannot actualize just any world with moral good and moral evil. But it is also true God cannot actualize just any on balance good world that includes moral good and moral evil. Suppose, for instance, that every world with moral good and moral evil is worse than some world with no moral evil. A perfectly good being would in that case actualize a world with no moral evil and no moral good. Presumably God would actualize a world that included no significantly free creatures at all.

It is not obvious that R2 is consistent with God's perfect goodness, but we can do better. Consider replacing R2 with R3.

> R3.  God actualizes a world that is on balance good and it is not within God's power to actualize a world containing moral good but no moral evil.

It seems consistent with God's perfect goodness that he actualizes a world with moral evil if some actualizable world with moral good and moral evil is better than any actualizable world with no moral evil. The additional axiological assumption is also suggested in the story above.

A world containing creatures who are sometimes significantly free (and freely perform more good than evil actions) is more valuable, all else equal, than a world containing no free creatures at all.[31]

So, R3 seems consistent with God's moral perfection. R3 and (1) also seem consistent. And R3 and (1) clearly entail (2). If God actualizes an on

---

[31] See Plantinga, *The Nature of Necessity*, op. cit. p. 167.

balance good world and it is not in his power to actualize a world with moral good but no moral evil, then God actualizes a world that contains some evil.

Notice that if R3 and (1) are consistent, then (3.3)–(3.5) are all false. (3.3)–(3.5) each entail that there are no possible worlds that include any evil states of affairs. Either necessarily God actualizes the best possible world or necessarily God actualizes the best actualizable world or necessarily God actualizes a good enough world. And, according to (3.3)–(3.5), none of those worlds includes any evil states of affairs.

Propositions R3 and (1) are consistent, of course, if and only if R3 is possible. Plantinga's argument from the possibility of universal transworld depravity is an attempt to show that the second conjunct in R3 is possibly true. But there is no argument forthcoming for the possibility of the first conjunct in R3. The argument from universal transworld depravity attempts to establish that, possibly, it is not within God's power to actualize a world containing moral good but no moral evil. But something stronger has to be shown to establish that R3 is possibly true. It has to be shown that, possibly, God actualizes a world that is on balance good and it is not within God's power to actualize a world containing moral good but no moral evil.

## 2.5  Transworld Depravity

It is fundamental to the thesis of universal transworld depravity that created beings are free if and only if they are libertarian free. The thesis does not depend on any specific account of libertarian freedom.[32] Let U be the state of the universe—including every state of affairs that obtains—prior to a time t. As a first pass we might say that an agent S is libertarian free with respect to an action A at time t if and only if U is consistent with S performing A at t and U is consistent with S performing $\sim$A at t.[33] So, if S is libertarian free with respect to A at t then the states of affairs in U do

---

[32] The competing accounts of libertarian freedom include, among others, agent causal accounts, event causal accounts, and non-causal accounts.

[33] Of course, some actions A are possible at t and such that, were A performed then U would have to have been different. These actions are possible but not consistent with U. So the analysis is inaccurate left to right.

not deterministically cause S to perform A at t and do not deterministically cause S to perform ∼A at t.[34]

The state of the universe includes, among other things, every state of affairs that God causes to obtain up to a time t. Let a world W include every state of affairs that God causes to obtain at any time. God causes it to be the case that contingent individuals exist and that they exemplify a certain set of contingent properties. God causes you to exist, for instance, and causes it to be the case that you exemplify the properties of being right-handed and bipedal. God thereby causes the state of affairs to obtain of your being right-handed and bipedal. It seems certain that God might have instantiated an individual essence of yours that is left-handed instead, since the property of being left-handed is paradigmatically contingent and, in most cases, not freely chosen. Perhaps, too, he could have instantiated an individual essence of yours that has the exotic contingent properties of being scaled and reptilian.[35]

On this account, God creates all of the contingent natural and non-natural objects and causes to be instantiated most of the exemplified natural and non-natural properties. The states of affairs in W that God causes to obtain are the *strongly actualized* states of affairs in W.

There are some contingent properties that God cannot cause any individual to exemplify. For instance, God cannot cause any individual to exemplify the contingent property of freely performing an action or freely doing what is right. If there are genuinely chancy events in the world, then God cannot cause a chancy event.[36] If radon decay and coin tosses are genuinely chancy events, for instance, then God does not cause radon to emit alpha particles or coins to fall heads. Events that God causes to occur are not genuinely chancy.[37] God can create a coin whose propensity to fall heads he foreknows, but he cannot change the propensity of a particular coin's falling tails, if that is a genuinely chancy event, and he cannot change the rate of a particular radon atomn's decaying, if that is genuinely chancy. If there are genuinely chancy events and genuinely free

---

[34] The state of affairs U might be stochastically related to A. It might be the case that S is libertarian free with respect to A in U and the chances are high that S does A in U (but the chances are not high that S does A in U').

[35] See Plantinga, *The Nature of Necessity*, op. cit. sect. IV, 12.

[36] There is a sense in which God can probabilistically cause a chancy event. God can so act that the chances that a chancy event occurs goes from 0 to p, for some positive p. God can actualize a world in which he creates radon atoms, for instance, and thereby raises the chances of there being radon decay.

[37] Perhaps God can *direct* chancy events in other ways.

events in W, then there are states of affairs in W that God does not cause to obtain. The states of affairs that obtain in W, but that God does not cause to obtain, are the *weakly actualized* states of affairs in W.[38]

If a person S suffers from transworld depravity then God could not have created S with the contingent property of being significantly free with respect to some actions and without the contingent property of being transworld depraved. A person S exemplifies the contingent property of being transworld depraved if and only if S satisfies the conditions in TD.

> TD. A person S suffers from transworld depravity iff for every world
> W such that S instantiates the properties *is significantly free* in W and
> *always does what is right* in W, there is a state of affairs T and an
> action A such that,
> (1) T is the largest state of affairs God strongly actualizes in W;
> (2) A is morally significant for S in W;
> (3) if God had strongly actualized T, S would have gone wrong
>     with respect to A.

For each person S, there is a set of worlds W such that S instantiates the essential properties *is significantly free* in W and *always does what is right* in W.[39] Call that set of worlds the *S-perfect worlds*. Call the set of worlds that God can weakly actualize the set of *feasible* worlds. A possible world W is among the feasible worlds if and only if there is some largest state of affairs T that God can strongly actualize such that T ≠ W and were God to strongly actualize T then W would obtain. If S is possibly transworld depraved then, possibly, God cannot actualize an S-perfect world or, possibly, the set of feasible worlds includes no S-perfect worlds.

The set of S-perfect worlds exhaust the possible worlds in which God creates S and S always goes right. In each of these worlds S is created with a particular profile of contingent properties; S is created in a set of circumstances, at a particular place and time, and with a set of intrinsic properties. In worlds where S is transworld depraved God can strongly actualize any largest state of affairs T such that T is actualized in some S-perfect world.

---

[38] See Plantinga, *The Nature of Necessity*, op. cit. pp. 172–3. If T is a largest state of affairs that God can strongly actualizes and W ≠ T then if God were to strongly actualize T, then W is the largest state of affairs that would obtain, then W is the largest state of affairs that God weakly actualizes.

[39] The set of worlds might be empty. I restrict attention here to non-empty sets of S-perfect worlds.

But, for each profile of properties P such that S instantiates P in an S-perfect world, God cannot strongly or weakly actualize a state of affairs T such that S instantiates P in T.

It is useful to contrast S-perfect worlds with morally perfect worlds, naturally perfect worlds, and best worlds.

M. Let a world W be a morally perfect world or an M-world if and only if (i) there are significantly free beings in W (ii) every significantly free being in W performs some morally significant action A in W and (iii) and every significantly free agent in W goes morally right with respect to each morally significant action A.

There are no trivial ways in which worlds might satisfy M. A world that includes no moral agents at all, or no significantly free beings, is not morally perfect. A world in which significantly free beings perform no significant actions is not a morally perfect world.

N. Let a world W be a naturally perfect world or an N-world if and only if (i) there are natural objects and sentient beings in W and (ii) W contains no naturally evil states of affairs.

According to N, there are no trivially perfect worlds among the naturally perfect worlds. Worlds in which God creates no natural objects and no sentient beings are not naturally perfect worlds. Otherwise worlds that include no natural disasters, no bad natural events, and in general no natural evils are naturally perfect worlds. It is evident that some naturally perfect worlds are morally perfect worlds. Many worlds that include no natural evils and no moral evils are morally and naturally perfect.

B. Let a world W be a best world or a B-world if and only if there is no possible world $W'$ such that the overall value of $W'$ exceeds the overall value of W.[40]

Presumably, some S-perfect worlds are M-worlds. In particular, the S-perfect world in which S is the only free and rational agent is an M-world. But certainly other significantly free agents in many S-perfect worlds go wrong. So, S-perfect worlds are not in general M-worlds.

---

[40] Note that (3.3) entails that all B-worlds are M-worlds. Since there is considerable question about (3.3), I do not assume that it is true here.

Similarly, it seems that some S-perfect worlds are N-worlds, since some worlds in which S never goes wrong are worlds in which there is no natural evil. But the fact that S never goes wrong seems consistent with the existence of natural evil. So some S-perfect worlds are not N-worlds.

S might not exist in any B-worlds, so we don't know that any S-perfect world is among the best worlds. But surely some S-perfect worlds are not B-worlds. Other agents in S-perfect worlds might go terribly wrong and the states of affairs in S-perfect worlds might not be the best possible or the best feasible states of affairs.

It does seem true that, possibly, some person S satisfies the conditions in TD. But that's insufficient to establish the second conjunct of R3 unless, possibly, S is transworld depraved and *S exists in every feasible world in which there is any moral good*. And it is more difficult to determine whether that is possible. Recall that the second conjunct of R3 states that it is not within God's power to actualize a world containing moral good but no moral evil. Some rational and free beings have the essential property of existing in every feasible world in which there is moral good. God has that essential property, for instance. But it's not so obvious that any significant beings might have the contingent property of existing in every feasible world in which there is moral good.[41]

It is the possibility of *universal transworld depravity* that Plantinga uses to establish the second conjunct of R3. If it is true that, possibly, every creatable rational and free being suffers from transworld depravity then, possibly, it is not within God's power to actualize a world containing moral good but no moral evil.

## 2.6 Individual Essences, Haecceities, and Depravity

The individual essence or haecceity E of a person S is just the set of properties that S alone exemplifies in every world in which S exists.[42]

---

[41] But it might be true in every feasible world in which there is moral good that an ancestor of every existing free and rational being is transworld depraved.

[42] See Alvin Plantinga, "De Essentia" *Grazer Philosophische Studien* (1979) 101–21. And his *The Nature of Necessity*, op. cit. p. 70 ff. Plantinga identifies haecceities and individual essences and does not specify that haecceities must be non-qualitative properties.

Each rational and free being God creates is the instantiation of his or her individual essence or haecceity in each world in which he exists.

Individual essences exist in every possible world and themselves exemplify essential properties. There is the property of being the essence of S, for instance, which is a property an essence E has in every world simpliciter. There is the property of necessarily existing and the property of being a property, both of which E has in every possible world. Some individual essences have the essential property of being uninstantiated. The essence of anything that exists in no world at all will be essentially uninstantiated. These properties are part of the individual essence E′ of some essence E. In general, every individual essence and haecceity themselves have individual essences and haecceities and those haecceities, too, have individual essences and so on upward.

Individual essences also have contingent properties. It is a contingent property of some individual essence E that it is unexemplified. It is a contingent property of some individual essence that it is, for instance, among ten exemplified essences.

Not every property of an essence E is a property of E's instantiation S. There are worlds in which E has the contingent property of being exemplified. But it is false that S is exemplified in any world. S either exists or does not exist, but in no world does S have the property of being exemplified. E is necessarily the essence of S. But in no world is S an essence of anything. E is necessarily a property. But in no world is S a property.[43]

There are also properties that S can instantiate but S's haecceity or individual essence cannot. S might instantiate the property of being 6′ tall or left-handed. But an unexemplified essence E can be neither 6′ tall nor left-handed. In every case where S can instantiate a property P that E cannot, God can cause S to *coexemplify* P and E. And there are infinitely

---

[43] Compare Christopher Menzel, "Actualism" *The Stanford Encyclopedia of Philosophy* (December 2008), Edward N. Zalta (ed.), URL = <http://plato.stanford.edu/entries/actualism/index.html#Haecceitism>.

After all, it is not haecceities to which predicates apply at worlds, it is the things that exemplify them; [*being an Alien*], if it were exemplified, would not be a property of essences, but of individuals. Plantinga's trick is to talk, not about exemplification, but coexemplification.

But as noted there are predicates that apply to haecceities and not to the things that exemplify them.

many different sets of contingent properties that God might cause S to coexemplify with E.

There are some properties that *both* individual essences and their instantiations can exemplify. Transworld depravity, for instance, is a contingent property of persons S and a contingent property of individual essences E. It is characteristic of transworld depravity that an essence E has that contingent property only if any instantiation S of E that is significantly free with respect to some actions has that contingent property.

Transworld depravity is a property that the *unexemplified* property E contingently instantiates. But transworld depravity differs from other properties that the unexemplified property E instantiates. The unexemplified property E also has the contingent property of being unexemplified, for instance, but God can *cause* E to instantiate the property of being exemplified. But if the unexemplified property E has the contingent property of being transworld depraved, then God cannot cause E to instantiate the contingent property of being significantly free with respect to some actions and not transworld depraved.

Transworld depravity also differs from properties that God can cause to be coexemplified with E in an instantiation S. The property of being left-handed is a property that God can cause to coexemplify with E in S. The contingent state of affairs of S being left-handed is the result of God's causal activity. And the property of being right-handed is a property that God can cause to coexemplify with E in S. The contingent state of affairs of S being right-handed is the result of God's causal activity. But the contingent state of affairs of E being transworld depraved obtains prior to God's causal activity. In that state of affairs E exemplifies what we might call a *prevolitional property*: it is a property that E exemplifies in a world W prior to anything God does in W.

It can be difficult to see how a contingent state of affairs could obtain prior to God's creative activity. J. L. Mackie advances this objection against the possibility that some person or essence might be transworld depraved.

As I have argued, it is not logically impossible that even a created person should always act rightly; the supposed limitation of the range of possible persons is therefore logically contingent. But how could there be logically contingent states of affairs *prior to the creation and existence of any created beings with free will* which an omnipotent God would have to accept and put up with? The suggestion is simply incoherent. Indeed, by bringing in the notion of individual essences which determine—presumably non-causally—how Curley Smith, Satan and the rest of us would choose freely or would act in each hypothetical situation, Plantinga has not rescued the free will defense but made its weakness all too clear. The concept of individual essences concedes that even if free actions are not causally determined, even if freedom in the important sense is not compatible with causal determination, a person can still be such that he will freely choose this way or that in each specific situation. Given this, and given the unrestricted range of all logically possible creaturely essences from which an omnipotent and omniscient god would be free to select whom to create, it is obvious that my original criticism of the free will defense holds good: had there been such a god, it would have been open to him to create beings such that they would always freely choose the good.[44]

There exist lots of contingent states of affairs *prior to* the creation of any contingent object or being. There is the contingent state of affairs, for instance, of there being no trees, animals, finite rational beings, or mountains. But these contingent states of affairs do not constrain what an omnipotent and omniscient being can create. God can create trees, animals, rational beings, and mountains and thereby strongly actualize the contingent state of affairs of there being trees, animals, rational beings, and mountains to obtain.

In the domain of each possible world there are also uncreated and unexemplified individual essences.[45] What Mackie overlooks is that uncreated and unexemplified properties can themselves exemplify contingent properties prior to God's creative activity. Uncreated and unexemplified haecceities have contingent properties prior to God's creative activity. Some of those contingent properties impose some constraints on what God can do. Among the contingent properties of unexemplified individual essences that constrain what God can do is the property of being transworld depraved. But there are many others. There is the property of being such that one's first free action is morally wrong and of course the full range of properties due to one's free choices and actions.

Just as instantiated essences or persons might contingently exemplify the property of being transworld depraved so uninstantiated individual essences might contingently exemplify the property of being transworld depraved.

---

[44] J. L. Mackie advances this objection against the possibility that *every* creature essence is transworld depraved, but the argument holds just as well in the case of one essence being transworld depraved. See J. L. Mackie, *The Miracle of Theism*, op. cit. p. 174 ff.

[45] Plantinga calls the set of essences that would have been exemplified had w been actual the essential domain of w. In addition to the essential domain, there is in the domain of w a set of essences that would not have been exemplified, had w been actual. These essences have properties too.

TD★. An essence E suffers from transworld depravity iff for every world W such that E instantiates the properties *is significantly free* in W and *always does what is right* in W, there is a state of affairs T and an action A such that,

(1) T is the largest state of affairs God strongly actualizes in W;

(2) A is morally significant for E's instantiation in W;

(3) if God had strongly actualized T, E's instantiation would have gone wrong with respect to A.[46]

Transworld depravity is a *dispositional property* of unexemplified essences. An unexemplified essence E has the property of transworld depravity if and only if E's instantiation would freely go wrong with respect to some action were E coexemplified with the property F of being significantly free with respect to some actions.

Let a *strict disposition* be any disposition that satisfies (a restricted form of) strengthening antecedents. S has a strict disposition to do A if S is such that, for essence E of S, and for some property F and any property P, were E + F coexemplified in S then performing A would be exemplified in S *only if* were E + F + P coexemplified in S then performing A would be exemplified in S.

The property of transworld depravity is a strict dispositional property. Let F be the property of being significantly free with respect to some actions and let P be any other property that S might instantiate. If an unexemplified essence E is transworld depraved then there is no property P such that E's instantiation would never go wrong were God to coexemplify E + F + P. But then transworld depravity clearly constrains God's creative activity. Of course, God can fail to exemplify E altogether or exemplify E without the property of being significantly free with respect to some actions. But God cannot prevent E's instantiation from going wrong if that instantiation is significantly free with respect to some actions.

There is another way to see that transworld depravity is a strict dispositional property. Suppose E is transworld depraved and W′ the set of worlds in which E is instantiated and goes right with respect to every significantly free action. For each W ∈ W′ there is a largest state of affairs T that God causes to obtain in W and profile of properties C that God causes E's instantiation to exemplify in T. As we noted above, C does not exhaust

---

[46] See Plantinga, *The Nature of Necessity*, op. cit. p. 188.

the properties that E's instantiation exemplifies, since there are properties—both contingent properties and essential properties—that God cannot cause E's instantiation to exemplify. By TD⋆ we know that there is no profile of properties C and state of affairs T of W ∈ W′ such that God causes E's instantiation that exemplifies C in T and E's instantiation never goes wrong. Were there such a profile of properties, E would not be transworld depraved.

Now consider another set of worlds W⋆ in which E is instantiated and E's instantiation does not go right with respect to every significantly free action. W′ and W⋆ are disjoint and exhaust the worlds in which E is instantiated and significantly free. For each W ∈ W⋆ there is a largest state of affairs T that God causes to obtain in W and profile of properties C⋆ that God causes E's instantiation to exemplify in T. Since no W in W⋆ is morally perfect we know that there is no profile of properties C⋆ and state of affairs T of W ∈ W⋆ such that God causes E's instantiation to exemplify C⋆ in T and E's instantiation always goes right.

The profiles in C and C⋆ are all of the properties that God can cause E's instantiation to exemplify in worlds where E's instantiation is significantly free. Since there is no profile of properties that God causes E's instantiation to exemplify in any state of affairs T such that E's instantiation in T never goes wrong, transworld depravity is a strict dispositional property of E. Since transworld depravity is a strict dispositional property, E's exemplification of transworld depravity constrains God's creative activity.

## 2.7  Universal Transworld Depravity is Not Enough

The thesis of universal transworld depravity states that, possibly, *every* individual essence or haecceity has the strict dispositional property of being transworld depraved.

Now the interesting fact here is this: it is possible that every creaturely essence suffers from transworld depravity. But suppose this is true. God can create a world containing moral good only by creating significantly free persons. And, since every person is an instantiation of an essence, he can create significantly free persons only by instantiating some creaturely essences. But if every such essence suffers from transworld depravity, then no matter which essences God instantiated, the resulting persons, if free with respect to morally significant actions, would always perform at least some wrong actions. If every creaturely essence suffers from transworld depravity, then it was beyond the power of God to create a world but no moral evil.[47]

The argument that, possibly, every creaturely essence is transworld depraved is nothing more than a direct appeal to modal intuition. And indeed it does seem possible that every creaturely essence is transworld depraved. But if the thesis of universal transworld depravity is true, then we are close to a solution to the logical problem of evil.

The thesis of universal transworld depravity entails that, possibly, it is not within God's power to actualize a world containing moral good but no moral evil. So, universal transworld depravity entails the second conjunct of R3.

R3.  God actualizes a world that is on balance good and it is not within God's power to actualize a world containing moral good but no moral evil.

But it is not difficult to see that the possibility of universal transworld depravity does not alone entail that R3 is possible. R3 together with the proposition that (1) God is omnipotent, omniscient, and wholly good entails the proposition that (2) evil exists. But the possibility of universal transworld depravity together with (1) *does not* entail (2).[48] The thesis of universal transworld depravity is consistent with the thesis of *universal transworld ultra-depravity*.

UD.  An essence E suffers from transworld ultra-depravity iff for every world W such that E instantiates the property *is significantly free* in W there is a state of affairs T such that for *every action* A,

[47]  Ibid. pp. 188–9.
[48]  See *The Nature of Necessity*, op. cit. p. 189. Contrary to a very common misunderstanding of the argument, Plantinga concurs that the possibility of universal transworld depravity is not enough to establish that (1) is consistent with (2).

What we have just seen is that (31) [Every essence suffers from transworld depravity] is consistent with God's omnipotence. But then it is clearly consistent with (1). So we can use it to show that (1) is consistent with (2). For, consider the conjunction of (1), (31) and (32) [God actualizes a world containing moral good]. This conjunction is evidently consistent. But it entails (2) [There is evil]. Accordingly, (1) is consistent with (2); the Free Will Defense is successful.

What Plantinga does not attempt to establish is that (32) is consistent with God's perfect goodness. Plantinga would no doubt agree that (32) is not consistent with God's perfect goodness if every actualizable world with moral good and moral evil is worse than some actualizable world with no moral evil.

(1)  T is the largest state of affairs God strongly actualizes in W;

(2)  A is morally significant for E's instantiation in W;

(3)  if God had strongly actualized T, E's instantiation would have gone wrong with respect to A.

If every unexemplified essence is transworld ultra-depraved then any instantiation of those essences, in any state of affairs T, would go wrong with respect to every morally significant action. But suppose every world in which every essence is transworld depraved is a world in which every essence is transworld ultra-depraved. It follows that, possibly, it is not within God's power to actualize a world containing any moral good at all. But then we cannot conclude that possibly God actualizes a world with moral evil.

Universal transworld depravity shows that it is consistent with God's *omnipotence* that he actualizes a world with moral evil. To establish R3 it also must be consistent with God's *perfect goodness* that he actualizes a world with moral evil. To establish R3 it must be shown that, possibly, every individual essence is transworld depraved and that God actualizes a world that is on balance good. But it is evident that God cannot actualize a world that is on balance good if every actualizable world with moral good and moral evil is worse than some actualizable world with no moral evil. In that case no actualizable world contains more moral good than moral evil.

But surely there are other possibilities. God can actualize a world that is on balance good if some actualizable world with moral good and moral evil is better than any actualizable world with no moral evil. Plantinga elicits a strong and widely shared moral intuition that it does not in general diminish the moral goodness of an agent that he fails to eliminate certain evil states of affairs.

One of [your] bruises is very painful. You mention it to a physician friend, who predicts that the pain will leave of its own accord in a day or two. Meanwhile, he says, there's nothing he can do short of amputating your leg above the knee, to remove the pain. Now the pain in your knee is an evil state of affairs. All else equal, it would be better if you had no such pain. And it is within the power of your friend to eliminate this evil state of affairs. Does his failure to do so mean that he is not a good person? Of course not; for he could eliminate this evil state of affairs only by bringing about another, much worse evil. . . . It is entirely possible that a good person fail to eliminate an evil state of affairs he knows about and can eliminate. This would take place if, as in the present example, he couldn't eliminate the evil without bringing about a greater evil.[49]

---

[49]  See Plantinga, *God and Other Minds*, op. cit. p. 19.

A perfectly good being might fail to actualize a world with no moral evil if some actualizable world with moral good and moral evil is better than any world with no moral evil.

Suppose it is possible that every essence is transworld depraved and that some actualizable world with moral good and moral evil is better than any actualizable world with no moral evil. It follows that R3 is possible. R3 is consistent with (1) and R3 & (1) entail (2). We then have an argument that the existence of an omniscient, omnipotent, and wholly good being is consistent with the existence of evil.

## 2.8 Concluding Remarks

There is good reason to believe that (1) and (2) are not broadly, logically consistent.

1. God is omnipotent, omniscient, and wholly good.
2. Evil exists.

Each of the theses in (3.3)–(3.5) together with (1) entail that (2) is false. So there are three inconsistent sets of propositions and three ways that the logical problem of evil might succeed. Mackie argued that anyone committed to (1) is committed to (3.3). But the weaker theses in (3.4)–(3.5) also generate a logical problem of evil.

3.3. Necessarily, an omnipotent, omniscient, wholly good being brings about *the best possible world* and the best possible world includes no evil states of affairs at all.

3.4. Necessarily, an omnipotent, omniscient, wholly good being brings about *the best actualizable world* and the best actualizable world includes no evil states of affairs.

3.5. Necessarily, an omnipotent, omniscient, wholly good being brings about *a good enough world* and a good enough world includes no evil states of affairs.

If the thesis in R3 is possible, then (1) and (2) are consistent and all of (3.3)–(3.5) are false. If the thesis in R3 is possible, then it is possible that God actualizes a world with moral good and moral evil. So, there is some world in which (3.3)–(3.5) are all false.

But if it is possible that God actualizes a world with moral good and moral evil, we cannot conclude that the first conjuncts in (3.3)–(3.5) are all false. Perhaps the second conjuncts are all false. For each individual essence E, there is a set of worlds W such that E instantiates the essential properties *is significantly free* in W and *always does what is right* in W. Call that set of worlds the *E-perfect worlds*. The thesis of universal transworld depravity states that, possibly, God cannot actualize an E-perfect world. But it does not follow that possibly God does not actualize the best actualizable world. Possibly, the best actualizable world is not an E-perfect world.

Among the E-perfect worlds are possible worlds in which *every* instantiated essence always goes right. Call a world in which every instantiated essence always goes right an E*-perfect world. If universal transworld depravity is possible then, possibly, God cannot actualize an E*-perfect world. But it does not follow that possibly God cannot actualize the best possible world. The best possible world might not be an E*-perfect world. It might be true that some possible world in which some free and rational agents sometimes go wrong is better than any world in which every free and rational agent always goes right. It is consistent with R3 that some haecceities are *necessarily* transworld depraved. If so then necessarily any world in which any one of these haecceities is instantiated includes moral evil. It is consistent with R3, and by my lights quite credible, that necessarily, some haecceities or other are such that they would bring about moral evil, were they instantiated, but would bring about more moral good than moral evil. The best possible world would then include an instantiated haecceity that brings about moral evil, but also brings about more moral good than moral evil.

If universal transworld depravity is possible, then possibly God cannot actualize an E*-perfect world. But it does not follow that God cannot actualize a good enough world. The good enough worlds might not be E*-perfect worlds. Certainly good enough worlds might include free and rational agents that sometimes go wrong.

The main conclusion from R3 is that (3.3)–(3.5) are all false, and (1) is consistent with (2). But R3 does not entail that God does not actualize the best possible world or the best actualizable world or a good enough world. Of course R3 is not the only thesis consistent with (1) that entails (2).[50] Indeed R3 is a much stronger thesis than necessary to resolve the logical problem of evil.

---

[50] Plantinga makes a similar observation. See *The Nature of Necessity*, op. cit. pp. 189–90.

# 3

# Three Important Objections

## 3.0 Introduction

The aim of the free will defense is to prove the broad logical consistency of the existence of evil and the existence of an omnipotent, omniscient, wholly good being. The structure of the argument is deductive and the argument is clearly valid. But there are three well-known objections to the free will defense that are designed to display some serious flaws in that argument.

I show in this chapter that the three well-known objections to the free will defense severely underestimate the resources available to that argument. The *Problem of Sanctified Agents* introduces the modal thesis that, possibly, it is necessary that some essence or other is transworld sanctified.[1] Transworld sanctified essences are such that there are some worlds in which their instantiations *might* always go right.[2] So, it is possible that, necessarily, some essence or other is transworld sanctified only if the thesis of universal transworld depravity is false. Indeed, it is possible that, necessarily, some essence or other is transworld sanctified only if the thesis of universal transworld depravity is *necessarily* false.

---

[1] The notion of possibility here is epistemic possibility of a sort taken up in the forthcoming criticisms.

[2] What we might have expected is that transworld sanctified essences are such that God could not actualize a world in which they go wrong. That would be the natural analogue for transworld depravity and would be defined as follows.

TS$^+$  An essence E enjoys transworld sanctity iff for every world W such that E instantiates the properties *is significantly free* in W and *does at least one thing wrong* in W, and for every state of affairs T and action A such that,

    (1) T is the largest state of affairs God strongly actualizes in W;

    (2) A is morally significant for E's instantiation in W;

    (3) if God had strongly actualized T, E's instantiation would not have gone wrong with respect to A.

The *Problem of Sanctified Agents* is seriously hampered by the implicit assumption that there is a single proposition R suitable to the consistency proof in the free will defense. The problem focuses on a single proposition R as though R alone showed that God's existence is consistent with the existence of evil. In fact there are several modal theses available to the free will defense that are much weaker than the thesis of universal transworld depravity and that are sufficient to resolve the logical problem of evil. The thesis of *intraworld depravity*, for instance, and the thesis of *multiworld depravity* are sufficient to resolve the logical problem of evil. The theses of intraworld depravity and multiworld depravity are much weaker than the thesis of universal transworld depravity and, in addition, are consistent with the thesis of transworld sanctity. They are also consistent with the theses of multiworld sanctity and intraworld sanctity. So the *Problem of Sanctified Agents* has no hope of making it reasonable to refrain from believing that the existence of God is inconsistent with the existence of evil.

The *Problem of Transworld Untrustworthy Agents* advances the stronger modal thesis that, possibly, some essence is necessarily not transworld depraved. The thesis is incompatible with the thesis of universal transworld depravity, but it is consistent with the thesis of intraworld depravity and multiworld depravity. The objection again sorely underestimates the resources available to the free will defense. We can agree that some essence is necessarily not transworld depraved and easily retain the resources to show that the existence of God is consistent with the existence of evil.

The *Problem of Selective Freedom* asserts that, necessarily, God can cause significantly free essences to exemplify the property of *selective significant freedom*. If, necessarily, God can cause an essence to exemplify the property of restricted significant freedom, then, necessarily, God can weakly actualize a *quasi-E-perfect world*. It follows that the thesis of universal transworld depravity is false.

Let an essence E exemplify the property of selective significant freedom in world W if and only if (i) E's instantiation goes right with respect to every significantly free action A in W and (ii) E's instantiation is not libertarian free with respect to some actions A' in W. A possible world W is quasi-E-perfect if and only if E exemplifies selective significant freedom in W.

According to the *Problem of Selective Freedom*, God does not decide once and for all whether his creatures are significantly free. God can make a creature that is free on some occasions and not free on others. Since God knows by foreknowledge or middle knowledge what a creature will do or what he would do were he to freely act on a given occasion, God can grant freedom to a creature when and only when he knows that freedom will not be misused.[3]

Selective significant freedom is supposed to be inconsistent with the thesis of universal transworld depravity. It is also supposed to be inconsistent with the thesis of intraworld depravity and multiworld depravity. But the objection underestimates the resources available to the free will defense. We can agree that God can cause significantly free essences to instantiate the property of selective significant freedom and retain the resources to show that the existence of God is consistent with the existence of evil.

I conclude that these three well-known objections to the free will defense seriously underestimate the argument. The free will defense is a consistency proof. It aims to show that the existence of God is broadly logically consistent with the existence of evil. The best known objections to the free will defense fail to appreciate the number of ways in which the consistency proof can succeed.[4]

## 3.1 The Problem of Sanctified Agents

John Hawthorne and Daniel Howard-Snyder advance an intriguing epistemological argument that we can reasonably refrain from believing that (1) and (2) are consistent.

---

[3] See David Lewis, "Evil for Freedom's Sake" in his *Papers in Ethics and Social Philosophy* (Cambridge: Cambridge University Press, 2000) 119 ff. See also M. J. Almeida, "Transworld Enablers" unpublished manuscript.

[4] It is surprising that the best objections to the free will defense fail to appreciate the variety of ways that the consistency proof can succeed, since Plantinga has been explicit about this. See *The Nature of Necessity* ( Oxford: Oxford University Press, 1974) 189–90.

Of course the conjunctions of (31) [every essence suffers from transworld depravity] with (32) [God actualizes a world containing moral good] is not the only proposition that can play the role of R in the Free Will Defense. Perhaps, for example, it was within the power of God to actualize a world including moral good but no moral evil, but not within his power to actualize one including no moral evil and including as much moral good as the actual world contains. So (33)—for any world W, if W contains no moral evil and W contains as much good as $\alpha$ contains, then God could not have actualized W—(which is weaker than (31)) could be used in conjunction with (34)—God actualizes a world containing as much good as the actual world contains—to show that (1) [God exists] and (2) [there is evil] are consistent.

But of course there are many other possibilities including the thesis of intraworld depravity that are sufficient to prove the consistency.

1. God is omnipotent, omniscient, and wholly good.
2. Evil exists.

According to Hawthorne and Howard-Snyder, the argument that (1) and (2) are consistent depends on the possibility that R is true and consistent with (1).

R. God created a world containing moral good and it was not within his power to create a world containing moral good without creating one containing moral evil.[5]

Hawthorne and Howard-Snyder aim to show that we can reasonably refrain from believing that R is possible and so we can reasonably refrain from believing that (1) and (2) are consistent.

### 3.1.1 Three Problems in Formulation

There are three immediate problems with Hawthorne and Howard-Snyder's epistemological argument that we can reasonably refrain from believing that (1) and (2) are consistent. The initial problem is their choice of a proposition to play the role of R. For all we know, R and (1) are *not* consistent. Suppose R is true and every world with moral good and moral evil is worse than some world with no moral evil. Presumably only a morally imperfect being could actualize an on balance morally bad world with moral good. Since God is essentially not morally imperfect, R and (1) are inconsistent. So, the possibility that R is true is compatible with the fact that R and (1) are not consistent. What must be shown to be possible is not Hawthorne and Howard-Snyder's R but R3.

R3. God actualizes a world that is on balance good and it is not within God's power to actualize a world containing moral good but no moral evil.

If R3 is possible then, possibly, God actualizes a world with moral good and moral evil that is better than any actualizable world with no moral evil. And that seems consistent with God's perfect goodness. Further, R3 and (1) clearly entail (2). If God actualizes an on balance good world and it is

---

[5] See John O'Leary-Hawthorne and Daniel Howard-Snyder, "Transworld Sanctity and Plantinga's Free Will Defense" *International Journal for Philosophy of Religion* (1999) 1–21. On page 4 the claim is a conjunction, but literally they write,

R. God created a world containing moral good; however, it was not within His power to create a world containing moral good without creating one containing moral evil.

not in his power to actualize a world with moral good but no moral evil, then God actualizes a world that contains some evil.

The second problem is that Hawthorne and Howard-Snyder overlook the fact that there are several other propositions that might play the role of R. Each of these propositions is consistent with (1) and together with (1) entail (2). The point really should not have been missed, since Plantinga makes the same observation.

Of course the conjunction of (31) [it is not within God's power to actualize a world containing moral good but no moral evil] and (32) [God actualizes a world that contains moral good] is not the only proposition that can play the role of R in the Free Will Defense. Perhaps, for example, it was within the power of God to actualize a world including moral good but no moral evil, but not within his power to actualize one including no moral evil and including as much moral good as the actual world contains. So,

(33) For any world W, if W contains no moral evil and W includes as much moral good as ∝ contains, then God could not have actualized W.
(which is weaker than (31)) could be used in conjunction with (34),

(34) God actualizes a world containing as much moral good as ∝ contains to show that (1) and (2) are consistent.[6]

Hawthorne and Howard-Snyder's argument fails to observe that there are several other propositions that are consistent with (1) and that, together with (1), entail (2). Presumably, the line of argument is that if it is reasonable to refrain from believing R, then it is reasonable to refrain from believing that (1) is consistent with (2).[7] But that's clearly false.

Finally the epistemological standards that Hawthorne and Howard-Snyder stipulate are too high.

So what's our worry? This: to *show* that [(1)] is compatible with [(2)] is in part an epistemological task; thus, one succeeds at it only if the claims that constitute one's

---

[6] Plantinga, *The Nature of Necessity*, op. cit. pp. 189–90.

[7] See O'Leary-Hawthorne and Howard-Snyder, "Transworld Sanctity and Plantinga's Free Will Defense" op. cit. p. 3.

4. [R3] is possible.
The epistemic amendment implies that a Plantinga-style defense fails if it is reasonable to refrain from believing claim 4, and hence claim 2. The crux of our objection to Plantinga's Free Will Defense is that it is indeed reasonable to refrain from believing his candidate for claim 4.

They are somewhat more cautious in arguing for the claim that it is reasonable to refrain from believing R3. They argue that it is reasonable to refrain from believing R3 if it is reasonable to refrain from believing that universal transworld depravity is possible and the possibility of universal transworld depravity is one's exclusive basis for believing R3.

defense meet certain epistemic standards. Without argument, we lay down this minimal standard: One shows that [(1)] is compatible with [(2)] by deploying a Plantinga-style defense only if *it is not reasonable to refrain* from believing those claims that constitute it.

Call this the *epistemic amendment*.

Hawthorne and Howard-Snyder stipulate without argument that a Plantinga-style defense must meet the "minimal" epistemic standard in (S0).

> S0. It is not reasonable to believe that there is no possible world that includes an omniscient, omnipotent, wholly good being, and an evil state of affairs.

But the hypothesis that there is some world that includes an omniscient, omnipotent, wholly good being, and an evil state of affairs might meet the strong epistemic conditions in (EC0) and still not satisfy the standard in (S0). It depends on the epistemic probability and significance given to alternative hypotheses.[8]

> EC0. It is epistemically much more probable than not that there is some possible world that includes an omniscient, omnipotent, wholly good being and an evil state of affairs.

Improbable modal hypotheses are not hard to imagine. As we have mentioned, it is not difficult to imagine a possible world that includes an *antitheos*. Let an antitheos exist in any world in which there is an evil state of affairs and in no world where there exists an omniscient, omnipotent, and wholly good being. It seems unlikely that an antitheos is possible but I do not *know* that an antitheos is not possible. And since I do not know that an antitheos is not possible, I can reasonably refrain from believing that some possible world includes an omniscient, omnipotent, wholly good being, and an evil state of affairs.

The antitheos hypothesis is a kind of skeptical hypothesis. But so is the hypothesis that, possibly, it is necessary that some essence of other is a transworld sanctified. The transworld sanctified hypothesis is true only if there is no world in which every essence is transworld depraved. But no evidence is adduced for the hypothesis that there might be such an essence in every world other than that we do not know that the transworld sanctified hypothesis is false. It does not seem likely that, possibly, there

---

[8] Compare Chapter 2, Section 2.2.

is a transworld sanctified essence in every world but I do not *know* that the transworld sanctified hypothesis is not true. And since I do not know that transworld sanctified essences do not exist in every world, I can reasonably refrain from believing that there is some possible world in which every essence is transworld depraved.

As we have noted, the skeptic argues that we have no knowledge of the world because we don't know that we are not being massively deceived. It seems extremely unlikely that we are being massively deceived but, on reflection, we do not know that we are not being deceived. But then we can reasonably refrain from believing highly motivated propositions that seem probable. The argument from the possibility of transworld sanctified agents is similarly skeptical. The thesis of universal transworld depravity is well-motivated and probable. But the transworld sanctified hypothesis provides a reason to refrain from believing it.

But then only the highest epistemic probability will ensure that it is unreasonable not to believe that some world includes an omniscient, omnipotent, wholly good being, and an evil state of affairs. There are always imaginable modal hypotheses that function as skeptical hypotheses and make it not unreasonable not to believe there is such a world.

In contexts where skeptical modal hypotheses are introduced, the epistemic standard in (S0) is far too high. Therefore the standard expressed in the epistemic amendment is far too high. No theistic defense could establish with certainty that some world includes an omniscient, omnipotent, wholly good being, and an evil state of affairs.

## 3.2  Sanctified Essences and Depraved Essences

According to Hawthorne and Howard-Snyder the argument for R3 depends on the thesis of universal transworld depravity. But of course, R3 depends on more than the thesis of universal transworld depravity. Universal transworld depravity, as observed above, is consistent with universal transworld ultra-depravity. And every world where universal transworld ultra-depravity is true is a world where R3 is false. An omnipotent, omniscient, wholly good being would create no free and rational beings at all were every individual essence transworld ultra-depraved.

The argument implicitly assumes that if universal transworld depravity is not possible, then R3 is not possible. And it can be difficult to see how the second conjunct of R3 might be true if universal transworld depravity is impossible. According to Hawthorne and Howard-Snyder, if it is possible that, necessarily, some essence or other is transworld sanctified, then it is impossible that every essence is transworld depraved. Transworld sanctification is defined on analogy with transworld depravity.

> TS*. An essence E enjoys transworld sanctity iff for every world W such that E instantiates the properties *is significantly free* in W and *always does what is right* in W, there is no state of affairs T and no action A such that,
>
> (1) T is the largest state of affairs God strongly actualizes in W;
> (2) A is morally significant for E's instantiation in W;
> (3) if God had strongly actualized T, E's instantiation would have gone wrong with respect to A.

"Transworld sanctification" is an unusual name for the property described in TS*. Transworld sanctified essences are not such that their instantiations would always go right in any world in which they were actualized. Transworld sanctification is a contingent property. Let E be a transworld sanctified essence. There are worlds W such that T is the largest strongly actualizable state of affairs in W, God instantiates E in T, and E's instantiation does nothing but terrible wrongs. E is such that there are *some worlds* in which its instantiations *might* always go right.[9] This is consistent with the instantiations of transworld sanctified essences not being especially good even in worlds where they never go wrong and with their instantiations exemplifying extreme evil in other worlds. So the sanctification of such essences need not be in any ordinary sense *transworld*.

As we observed above, for each individual essence E, there is a set of worlds W such that E instantiates the essential properties *is significantly free*

---

[9] What we might have expected is that transworld sanctified essences are such that God could not actualize a world in which they go wrong. That would be the natural analogue for transworld depravity and would be defined as follows.

> TS+ An essence E enjoys transworld sanctity iff for every world W such that E instantiates the properties *is significantly free* in W and *does at least one thing wrong* in W, and for every state of affairs T and action A such that,
>
> (1) T is the largest state of affairs God strongly actualizes in W;
> (2) A is morally significant for E's instantiation in W;
> (3) if God had strongly actualized T, E's instantiation would not have gone wrong with respect to A.

*in W* and *always does what is right in W*. We called that set of worlds the *E-perfect worlds*. The thesis of universal transworld depravity states that, possibly, every essence is transworld depraved. The thesis of universal transworld depravity entails that, possibly, God cannot actualize an E-perfect world. Slightly more technically, universal transworld depravity states that, possibly, for all maximal states of affairs T that God can strongly actualize, and for all E-perfect worlds $W_E$, it is true that $T \; \square \rightarrow \; \sim W_E$.

It should be borne in mind that among the E-perfect worlds in $W_E$ there is a set of morally imperfect worlds $W_I$ where perhaps one or two instantiated essences always go right, and all others always go terribly wrong. Among the E-perfect worlds W there is also a set of morally perfect worlds $W_P$ where *every* instantiated essence always does what is right. The thesis of universal transworld depravity entails that possibly no E-perfect world—whether that world is morally perfect or morally imperfect—is such that it is within God's power to actualize it.

The thesis of transworld sanctity states that, possibly, it is necessary that some essence or other enjoys transworld sanctity. The thesis of transworld sanctity entails that, necessarily, it is not the case that God cannot actualize an E-perfect world.[10] Again, slightly more technically, the thesis of transworld sanctity entails that, necessarily, for some state of affairs T and E-perfect world $W_E$, $\sim(T \; \square \rightarrow \; \sim W_E)$. So the thesis of transworld sanctity is inconsistent with the thesis of universal transworld depravity. But it's another question altogether whether the thesis of transworld sanctity entails that God can actualize a world containing moral good and no moral evil.

The second conjunct of R3, recall, states that it is not within God's power to actualize a world containing moral good and no moral evil. Any world that contains moral good and no moral evil is among the E-perfect worlds, but of course the converse does not hold. There are E-perfect worlds that are among the morally imperfect worlds. It is not within God's power to actualize a world containing moral good and no moral evil if and only if, for all maximal states of affairs T that God can strongly actualize, and for all morally perfect worlds $W_P$, it is true that $\sim(T \; \square \rightarrow \; W_P)$. It is within God's power to actualize a world containing moral good and no moral evil just in case there is some maximal state of affairs T that God can

---

[10] Since we are assuming a version of S5 (a version of S5 that does not validate the Barcan Formula) we know that whatever is possibly necessary is necessary.

strongly actualize such that for some morally perfect world $W_P$ it is true that $T \: \square \rightarrow W_P$.

This result follows from a strengthened version of Lewis's Lemma where $T(W)$ is the largest state of affairs that God can strongly actualize in W and "$G(T(W))$" expresses the proposition that God strongly actualizes T of W.

L. For every world W in which God exists, God could have actualized W if and only if $G(T(W)) \: \square \rightarrow W$.[11]

In the special case we are discussing, it follows from strengthened Lewis's Lemma that God can actualize $W_P$ just in case $G(T(W_P)) \: \square \rightarrow W_P$.

The thesis of transworld sanctity entails that, necessarily, for every state of affairs T and morally perfect world $W_P$, $\sim(T \: \square \rightarrow \sim W_P)$. And in at least Lewis's logics for counterfactuals $\sim(T \: \square \rightarrow W_P)$ is compatible with $\sim(T \: \square \rightarrow \sim W_P)$.[12] It might be true, for instance, that both $(T \: \diamond \rightarrow W_P)$ and $(T \: \diamond \rightarrow \sim W_P)$. So there is some reason to believe that the thesis of transworld sanctity provides no reason to reject R3. The thesis of transworld sanctity is inconsistent with the thesis of universal transworld depravity, but the thesis of universal transworld depravity is stronger than any thesis necessary to establish the second conjunct of R3.

There is in Robert Stalnaker and Richmond Thomason's logic for counterfactual conditionals the principle of conditional excluded middle which states that $(\phi \: \square \rightarrow \psi) \lor (\phi \: \square \rightarrow \sim \psi)$.[13] Since the thesis of transworld sanctity entails that $\sim(T \: \square \rightarrow \sim W_P)$, it follows from the principle of conditional excluded middle that $(T \: \square \rightarrow W_P)$. And from Lewis's Lemma it follows that God can actualize a world that contains moral

[11] See James E. Tomberlin and Peter van Inwagen, *Profiles: Alvin Plantinga* (Dordrecht-Holland: D. Reidel Publishing Co., 1985). In Part I, pp. 50–1, Plantinga provides a proof for the weak version of Lewis's Lemma which states that for every world W in which God exists, God could have weakly actualized W only if $G(T(W)) \: \square \rightarrow W$. The proof left to right assumes that for some A, $G(A) \: \square \rightarrow W$. Since W entails $G(T(W))$, it follows that $G(A) \: \square \rightarrow G(T(W))$ and W includes A. But then $G(T(W)) \: \square \rightarrow G(A)$. And so $G(T(W)) \: \square \rightarrow W$. For right to left we need only assume that $G(T(W))$ does not entail W. To complete a proof for the strengthened version of Lewis's Lemma we only add for our proof right to left that either $G(T(W))$ does not entail W or $G(T(W))$ does entail W. If $G(T(W))$ does not entail W then God can weakly actualize W and if $G(T(W))$ does entail W then God can strongly actualize W.

[12] David Lewis, *Counterfactuals* (Cambridge, Mass.: Harvard University Press, 1973).

[13] Robert Stalnaker, "A Theory of Conditionals" in W. Harper, R. Stalnaker, and G. G. Pearce (eds.) *Ifs* (Dordrecht-Holland: D. Reidel Publishing Company, 1981) 1–56; and Robert Stalnaker and Richmond Thomason, "A Semantic Analysis of Conditional Logic" *Theoria* 36 (1970) 23–32.

good and no moral evil. Since R3 entails $\sim(T \:\square\!\!\rightarrow W_P)$, it is evident that the thesis of transworld sanctity together with the principle of conditional excluded middle is inconsistent with R3. So, we can generate an inconsistency between the thesis of transworld sanctity and R3 if the principle of conditional excluded middle is true.

Plantinga seems to favor the Stalnaker and Thomason analysis of counterfactuals and offers this intuitive argument for the principle of conditional excluded middle.

> We do not know, after all, whether Curley would have accepted the bribe,—it is a fairly small one and perhaps his pride would have been injured. Let us ask instead whether he would have accepted a bribe of $36,000, everything else being as much as possible like the actual world. Here the answer seems fairly clear: indeed he would have. And this despite the fact that for any possible world W as close as you please to $a$ where Curley takes the bribe, there is a world $W^\star$ that shares the appropriate initial segment with W in which he manfully refuses it.[14]

Whatever the merits of the argument for conditional excluded middle, Hawthorne and Howard-Snyder don't need anything that strong to generate an inconsistency between transworld sanctity and R3. If conditional excluded middle is not a theorem in the logic of counterfactuals, but holds *contingently* for the sorts of cases under consideration, then transworld sanctity will be inconsistent with R3. We have the counterfactual theorem, $[((\phi \:\square\!\!\rightarrow \psi) \vee (\phi \:\square\!\!\rightarrow \sim\!\psi)) \: \& \: \sim\!(\phi \:\square\!\!\rightarrow \sim\!\psi)] \:\square\!\!\rightarrow (\phi \:\square\!\!\rightarrow \psi)$ which makes the inference from contingent conditional excluded middle $(T \:\square\!\!\rightarrow W_P) \vee (T \:\square\!\!\rightarrow \sim\!W_P)$ and transworld sanctity $\sim\!(T \:\square\!\!\rightarrow \sim\!W_P)$ to $(T \:\square\!\!\rightarrow W_P)$ valid. So, if conditional excluded middle is contingently true—true in at least the worlds relevant to the objection from transworld sanctity—then it is within God's power to actualize a world containing moral good but no moral evil. And it follows that R3 and the thesis of universal transworld depravity are both false.

Of course it is not obvious that contingent conditional excluded middle is true, either. In general we know that a transworld sanctified agent might go right with respect to each morally significant action A, so it is false that they would go wrong with respect to A. But why believe that in general transworld sanctified agents would go right with respect to each morally significant action A? Agents that would go right with respect to each morally significant action A are perhaps better characterized as *transworld super-sanctified agents*.

---

[14] Plantinga, *The Nature of Necessity*, op. cit. p. 176 ff.

According to Hawthorne and Howard-Snyder it is not unreasonable to believe the thesis of transworld sanctity. On the assumption of conditional excluded middle, the thesis of transworld sanctity is inconsistent with R3 and the thesis of universal transworld depravity. So they conclude that it is not unreasonable to refrain from believing the thesis of universal transworld depravity. And so, by the epistemic standards stipulated in the epistemic amendment, they reach the conclusion that Plantinga's defense against the logical problem of evil fails.

## 3.3  Universal Transworld Depravity, Super-Sanctified Essences, and the Challenge of Evil

The thesis that, possibly, it is necessary that some essence or other is transworld sanctified seems an improbable modal hypothesis. But on prevailing epistemic standards this improbable modal thesis entails that we can reasonably refrain from believing the thesis of universal transworld depravity. Of course, on these standards, we could reasonably refrain from believing the thesis of universal transworld depravity even if the probability of universal transworld depravity were very high. So certainly we could reasonably reject the epistemic standards encoded in the epistemic amendment.

If the thesis of transworld sanctity and the principle of conditional excluded middle are true, then, necessarily, God can actualize a morally perfect world. God can actualize a world in which the instantiation of a transworld sanctified essence is significantly free and always goes right. But, even conceding the principle of conditional excluded middle, the thesis of transworld sanctity does not entail that the proposition that (1) there is an omnipotent, omniscient, wholly good being is inconsistent with the proposition that (2) evil exists.

Suppose we could be assured that God can actualize a morally perfect world whether or not the principle of conditional excluded middle is true. Suppose that every transworld sanctified essence is a *transworld super-sanctified essence*. And suppose transworld super-sanctified essences all satisfy TSS.

TSS.  An essence E enjoys transworld super-sanctity if and only if for every world W such that E instantiates the properties *is significantly free* in W and *does at least one thing wrong* in W, and for every state of affairs T and action A such that,

(1) T is the largest state of affairs God strongly actualizes in W;

(2) A is morally significant for E's instantiation in W;

(3) if God had strongly actualized T, E's instantiation would have gone right with respect to A.[15]

We are assuming that all transworld sanctified essences are transworld super-sanctified essences. According to TSS, any world in which God instantiates a transworld super-sanctified essence E, E's instantiation always goes right. Call the set of worlds in which all and only transworld super-sanctified essences are instantiated E*-perfect worlds. We can combine the thesis of transworld sanctity with the auxiliary principle in P0 to prove the inconsistency of (1) and (2).

P0. Necessarily, *every* actualizable E*-perfect world is better than *any* actualizable non-E*-perfect world and an omniscient and wholly good being actualizes an E*-perfect world.

The thesis of transworld sanctity together with P0 does entail that (1) and (2) are inconsistent. Every actualizable E*-perfect world contains instantiations of all and only transworld sanctified essences, so every instantiation in any E*-perfect world always goes morally right. But P0 is surely false. Certainly it is possible that God can actualize some non-E*-perfect world that is better than some E*-perfect world he can actualize. Consider an E*-perfect world in which every instantiated sanctified essence brings about some small moral good. There might be some better non-E*-perfect world in which every instantiated essence brings about some small evil but otherwise brings about great goods. The thesis of transworld sanctity together with P0 does entail that (1) and (2) are inconsistent. But the principle in P0 is false.

But then consider the principle P1 according to which *some* actualizable E*-perfect world is better than *any* actualizable non-E*-perfect world.

P1. Necessarily, *some* actualizable E*-perfect world is better than *any* actualizable non-E*-perfect world and an omniscient and wholly good being actualizes an E*-perfect world.

---

[15] The notion of a transworld supersantified agent is due to Michael Bergmann. See his "Might-Counterfactuals, Transworld Untrustworthiness and Plantinga's Free Will Defense" *Faith and Philosophy* 16 (1999) note 15.

The thesis of transworld sanctification and P1 also entails that (1) and (2) are inconsistent. In some E★-perfect worlds instantiated essences always go right, but do not produce much moral good. On the other hand, certainly, some E★-perfect worlds include a great deal of moral good. It might be true that some E★-perfect worlds are among the best worlds.

Let's suppose some E★-perfect world is among the best worlds. The thesis of transworld sanctity—continuing with the assumption of transworld super-sanctity—ensures that, necessarily, some E★-perfect world is actualizable. But it does not ensure that, necessarily, *every* E★-perfect world is actualizable. In particular it does not ensure that a best world is actualizable. Since transworld sanctity is a contingent property it is perfectly possible that very few essences exemplify transworld sanctity. If, for instance, there is a single essence that is transworld sanctified, God cannot actualize an E★-perfect world in which more than one transworld sanctified essence is instantiated. There might be any number of actualizable non-E★-perfect worlds that are better than an E★-perfect world that includes a single instantiated transworld sanctified essence. So P1 is clearly false.

But certainly every world will include, in addition to transworld sanctified essences, *multiworld sanctified essences* or *intraworld sanctified essences*. Let the thesis of multiworld sanctified essences state that possibly, it is necessary that some essence or other is multiworld sanctified. Let a multiworld sanctified essence be an essence that satisfies the conditions in MS.

> MS. An essence E is multiworld sanctified if and only if for every world W such that E instantiates the properties *is significantly free* in W and *always does what is right* in W, there are *some* states of affairs T such that for *every* action A,
>
> (1) T is the largest state of affairs God strongly actualizes in W;
> (2) A is morally significant for E's instantiation in W;
> (3) if God had strongly actualized T, E's instantiation would have gone right with respect to A.

Under the assumption of transworld super-sanctification, all transworld sanctified agents are multiworld sanctified, but the converse does not hold. There might be several states of affairs T that meet condition (1) and (2) in MS but were God to instantiate a multiworld sanctified essence E in T, then the instantiated essence would go wrong with respect to A and many other actions. Let an essence E be *intraworld sanctified* just in case there is *some unique* state of affairs T such that T meets the condition in (1) and (2) and were E instantiated in T then E's instantiation would always go right.

In addition to the thesis of transworld sanctity, suppose the thesis of multiworld sanctity and the thesis of intraworld sanctity are both true. The thesis of multiworld (intraworld) sanctity states that, possibly, it is necessary that some essence or other is multiworld (intraworld) sanctified.

Now let $S_W$ be the set of worlds in which every instantiated essence is either transworld sanctified or intraworld sanctified or multiworld sanctified. There are some worlds in $S_W$ where every instantiated essence is intraworld sanctified and always goes right. There are also worlds in $S_W$ where some instantiated essences always go right and other instantiated essences do not. Call the worlds in which every intraworld, multiworld, and transworld sanctified essence always goes right $S_W$-*perfect worlds*.

Suppose that, necessarily, some $S_W$-perfect world is the *most valuable* world in which every instantiated sanctified essence always goes right.[16] Such worlds will often include the instantiation of multiworld, intraworld, and transworld sanctified essences. Call the most valuable worlds in which every instantiated sanctified essence always goes right, $S_W\star$-perfect worlds. There will in general be more sanctified essences in $S_W\star$-perfect worlds than $E\star$-perfect worlds.

The thesis of transworld sanctity together with the principle in P2 entails that (1) and (2) are inconsistent.

P2. Necessarily, *every* actualizable $S_W\star$-perfect world is better than *any* actualizable non-$S_W\star$-perfect world and an omniscient and wholly good being actualizes an $S_W\star$-perfect world.

According to P2, necessarily, God actualizes some $S_W\star$-perfect world or other. But P2 is false. The properties of being transworld sanctified or multiworld sanctified or intraworld sanctified are all contingent properties. So, possibly, some $S_W\star$-perfect world contains very few instantiated essences. It is perfectly possible that some $S_W\star$-perfect world contains very little moral value. It is perfectly possible that there are much better actualizable worlds that include some moral evil. So it is not necessary that

---

[16] We are assuming that, necessarily, there is no sequence of better and better $S_W$-perfect worlds.

*every* actualizable $S_W^\star$-perfect world is better than *any* actualizable non-$S_W^\star$-perfect world.

There is a weaker principle according to which, necessarily, *some* actualizable $S_W^\star$-perfect world is better than *any* actualizable non-$S_W^\star$-perfect world.

> P3.  Necessarily, *some* actualizable $S_W^\star$-perfect world is better than *any* actualizable non-$S_W^\star$-perfect world and an omniscient and wholly good being actualizes an $S_W^\star$-perfect world.

The thesis of transworld sanctity together with the principle in P3 entails that (1) and (2) are inconsistent. But the principle in P3 is also false. The best $S_W^\star$-perfect world might include very few instantiated essences that together produce a minimum amount of moral value. There may well be several non-$S_W^\star$-perfect worlds that include no instantiated essence that always goes right, but that are overall much better worlds.

The principles P0–P3 each state that, necessarily, an omniscient, omnipotent, wholly good being actualizes a world containing moral good and no moral evil. The thesis of transworld sanctity together with each of the principles P0–P3 entails that the proposition that (1) there is an omnipotent, omniscient, wholly good being is inconsistent with the proposition (2) evil exists. But each of the principles in P0–P3 is false. We should conclude that the thesis of transworld sanctity does not entail (1) is inconsistent with (2). And the addition of transworld super-sanctified agents, multiworld sanctified agents, and intraworld sanctified agents gets us no closer to showing that (1) and (2) are inconsistent.

## 3.4  Intraworld Depravity and the Challenge of Evil

Let the thesis of intraworld depravity state that possibly, some essences are intraworld depraved. Let's define intraworld depravity as follows.

> ID.  An essence E suffers from *intraworld depravity* iff for some world W such that E instantiates the properties *is significantly free* in W and *always does what is right* in W, there is *some* state of affairs T and *some* action A such that,

(1) T is the largest state of affairs God strongly actualizes in W;

(2) A is morally significant for E's instantiation in W;

(3) if God had strongly actualized T, E's instantiation would have gone wrong with respect to A.

An individual essence E is intraworld depraved just in case there is some maximal state of affairs T and some action A such that A is morally significant for E's instantiation, and were God to actualize T, E's instantiation would go wrong with respect to A. The thesis of intraworld depravity is consistent with the theses of transworld sanctity, multiworld sanctity, and intraworld sanctity. Certainly, there are worlds in which some essences are intraworld depraved.

Let $S_{BI}$ be the set of best worlds at which some instantiated essence is intraworld depraved and goes wrong with respect to some action. Let $S_{BE}$ collect together the best worlds in which every instantiated essence goes right with respect to every action. Every instantiated essence in $S_{BE}$ is either transworld sanctified or intraworld sanctified or multiworld sanctified.

Let's prove the proposition that (1) there is an omnipotent, omniscient, wholly good being is consistent with the proposition that (2) evil exists. (1) and (2) are consistent if there is some proposition that is consistent with (1) and together with (1) entails (2). Consider R4.

R4. God actualizes a world that includes moral evil and it is not within God's power to actualize a better world containing moral good and no moral evil.

Proposition R4 is possibly true and consistent with (1). It is possible that some actualizable world in which some instantiated essence does at least one thing wrong is better than any actualizable world in which no instantiated essence does anything wrong. It is possible that some actualizable world in $S_{DI}$ is better than any actualizable world in $S_{BE}$. But then clearly R4 and (1) entail (2) that evil exists.

The thesis that possibly some essences are intraworld depraved is obviously much weaker than the thesis that possibly every essence is transworld depraved. But the thesis of intraworld depravity is sufficient to show that the existence of evil is compatible with the existence of an omniscient, omnipotent, wholly good being. The weak thesis of intraworld depravity provides an excellent reason for God to actualize a world that includes moral good and moral evil. And that is all the free will defense needs to resolve the logical problem of evil.

## 3.5  Intraworld Depravity and Untrustworthy Essences

There are propositions other than the thesis of transworld sanctity that are inconsistent with the thesis of transworld depravity. The thesis in T0 has been advanced as at least epistemically possible.[17] The possibility described in T0 is a metaphysical possibility.

> T0.  Possibly, some essence is necessarily not transworld depraved.

The thesis in T0 is of course stronger than the thesis of transworld sanctity. It states that possibly, there is some essence that has the essential property of not being transworld depraved. Since individual essences exist in every world, T0 is equivalent to the claim that necessarily there is some essence that is essentially not transworld depraved and also equivalent to the claim that there is some essence that is essentially not transworld depraved.[18]

The thesis in T0 does present a problem for the free will defense, since it is clearly inconsistent with the thesis of universal transworld depravity. And the thesis of universal transworld depravity is the basis for R3. But the thesis in T0 presents no problem at all for the thesis of intraworld depravity. The thesis of intraworld depravity states that possibly some essence or other is intraworld depraved. Given the thesis of intraworld depravity, we know that R4 is possible and that the proposition that (1) there is an omnipotent, omniscient, wholly good being is consistent with the proposition that (2) evil exists.

But consider the much stronger thesis in T1 that, possibly, every significantly free essence is necessarily transworld untrustworthy. The possibility in T1 is metaphysical possibility.

> T1.  It is possible that every significantly free essence is necessarily transworld untrustworthy.

The proposition that, possibly, every significantly free essence is essentially transworld depraved is equivalent to the proposition that, necessarily, every significantly free essence is essentially transworld depraved. This is

---

[17] See Michael Bergmann, "Might-Counterfactuals, Transworld Untrustworthiness and Plantinga's Free Will Defense" *Faith and Philosophy* 16 (1999) 336–51.
[18] Given S5 and the fact that E necessarily exists, we get the following equivalences: necessarily [E is necessarily F ≡ possibly E is necessarily F ≡ necessarily E is necessarily F].

because every possible essence exists in every world. Let's say that an individual essence is transworld untrustworthy just in case it meets the conditions in TU.[19]

> TU. An essence E is transworld untrustworthy if and only if for every world W such that E instantiates the properties *is significantly free* in W and *always does what is right* in W, there is a state of affairs T and an action A such that,
> (1) T is the largest state of affairs God strongly actualizes in W;
> (2) A is morally significant for E's instantiation in W;
> (3) if God had strongly actualized T, E's instantiation *might have* gone wrong with respect to A.

Proposition T1 is inconsistent with the thesis of intraworld depravity. If T1 is true then, necessarily, no individual essence is intraworld depraved. The thesis in T1 is an extremely strong modal claim, but there are some interesting reasons that might be adduced in support of T1.

### 3.5.1 *Libertarian Freedom and Counterfactuals of Freedom*

A moral agent has significant freedom in doing A at a time t if and only if A is morally significant for the agent and the agent's options at t are not logically entailed by any set of propositions describing facts or causal laws holding antecedent to t.[20] A moral agent has significant freedom in doing A at t only if the agent is libertarian free with respect to A. It is not causally determined that the agent performs A and not causally determined that the agent performs ~A.[21]

A morally significant action is simply one that it would be right for the agent to perform and wrong for the agent not to perform, or vice versa.[22] We'll say that Adam has significant freedom in keeping a promise, for instance, if the state of the universe prior to his action does not entail that Adam keeps his promise or that Adam breaks his promise. If U describes

---

[19] Bergmann, "Might-Counterfactuals," op. cit. p. 38 ff.

[20] There are important restrictions on this analysis of significant freedom. These are discussed in what follows.

[21] I do not here assume any specific sort of libertarian freedom: e.g., event-causal, deliberative, agent causal, etc. For a full discussion of the alternatives, see Randolph Clarke, *Libertarian Accounts of Free Will* (Oxford: Oxford University Press, 2003).

[22] See M. J. Almeida, "A Paradox for Significant Freedom" *International Journal for Philosophy of Religion* (2003) 175–84.

the total state of the universe holding up until time t in a world w then the general conditions of significant freedom in w are given in S0.

S0:   S has significant freedom in doing A at t if and only if (i) A is morally significant for S at t and (ii) $\sim\Box$(U $\supset$ S does A at t) & $\sim\Box$(U $\supset$ S does $\sim$A at t).

According to S0, S has significant freedom in doing A just in case the state of the universe at t does not entail that S does A at t and the state of the universe at t does not entail that S fails to do A at t. In short, S's doing A at t and S's failing to do A at t are both compatible with a single past summed up in U.

We'll say that God creates a moral agent that has significant freedom in doing A at t if and only if A is morally significant for the agent and the agent's options at t are not logically entailed by the largest state of affairs that God can strongly actualize. If God strongly actualizes the largest state of affairs T, for instance, and Adam freely breaks his promise, then there is some world in which God strongly actualizes the same state of affairs T and Adam keeps his promise. If T is the largest state of affairs that God strongly actualizes in a world W then the general conditions of significant freedom in W are given in S1.

S1.   S has significant freedom in doing A at t if and only if (i) A is morally significant for S at t and (ii) $\sim\Box$(God actualizes T $\supset$ S does A at t) & $\sim\Box$(God actualizes T $\supset$ S does $\sim$A at t).

According to S1 a moral agent S has significant freedom to do A at t if and only if God's actualizing T does not entail that S does A at t and God's actualizing T does not entail that S does $\sim$A at t. Suppose we enumerate the worlds in which God actualizes T as follows $W_0$, $W_1$, $W_2, \ldots, W_n$. Call these possible worlds T-worlds. Each T-world also contains a largest state of affairs F that includes the free actions of agents in those worlds. For each T-world, then, there is the largest state of affairs that God can cause T and the largest state of affairs resulting from the free actions of agents F. Let's assume that S0 and S1 are correct and that moral agent S has significant freedom to do A at t. Since S has significant freedom we know there is some T-world $W_0$ in which S does A at t and another T-world $W_1$ in which S does $\sim$A at t.

The worlds $W_0$ and $W_1$ are exactly alike with respect to the states of affairs T that God strongly actualizes. And worlds $W_0$ and $W_1$ are exactly alike with respect to the state of universe U obtaining prior to t in each world. We will say that $W_0$ and $W_1$ are worlds that branch off the same past at t. So it certainly seems that, just prior to t, $W_0$ is as similar as $W_1$—and generally as similar as any other T-world—to the actual world $a$. But then the counterfactuals of freedom in C0 and C1 both seem false.

C0.  God strongly actualizes state of affairs T $\square\!\rightarrow$ S freely does A at t.
C1.  God strongly actualizes state of affairs T $\square\!\rightarrow$ S freely does ~A at t.

The counterfactual C0 is true if and only if all of the most similar T-worlds to $a$ are also (perhaps according to some salient similarity relation) A-worlds. C1 is true if and only if all of the most similar T-worlds to $a$ are also (again, perhaps according to some salient similarity relation) ~A-worlds. But it seems that some of the most similar T-worlds to $a$ are A-worlds and some of the most similar T-worlds to $a$ are ~A-worlds. So neither C0 nor C1 are true. The conclusion holds generally. So, necessarily, for all states of affairs T, libertarian free agents S and significantly free actions A, C0 and C1 are false.

But if, necessarily, for all states of affairs T, free agents S and significantly free actions A, C0 and C1 are false, then there is no possible world in which any individual essence is intraworld depraved or, for that matter, transworld depraved or multiworld depraved. Thesis T1 is true and every significantly free essence is necessarily transworld untrustworthy. But then the thesis of universal transworld depravity is necessarily false and so is the thesis of intraworld depravity.

## 3.5.2 Chance and Counterfactuals

There are chancy propositions that do not involve God's foreknowledge. Consider the case of Fred who always takes his hat when it is raining.[23] It is raining today and he takes his hat. On days when it is not raining, there is a 0.5 chance that he takes his hat. Consider C2.

C2.  It was not raining $\square\!\rightarrow$ Fred took his hat.

It is difficult to tell whether C2 is true, since there is variation in the chances that Fred takes his hat depending on the particular states of affairs

[23] See Dorothy Edgington, "Counterfactuals and the Benefits of Hindsight" in Phil Dowe and Paul Noordhof (eds.) *Cause and Chance: Causation in an Indeterministic World* (London: Routledge, 2004). The Fred example is attributed to Paul Tichy, "A Counterexample to the Stalnaker–Lewis Analysis of Counterfactuals" *Philosophical Studies* (1976) 29: 271–3.

that obtain. There is no doubt a set of worlds in all or most of which it is not raining and Fred takes his hat. These might be those worlds where it is true that Fred is going to work or it is the weekend or it is a day on which Fred has a meeting to attend, etc. Suppose that on days when it is not raining and Fred is going to work, there is a 0.95 chance that he takes his hat, and suppose it is a work day. In that case C2 seems true, and that's enough to show that T1 is false.

The classical law of bivalence ensures that future contingent propositions, including chancy propositions, are either true or false.[24] A chancy proposition is roughly any proposition that has some objective probability of being true. God knows all true propositions including all true chancy propositions. So, the fact that there are chancy propositions does not diminish God's foreknowledge. But consider a world in which a very chancy proposition is true.

Suppose the chances that an exactly 6′ 2.23322″ Dane exists is approximately zero. But suppose it's true that tomorrow there will be a 6′ 2.23322″ Dane. Despite the chanciness of the consequent, we are not inclined to argue that the counterfactual in C3 is false.

C3.  Otto flies to Denmark tomorrow $\square\!\!\rightarrow$ there is a 6′ 2.233220″ Dane.

The proposition that there is a 6′ 2.233220″ Dane is extremely improbable. But that is insufficient to render C3 false. The well-known *Preface Paradox* yields a similar conclusion.

A meticulous historian writes a long book full of separate factual claims. Given human fallibility, it is almost inevitable that the book will contain errors somewhere or other, for any of which she apologizes in the preface. Nevertheless, she competently deduces the conjunction of all the separate claims in the book (excluding the preface) from its conjuncts and believes it on that basis. As it happens, she does in fact know each conjunct. Therefore, by closure, she knows the conjunction.[25]

It is very improbable that the closure of the conjuncts is true. But if it is true that the historian writes the book and true that the historian knows the closure of the conjuncts, then C4 is true.

---

[24] See Timothy Williamson, "Probability and Danger" *The Amherst Lecture in Philosophy* (2009) 4: 1–35.

[25] See Timothy Williamson, "Replies to my Critics" in Patrick Greenough and Duncan Pritchard (eds.) *Williamson on Knowledge* (Oxford: Oxford University Press, 2009) 279–304.

C4.  The historian writes the book $\square \rightarrow$ the closure of the conjuncts is true.

The closest worlds where she writes the book can include no gratuitous differences from the actual world. But in the actual world she writes the book and makes no mistake in any conjunct. Worlds where she makes a mistake in writing the book include gratuitous differences from the actual world. So there is no closest world where the historian does not know the closure of the propositions forming her book.

We should reach similar conclusions for more familiar indeterministic events. Consider C5.

C5.  I toss the die $\square \rightarrow$ it comes up 5.

There is perhaps some intuition that if I toss the die and it does come up 5, C5 is nonetheless false. Plantinga expresses some reservations about C5.

I toss the die. It comes up 5. That is not sufficient to entail that if I had tossed the die, it would have come up 5.[26]

But what affects intuitions about C5 is the fact that "tossing the die" belongs to various reference classes.[27] If we abstract away from various properties of the toss—for instance, the velocity, angle, spin, and direction of the toss—then the reference class of tossing the die includes many instances of tossing the die that are not a instances of throwing 5. But if I actually toss the die and it comes up 5, then the reference class of tossing the die includes all of the actual properties of the toss—for instance, the actual velocity, angle, spin, and direction of the toss. In that reference class the toss (nearly) always has the property of being a throwing of 5. Indeed, it is perfectly possible to design a machine that tosses fair die that always (or nearly always) come up 5. Worlds where the die does not land 5 include gratuitous differences from the actual world. So there is no closest world where I toss the coin precisely as I in fact tossed it and it does not land 5.

There are two objections to the inference from A & B to A $\square \rightarrow$ B. One objection urges that, in cases where it is unintuitive to assert that A and B are counterfactually related, B might be false in some A-worlds that are more similar to the actual world than the actual world is to itself. This

[26] Alvin Plantinga, "*Respondeo*" in Jon Kvanvig (ed.) *Warrant in Contemporary Epistemology Essays in Honor of Plantinga's Theory of Knowledge* (Lanham: Rowman & Littlefield, 1996) 307–78.
[27] See Alan Hajek, "The reference class problem is your problem too" *Synthese* (2007) 563–85.

objection does not have much to recommend it. No world is *more* similar to any world than that world is to itself.

A second objection urges that, in cases where it is unintuitive to assert that A and B are counterfactually related, B might be false in some A-worlds that are as similar to the actual world as the actual world is to itself. To accommodate the second objection it is argued that we must make the assumption of weak centering in the semantics for counterfactuals according to which some worlds are as similar to the actual world as the actual world is to itself. But consider the counterfactual conditional in C6.

C6.  Smith plays baseball tomorrow $\Box \rightarrow$ Napoleon loses at Waterloo.

Suppose it is true that Smith plays baseball tomorrow. The second objection should deny that C5 is true on the grounds that Smith's playing baseball has no counterfactual relation to Napoleon losing at Waterloo. But even on weak centering the antecedent and consequent are true throughout all of the closest worlds. Why would it be non-gratuitously true in some of the closest worlds where Smith plays baseball tomorrow that Napoleon does not lose at Waterloo? So now the objection must include the reservation that some counterfactuals are not true even in cases where the consequent is true throughout all of the closest antecedent worlds. That is a different problem entirely. Whatever the second objection amounts to, it is not specifically an objection to the inference from A & B to A $\Box \rightarrow$ B.

There is no convincing argument that counterfactuals that include undetermined consequents are false. We found no reason to deny that the counterfactuals in C2–C6 are true, though they all include chancy consequents. We have no better reason to deny that either C0 or C1 is true, though each includes an undetermined consequent. But if we have no reason to deny that either C1 or C0 is true, then of course we have no compelling objection to the thesis of intraworld depravity.

## 3.6  The Problem of Selective Significant Freedom

According to the *Problem of Selective Freedom*, necessarily, God can cause significantly free essences to exemplify the property of *selective significant freedom*. Let an essence E exemplify the contingent property of selective significant freedom in world W if and only if (i) E's instantiation goes right with respect to every action A in W for which it is significantly free, (ii) E's instantiation is not libertarian free with respect to some morally significant actions A' in W and (iii) E's instantiation is significantly free with respect to some actions A in W.

Let the thesis of selective significant freedom state that, necessarily, God can cause every significantly free essence to exemplify the property of being selectively significantly free. Essences that exemplify the property of selective significant freedom are such that their instantiations are significantly free with respect to some morally significant actions and not significantly free with respect to other morally significant actions. If an essence E exemplifies selective significant freedom in world W then with respect to every action A that E's instantiation performs in W either A is morally right and God causes E's instantiation to perform A or A is right and E's instantiation is significantly free with respect to A. So, if an essence E exemplifies selective significant freedom in W then E's instantiation goes right (though not always freely) with respect to every morally significant action in W.

But if an essence E exemplifies selective significant freedom in W then W is not a morally perfect world. In morally perfect worlds no instantiated essence is such that God causes it to perform morally right actions or prevents it from performing morally wrong actions. Still we know that E exemplifies selective significant freedom in W only if E's instantiation always goes right in W. Call a world in which E is selectively significantly free a *quasi-E-perfect world*.

Selective significant freedom is incompatible with the thesis of universal transworld depravity. It is also incompatible with the thesis of intraworld depravity and multiworld depravity. God can instantiate essences that are significantly free on some occasions and that are not significantly free on other occasions. Since God knows either by foreknowledge or by middle knowledge what an instantiated essence would do were it to freely act on a given occasion, God can grant significant freedom to a creature when and only when that creature would go morally right.

*3.6.1 Selective Significant Freedom and Universal Transworld Depravity*

If, necessarily, God can cause every significantly free essence to exemplify the property of *selective significant freedom*, then the thesis of universal transworld depravity is false. But can it be shown that, necessarily, God can cause significantly free essences to exemplify the property of *selective significant freedom*?

Consider the following argument that possibly God *cannot* cause every significantly free essence to exemplify the property of selective significant freedom.

The counterfactuals of freedom say what the free creatures would do in various circumstances; and among the circumstances are God's granting and withholding freedom. They just might say that the more God withholds freedom so as to prevent evil, the more evil would be done on the remaining occasions when creatures are left free. For example, we could have a pattern of counterfactuals saying that a certain man would do evil on the first, and only the first, of the days when he is left free. It is useless then for God to withhold freedom on day one—that would only put off the evil day. Given this pattern, the only way God can prevent him from doing evil is to withhold freedom all the days of his life. Selective freedom doesn't work.[28]

The modal thesis in this argument is much stronger than the thesis of universal transworld depravity. The thesis of universal transworld depravity states that possibly, every significantly free essence E is such that were E instantiated in any maximal state of affairs T, E's instantiation would do something wrong. But this argument assumes that, possibly, every significantly free essence E is such that were E instantiated in any maximal state of affairs T, E's instantiation would go wrong with respect to the first, and only the first, day on which it is significantly free. Call that *Universal Day-One Depravity*. To ensure that each instantiation goes wrong on the first day on which it is significantly free, there must be infinitely many true counterfactuals of creaturely freedom for each essence whose antecedents specify every possible way in which its instantiation might fail to be significantly free and whose consequents state that it would go wrong on the very next day that it is significantly free.

To show that the thesis of universal day-one depravity is false, we need a situation C that God could have actualized in any world in which he exists and in which it is false for some significantly free essence E that were E instantiated in C, then E would go wrong on the first day. Let E be a significantly free essence and assume for reductio that E suffers from universal day-one depravity in world W. Let E be instantiated near the end of day one and let E's instantiation face one last morally significant

---

[28] See Lewis, "Evil for Freedom's Sake," op. cit. p. 19.

action. E's instantiation faces a thousand levers only one of which is such that, were the lever pulled downward, a thousand people would not be rescued. The remaining levers are such that were they pulled downward, everyone would be rescued. Imagine that if E's instantiation pulls no lever, then again everyone would be rescued. The choices are to randomly pull a lever or pull no lever at all. It is evidently false that were E's instantiation to act in this situation, then he would do something wrong.

There are other reasons to believe that the thesis of universal day-one depravity is false. Let a *transworld enabler* be someone or something that provides an occasion or opportunity for the wrongdoing of those who are transworld depraved. In the absence of transworld enablers, it is difficult to see how much of the wrongdoing of the transworld depraved could get accomplished. If Sam had not deliberately provoked Sue, Sue would never have dented his car. If Smith hadn't arrived drunk, Jones would never have punched him. The fact that there are transworld enablers generates a serious problem for the thesis of universal day-one depravity. Even if every essence is day-one transworld depraved, the proposition in D is necessarily true.

> D. There is a feasible world W in which there exists one significantly free being that performs a single wrong action near the end of day one.

But if D is necessarily true, then it seems universal day-one depravity is false.[29] That is, if necessarily there is an actualizable world W in which there exists just one significantly free being that performs a single wrong action near the end of his life, then God can actualize a world in which no one does anything wrong on day one.

Of course, we do not assume that God can actualize an essence that has the property of selective significant freedom. But God might interfere with the *non-significantly free actions* of transworld enablers. Consider the feasible world W under the assumption that every essence is day-one transworld depraved. Let W be a world in which God creates a single significantly free being—viz. Jim—that goes through most of day one doing nothing wrong. The only moral evil that happens in W is a harm to a sentient, non-human being. Toward the end of his life, Jim is lying in bed sleeping. A few feral dogs startle him out of a restful sleep. In an unusual fit of anger Jim rushes to the yard and kills the two dogs as the clock strikes 12 midnight.

---

[29] Still, a defender of universal transworld depravity should have a serious reservation about the argument to follow. See Section 3.6.3 below.

Now it is true in W that God might have interfered with the actions of the feral dogs. God might have delayed them or otherwise caused them to go in some direction away from Jim's home. God could have brought it about that the dogs did not awaken Jim. So C1 seems true in W.

>C1.  Had God caused the feral dogs not to awaken Jim, then Jim would have done nothing wrong on day one.

A defender of universal day-one depravity must deny C1. But there aren't any credible alternatives to C1. Consider C2.

>C2.  Had God caused the feral dogs not to awaken Jim, then it would have been true that Jim did something wrong earlier in the day.

The counterfactual C2 is a backtracking counterfactual. According to backtracking counterfactuals, the way things are in the past counterfactually depends on the way things are in the future. But backtracking counterfactuals are not true except in very special circumstances, and there are no special circumstances surrounding C2. So we have no reason to believe that it's true. But then consider A1.

>A1.  God could not have brought about the world W.

But the world W is perfectly consistent with the thesis of universal day-one depravity. So A1 also seems false. Consider A2.

>A2.  God could have brought about W, but God could not have interfered with the feral dogs.

There is no reason to believe that God could not have interfered with the feral dogs. So we have a case in which an essence E is significantly free on day one and E's instantiation performs no morally wrong actions on day one. The thesis of universal day-one depravity is false.[30]

But consider the thesis of *Universal Act-One Depravity*. Universal act-one depravity states that, possibly, every significantly free essence E is such that were E instantiated in any maximal state of affairs T, E's instantiation would go wrong with respect to the first, and only the first, action for which it is significantly free. Paraphrasing the argument above we might observe that,

---

[30]  If successful, this is also a counterexample to universal transworld depravity.

It is useless then for God to withhold freedom for the first action—that would only put off the evil action. Given this pattern, the only way God can prevent him from doing evil is to withhold freedom for every action. Selective freedom doesn't work.

But it is not credible that any essence should have the property of universal act-one depravity. The first action for which an essence is significantly free might not be one with respect to which E's instantiation would go wrong. God could place any two essences in an interpersonal dilemma, for instance, where each could go wrong by doing A and not both could go wrong by doing A. God might instantiate you and I, for instance, in circumstances where our first significantly free action involves either stealing the key to the office or not stealing the key. We can each steal the key, but we cannot both steal it.

So it is not possible that every significantly free essence E is such that were E instantiated in any maximal state of affairs T, E's instantiation would go wrong with respect to the first, and only the first, action for which it is significantly free. The thesis of universal act-one depravity is false.

The argument does not show that, possibly, God cannot actualize a world in which every essence exemplifies selective significant freedom. It aims to show instead that possibly every actualizable world containing only selectively significantly free essences is worse than some world containing some essences that are not selectively significantly free.

## 3.6.2 Selective Significant Freedom and R3

Suppose that, necessarily, God can cause any significantly free essence to exemplify the contingent property of selective significant freedom. Call that the thesis of *Selective Significant Freedom*. The problem of selective significant freedom states that the thesis of selective significant freedom is true and it is inconsistent with the theses of universal transworld depravity, multiworld depravity, intraworld depravity, and also inconsistent with the proposition in R3. Recall that the proposition in R3 states the following.

> R3. God actualizes a world that is on balance good and it is not within God's power to actualize a world containing moral good but no moral evil.

The thesis of selective significant freedom is inconsistent with R3, since necessarily God can actualize a quasi-E-perfect world in which there is moral good and no moral evil. But as we noted above, R3 is not necessary to the free will defense. R4 is also suitable for the free will defense and the thesis of selective significant freedom is consistent with R4.

> R4. God actualizes a world that includes moral evil and it is not within God's power to actualize a better world containing moral good and no moral evil.

Using R4 it is easy to prove that (1) there is an omnipotent, omniscient, wholly good being is consistent with (2) evil exists. R4 is consistent with (1) and together with (1) entails (2). But let's show that R4 is also consistent with the thesis of selective significant freedom.

It is possible that some actualizable world in which some instantiated essence does at least one thing wrong is better than any actualizable world in which no instantiated essence does anything wrong. Consider, for instance, a possible world in which at least some essences suffer from intraworld depravity. Recall that intraworld depraved essences satisfy the conditions in ID.

> ID. An essence E suffers from *intraworld depravity* iff for some world W such that E instantiates the properties *is significantly free* in W and *always does what is right* in W, there is *some* state of affairs T and *some* action A such that,
>
> (1) T is the largest state of affairs God strongly actualizes in W;
> (2) A is morally significant for E's instantiation in W;
> (3) if God had strongly actualized T, E's instantiation would have gone wrong with respect to A.

So, an intraworld depraved essence E is such that there is at least one E-perfect world W that God cannot actualize. This is of course consistent with there being lots of E-perfect worlds that God can actualize. Let $W'$ be an $E_1$-perfect world and an $E_2$-imperfect world in which $E_1$'s instantiation mercifully adopts an attitude of complete forgiveness for $E_2$'s grave transgression against him. It might be true that $W'$ is better than any other actualizable world that does not include the conjunctive state of affairs of $E_1$'s forgiving $E_2$'s transgression and $E_2$ transgressing against $E_1$.

If, possibly, $W'$ is better than any other actualizable world that does not include the conjunctive state of affairs of $E_1$'s forgiving $E_2$'s transgression and $E_2$ transgressing against $E_1$, then possibly R4 is true. God actualizes a world that includes moral evil and it is not within God's power to actualize a better world containing moral good and no moral evil. Since we have conceded the thesis of selective significant freedom, it is true at W' that God could have actualized a world W that includes moral good and no moral evil. But it is also true at W' that God could not have actualized a world W that is better than W' and that includes moral good and no moral evil. So the thesis of selective significant freedom presents no serious problem for the free will defense.

There are other possibilities. The thesis of selective significant freedom is consistent with a pattern of counterfactual dependence among essences that ensures that, for each selectively significantly free essence E, and any maximal state of affairs T in which E is instantiated, were God to instantiate E in T, E's instantiation $E_1$ would not bring about much good at all. So it might be true that some actualizable world W in which some individual essences are not selectively significantly free is better than any actualizable world W' in which every individual essence is selectively significantly free. It is true at W that God could have actualized a world W' that includes moral good and no moral evil. But it is also true at W that God could not have actualized a world W' that is as good as W and that includes moral good and no moral evil. So the thesis of selective significant freedom presents no serious problem for the free will defense.

### 3.6.3 A Final Argument Against Selective Significant Freedom

The thesis of universal transworld depravity entails that possibly every significantly free essence is transworld depraved. Recall that transworld depravity for essences is defined in TD★.

>   TD★. An essence E suffers from transworld depravity iff for every world W such that E instantiates the properties *is significantly free* in W and *always does what is right* in W, there is a state of affairs T and an action A such that,
>
>   (1) T is the largest state of affairs God strongly actualizes in W;
>   (2) A is morally significant for E's instantiation in W;
>   (3) if God had strongly actualized T, E's instantiation would have gone wrong with respect to A.

But TD★ entails that there is literally no maximal state of affairs T such that God strongly actualizes T and some essence instantiated in T always goes right. For every maximal state of affairs T there are infinitely many maximal states of affairs F such that T ∪ F is a possible world W. The states of affairs in F are those actualized by significantly free instantiated essences and also the result of undetermined events. If every significantly free essence is transworld depraved, then for each T that God can strongly actualize, there is no more than some proper subset of the maximal states of affairs $F^*$ of F that God can actualize. But it is also true that if every significantly free essence is transworld depraved, then for each maximal state of affair T that God can strongly actualize, there is no more than some proper subset $F^*$ of F that each instantiated essence $E_n$ can weakly actualize.

If universal transworld depravity is true, then for any maximal state of affairs T and for any essence $E_n$ instantiated in T, there is simply no state of affairs P in T such that were God to strongly actualize P in T then $E_n$ would never go wrong. But then it follows from universal transworld depravity that there is no pattern of *evil prevention* P such that were God to strongly actualize P in some maximal state of affairs T, some instantiated essence $E_n$ would never go wrong.

Further, if universal transworld depravity is true, then for any maximal state of affairs T, and for any essence $E_n$ instantiated in T, there is simply no state of affairs P in F such that were $E_n$ to strongly actualize P in F then $E_n$ would never go wrong. Under the assumption of universal transworld depravity, it does not matter how often $E_n$ prevents herself from going wrong—it does not matter what pattern of evil-prevention $E_n$ instantiates in F—$E_n$ would do something wrong. But then it follows from universal transworld depravity that there is no pattern of evil prevention P such that were $E_n$ to strongly actualize P in some maximal state of affairs F, $E_n$ would never go wrong. Universal transworld depravity entails that $E_n$ would do at least one thing wrong in F were God to instantiate $E_n$ in T.

According to the thesis of selective significant freedom, necessarily, God can cause every significantly free essence to exemplify the property of being selectively significantly free. If universal transworld depravity is possible, then the thesis of selective significant freedom is false. There are at least some worlds in which neither God nor any significantly free essence $E_n$ can actualize even a quasi-$E_n$-perfect world.

# 4

# Unrestricted Actualization, Freedom, and Morally Perfect Worlds

## 4.0 Introduction

In this chapter, I argue that, for all the resilience of the free will defense, the thesis of universal transworld depravity is necessarily false. And so are the weaker modal theses of multiworld depravity and intraworld depravity. It is a basic assumption in the free will defense that there are two senses in which God can bring it about that an instantiated essence $E_n$ performs an action A. God can *strongly actualize* the state of affairs of $E_n$ performing A. And God can *weakly actualize* the state of affairs of $E_n$ performing A.

It is true that, necessarily, God can strongly actualize the state of affairs of $E_n$ performing A. But if God strongly actualizes the state of affairs of $E_n$ performing A, then $E_n$ does not freely perform A. Paradigmatically God can cause $E_n$ to perform A by direct intervention or God can cause $E_n$ to perform A by putting $E_n$ in a deterministic universe where the laws and history cause $E_n$ to perform A. Presumably God could also cause $E_n$ to perform A by having other instantiated essences coerce or force $E_n$ to perform A or by installing a Frankfurt style device in $E_n$ that notifies a manipulator every time $E_n$ has decided to act wrongly.

It is also true that, possibly, God can weakly actualize the state of affairs of $E_n$ performing A. And if God weakly actualizes the state of affairs of $E_n$ performing A, then $E_n$ *freely performs* A. Paradigmatically God can create a significantly free being $E_n$ in an indeterministic world W where $E_n$ would freely perform A were God to strongly actualize the maximal state of affairs T in W.

But there are at least two other senses in which God can bring it about that an instantiated essence $E_n$ performs an action A. It is true that, possibly, God can strongly actualize a maximal state of affairs T which includes, for instance, God *announcing* that $E_n$ performed A yesterday. And, necessarily, God announces that $E_n$ performed A yesterday only if $E_n$ performed A. What's ruled out, it might be urged, is God's announcing that $E_n$ performed A yesterday in worlds where it is false that $E_n$ performed A.[1] Call that *restricted actualization*. Restricted actualization ensures that, possibly, God can strongly actualize a state of affairs T such that, necessarily, T only if God actualizes a morally perfect world. But God cannot strongly actualize T in every world unrestrictedly.

It is also true that, necessarily, God can strongly actualize the state of affairs T that includes the state of affairs of God's having *predicted or prophesied* that $E_n$ will perform A. But if, necessarily, God can predict that $E_n$ performs A, then it is true in every world that God can bring it about that $E_n$ performs A *without causing* $E_n$ to perform A. Call that *unrestricted actualization*. Unrestricted actualization ensures that God can strongly actualize a maximal state of affairs T such that, necessarily, T only if God actualizes a morally perfect world. And God can actualize T in every possible world unrestrictedly. If God can unrestrictedly actualize a morally perfect world, then it's evident that the thesis of universal transworld depravity is necessarily false. And so are the weaker modal theses of multiworld depravity and intraworld depravity. There is no world in which any essence, or set of essences E, is such that God cannot actualize an E-perfect world.

I argue in this chapter that the thesis that God can unrestrictedly actualize a morally perfect world is consistent with the Molinist position on the prevolitional truth of counterfactuals of creaturely freedom. The thesis that God can unrestrictedly actualize a morally perfect world does not entail that God can make some counterfactuals of freedom true.[2] I also

---

[1] Ric Otte, "Transworld Depravity and Unobtainable Worlds" *Philosophy and Phenomenological Research* (2009) 165–77. I'm unpersuaded that God cannot utter that S performed A yesterday in worlds where S did not perform A. Backtracking counterfactuals are true under certain unusual conditions, and the case of an omniscient being uttering "S performed A yesterday" seems like just the sort of case in which the backtracking counterfactual is true.

[2] See, for instance, Jon Kvanvig, "On Behalf of Maverick Molinism" *Faith and Philosophy* (2002) 348–57. Maverick Molinism denies that, necessarily, every counterfactual of creaturely freedom is prevolitionally true.

argue that the thesis that God can unrestrictedly actualize a morally perfect world is consistent with the significant freedom of creaturely essences. It is false that God predicts that every instantiated essence will always go right entails any troublesome form of theological fatalism.

## 4.1  A Counterexample to the Analysis of Transworld Depravity

There is an interesting counterexample to the original analysis of universal transworld depravity. The counterexample does not show that universal transworld depravity is impossible. It shows rather that the current analysis of universal transworld depravity is probably mistaken.[3]

Consider a possible world Wb in which Adam's first and only free choice is whether to kill himself (which is a morally bad action), and in which Adam makes the right choice not to kill himself; Wb is a world in which Adam only chooses the good. In this possible world, God strongly actualizes a situation in which Adam has the free choice to make, and after Adam decides not to kill himself, God announces that Adam has chosen the good and because of this he will make him ruler of Eden. What is important in this example is that the total state of affairs that God strongly actualizes after the good free choice is different from the total state of affairs that God could strongly actualize if Adam chose differently. If Adam chooses to kill himself, God cannot strongly actualize his making Adam ruler of Eden and announcing that Adam chose not to kill himself.[4]

It is a serious problem with the counterexample that the final conditional is false. It is false that Adam chooses to kill himself only if God cannot strongly actualize his making Adam ruler of Eden and announcing that Adam chose not to kill himself. Had God announced that Adam chose not to kill himself, it would have to have been true that Adam did not choose to kill himself. The special circumstances in which God makes such an announcement would surely make the backtracking counterfactual true. So if Adam chose to kill himself it would still be true that God could

[3] See Otte, "Transworld Depravity and Unobtainable Worlds," op. cit. Otte proposes an alternative analysis of transworld depravity that manages the counterexamples he offers. Plantinga takes the alternative analyses of transworld depravity to be successful. See Alvin Plantinga, "Transworld Depravity, Transworld Sanctity, and Uncooperative Essences" *Philosophy and Phenomenological Research* (2009) 178–91.

[4] Ibid. p. 167.

actualize his making Adam ruler and announcing that Adam chose not to kill himself.

The counterexample aims to show that, necessarily, there is some largest strongly actualizable state of affairs T of some Adam-perfect world such that it is impossible that God actualizes T and Adam goes wrong with respect to some action. T includes the fact that God announces that Adam has chosen the good. But since, necessarily, God announces that Adam chose the good only if Adam chose the good, it cannot be true that God makes the announcement and Adam goes wrong. The counterexample concludes that it is necessarily true that Adam is not transworld depraved. There is some Adam-perfect world W such that, necessarily, if God strongly actualizes T of W, then Adam would never go wrong.

The problem is not difficult to remedy. Let $E_n$ be the instantiation of essence E. An E-perfect world recall is one in which $E_n$ is significantly free but always does only what is right. Finally, let $Tw_t$ be the largest state of affairs God strongly actualizes in a world W up to time t. Consider the following revision to the original analysis of transworld depravity.[5]

> TDR.  An essence E suffers from transworld depravity iff for every E-perfect world W, there is an action A such that if God had strongly actualized $Tw_t$, $E_n$ would have gone wrong with respect to A.

There is a world in which God strongly actualizes the state of affairs T up to the time just prior to Adam's doing what is right, and Adam does what is wrong. So Adam might be transworld depraved on TDR.

It is likely that additional revisions to the analysis of transworld depravity will be required to secure the possibility of universal transworld depravity. But pursuing revisions to the analysis will ultimately prove unsuccessful. We can show that the thesis of universal transworld depravity is necessarily false and no revision in the analysis of the thesis can resolve the problem. We can show too that the weaker modal theses of multiworld depravity and intraworld depravity are necessarily false.

---

[5]  Otte, "Transworld Depravity and Unobtainable Worlds," op. cit. p. 171. Otte proposes another counterexample to this particular analysis. But the counterexample is not particularly plausible. The counterexample assumes that there is some Adam & Eve-perfect world in which Adam's exclusive moral choice is whether or not to kill himself. But surely Adam faces many moral choices in that world other than that, including killing Eve, rejecting God, blaspheming, acting cruelly, lying, insulting, wantonly destroying, etc. But even if we might generate a counterexample to the current analysis of transworld depravity, as I expect we could, it will not matter in any case for the discussion to come.

## 4.2 Predicting and Prophesying Perfect Worlds

Among the states of affairs that God can strongly actualize is the state of affairs of *predicting* that every (rational, creaturely) instantiated essence will always go right and the state of affairs of *prophesying* that every instantiated essence will always go right. God can also issue the fiat, *let it be that* every instantiated essence will always go right. But, necessarily, God predicts or prophesies or issues the fiat that every instantiated essence will always go right only if every instantiated essence always goes right. God is necessarily a perfect predictor. Consider, then, the following possible worlds.

Let $W_0$ be a morally perfect world and let T be the largest state of affairs that God strongly actualizes in $W_0$. It is possible that, before God instantiates any individual essences in T, he issues the fiat: let it be that every individual essence I instantiate will always go right. Suppose God then instantiates individual essences in T. Since, necessarily, God's fiats are always observed, it follows that, necessarily, every instantiated essence in T will always go right.

Now, of course, it is necessary that God can *strongly actualize* the state of affairs of having issued the fiat that it shall be that all individual essences will always go right. So it is necessarily possible that every instantiated essence will always go right. But, if God strongly actualizes the state of affairs of having issued the fiat that it shall be that all individual essences will always go right then it seems that none of the instantiated essences will be significantly free. When God issues a fiat such as *let there be light*, it does seem that God thereby causes there to be light. But it is impossible to cause significantly free actions. We should conclude that necessarily God can strongly actualize the state of affairs of having issued the fiat, let it be that every instantiated essence always goes right, and therefore it is necessarily possible that no instantiated essence goes wrong. But should we also conclude that none of those instantiated essences would be significantly free?

When God issues the fiat, let it be that every instantiated essence always goes right, there exist no instantiated essences that stand in any causal relation to the event of God's issuing the fiat. And the fiat does not bring into existence any instantiated essences. God does cause every uninstantiated essence to exemplify the contingent property of being such that each instantiation will go right. But no uninstantiated essence has the contingent property of being such that each instantiation is caused to go right. So it is not obvious that if God issues the fiat, let it be that every instantiated essence always goes right, then no instantiated essences would be significantly free.

Compare possible world $W_1$. $W_1$ is a morally perfect world and T is the largest state of affairs that God strongly actualizes in $W_1$. It is possible that, before God instantiates any individual essences in T, he makes the following prediction: I predict that every individual essence instantiated in T will always go right. The prediction God makes is a strongly actualized state of affairs in T and it narrows down the states of affairs T that he could actualize. Suppose God makes that prediction and then instantiates significantly free individual essences in T. Since, necessarily, God's predictions are always correct, it follows that every instantiated essence always goes right.

Now of course God strongly actualizes the state of affairs of having predicted that all instantiated essences will always go right only if every instantiated essence always goes right. But if God strongly actualizes the state of affairs of having predicted that all instantiated essences will always go right, then it might also be true that all of the individual essences are significantly free. God's prediction does not prevent him from creating significantly free essences. When God makes a prediction that some state of affairs will obtain, God does not thereby cause that state of affairs to obtain. It is possible to predict that every instantiated essence will always go right and have every instantiated essence always *freely* go right.

There is no question that, necessarily, God can strongly actualize the state of affairs of having issued the fiat, let it be that every instantiated essence always goes right. So we might be moved to conclude also that, necessarily, God can strongly actualize the state of affairs of having predicted that every instantiated essence will always go right and having instantiated significantly free essences. If so, then necessarily God can strongly actualize a world in which no instantiated essence is transworld depraved and every instantiated essence is significantly free.

But there are some interesting arguments against the conclusion that, necessarily, God can strongly actualize the state of affairs of having predicted that every instantiated essence will always go right.[6] If it is false that,

---

[6] In some useful correspondence Alvin Plantinga denies that, necessarily, God can strongly actualize the state of affairs of having predicted that every instantiated essence will always go right. Plantinga's argument, as I understand it, assumes that possibly universal transworld depravity is true. It concludes that it is not necessary that God can strongly actualize the state of affairs of having predicted that every instantiated essence will always go right. But of course the question is whether it is true that were God to utter the prediction that every instantiated

necessarily, God can strongly actualize that state of affairs, then our counterexample to universal transworld depravity is unimportant. It requires no more than another modification to the analysis of transworld depravity. But if, necessarily, God can strongly actualize the state of affairs of having predicted that every instantiated essence will always goes right, then no modification to the analysis of transworld depravity will resolve the problem. It will follow that necessarily God can actualize a morally perfect world and that necessarily the thesis of transworld depravity is false.

### 4.2.1 Prediction De Re and Prediction De Dicto

There are two ways that God might predict that every instantiated essence will always go right. God might instantiate significantly free essences $E_1$, $E_2, \ldots, E_n$, in T and then strongly actualize the state of affairs S in T of having predicted, of $E_1, E_2, \ldots, E_n$, that each of these instantiated essences would always go right. The prediction in this case is de re, and were God to strongly actualize T then he would actualize a world in which each significantly free essence $E_1, E_2, \ldots, E_n$ always goes right.

It is difficult to see how the conclusion could be resisted that God can actualize a morally perfect world in which $E_1 \ldots E_n$ always go right, unless there is no such world. But there is no reason at all to believe that modal claim. The maximal state of affairs in T is certainly entertainable. And there is no possible world in which it is true that God strongly actualizes T and some instantiated essence $E_1, E_2, \ldots, E_n$ is not significantly free. But if God strongly actualizes T and $E_1, E_2, \ldots, E_n$ are significantly free, then $E_1$, $E_2, \ldots, E_n$ always go right. So, necessarily, God can actualize a morally perfect world.

God might strongly actualize the state of affairs S in T of having predicted that each instantiated essence would always go right and God might then instantiate significantly free essences $E_1, E_2, \ldots, E_n$, in T. The prediction in this case is de dicto. And were God to strongly actualize T then he would actualize a world in which each significantly free essence $E_1, E_2, \ldots, E_n$ always goes right. But of course it would not have mattered which free essences he instantiated. They would all have gone right.

essence will always go right then (1) it would be true that every instantiated essence will always go right or (2) it would be true that a contradiction obtains. It seems obvious to me that (1) is correct.

There is no obvious way to resist the conclusion that God can actualize a morally perfect world. The maximal state of affairs in T is entertainable. And there is no possible world in which it is true that God strongly actualizes T and some instantiated essence $E_1, E_2, \ldots, E_n$ is not significantly free. But if God strongly actualizes T and $E_1, E_2, \ldots, E_n$ are significantly free, then $E_1, E_2, \ldots, E_n$ always go right. So, again, necessarily, God can actualize a morally perfect world.

## 4.3 Which Worlds Could God have Created?

Alvin Plantinga has argued against the possibility that an omnipotent being can strongly actualize the state of affairs of there being an instantiated essence freely performing some action. At most, God can cause an instantiated essence to be free and know that, if he causes the instantiated essence to be free in certain circumstances, then that instantiated essence will freely perform or refrain from some action.[7]

Suppose we concede that not even God can cause it to be the case that I freely refrain from A. Even so, he *can* cause me to be free with respect to A, and to be in some set S of circumstances including appropriate laws and antecedent conditions. He may also know, furthermore, that if he creates me and causes me to be free in these circumstances, I will refrain from A. If so, there is a state of affairs he can actualize, cause to be actual, such that, if he does so, then I will freely refrain from A.[8]

As we have noted, according to Plantinga, there are two senses, in which God can bring it about that an instantiated essence $E_n$ performs an action A. God can strongly actualize the state of affairs of $E_n$ performing A and God can weakly actualize the state of affairs of $E_n$ performing A. Let's consider the strict formulations of strong actualization and weak actualization in B0 and B1 respectively.

B0. Necessarily God can strongly actualize a state of affairs T including the instantiation $E_n$ of essence E such that, (i) necessarily, God strongly actualizes T only if $E_n$ performs action A and (ii) God causes the state of affairs of $E_n$'s performing A.

---

[7] See Alvin Plantinga, "Which Worlds Could God Have Created?" *The Journal of Philosophy* LXX/11 (1973) 539–52. See also Plantinga, *The Nature of Necessity* (Oxford: Oxford University Press, 1974) ch.r IX, sect. 4.

[8] See Plantinga, *The Nature of Necessity*, op. cit. p. 171.

According to B0, necessarily, God can strongly actualize the state of affairs of $E_n$ performing A. We of course have been assuming all along that $E_n$ is free if and only if $E_n$ is libertarian free. So if God strongly actualizes the state of affairs of $E_n$ performing A then $E_n$ does not freely perform A. As we have noted God can cause $E_n$ to perform A by some sort of direct intervention. But God can also cause $E_n$ to perform A by putting $E_n$ in a deterministic universe where the laws and history cause $E_n$ to perform A.

> B1. Possibly, God can strongly actualize a state of affairs T including the instantiation $E_n$ of essence E such that (i) possibly, God strongly actualizes T and $E_n$ does not perform A, (ii) were God to strongly actualize T then $E_n$ would perform action A and (iii) God does not cause the state of affairs of $E_n$'s performing A.

According to B1, possibly, God can weakly actualize the state of affairs of $E_n$ performing A. And if God weakly actualizes the state of affairs of $E_n$ performing A, then $E_n$ freely performs A. God can for instance create a significantly free being $E_n$ in an indeterministic world where $E_n$ would freely perform A.

We have observed that there are at least two other senses in which God can bring it about that an instantiated essence $E_n$ performs an action A. Let's consider the strict formulation of restricted actualization and unrestricted actualization in B2 and B3 respectively.

> B2. Possibly God can strongly actualize a state of affairs T including the instantiation $E_n$ of essence E such that (i) necessarily, God strongly actualizes T only if $E_n$ performs action A and (ii) God does not cause the state of affairs of $E_n$'s performing A.

God can strongly actualize a state of affairs T which includes, for instance, God announcing that $E_n$ performed A yesterday. And, necessarily, God announces that $E_n$ performed A yesterday only if $E_n$ performed A. Indeed, it is hard to see how we might resist the conclusion that, necessarily, God can strongly actualize the state of affairs of announcing that $E_n$ performed A yesterday. There are actions we can perform now which are such that, were we to perform them, the past would have to have been different. So it would be strange if there were nothing God could do now such that, were he to do it, it would have to have been the case that $E_n$ performed A yesterday. Plantinga notes this possibility.

It is possible (though no doubt unlikely) that there is something you can do such that, if you were to do it, then Abraham would never have existed. For perhaps you will be confronted with a decision of great importance—so important that one of the alternatives is such that if you were to choose *it*, then the course of human history would have been quite different from what in fact it is.[9]

But suppose that in such circumstances God cannot announce that $E_n$ performed A yesterday in worlds where it is false that $E_n$ performed A. Call that *restricted actualization*. Restricted actualization ensures that God can strongly actualize a state of affairs T such that necessarily, T only if God actualizes a morally perfect world. But God cannot strongly actualize T in every world unrestrictedly.

> B3. Necessarily God can strongly actualize a state of affairs T including the instantiation $E_n$ of essence E such that (i) necessarily, God strongly actualizes T only if $E_n$ performs action A and (ii) God does not cause the state of affairs of $E_n$ performing A.

God can strongly actualize the state of affairs T that includes the state of affairs of God's having predicted or prophesied that $E_n$ will perform A. But if it is true that, necessarily, God can predict that $E_n$ performs A, then it is true in every world that God can bring it about that $E_n$ performs A without causing $E_n$ to perform A. Call that *unrestricted actualization*. Unrestricted actualization ensures that God can strongly actualize a state of affairs T such that, necessarily, T only if God actualizes a morally perfect world. And God can actualize T in every possible world unrestrictedly.

According to Plantinga, God can weakly actualize a morally perfect world and God can also restrictedly actualize a morally perfect world. But God cannot unrestrictedly actualize a morally perfect world. God can unrestrictedly actualize a morally perfect world only if UA is true.

---

[9] See Alvin Plantinga, "On Ockham's Way Out" *Faith and Philosophy* (1986) 235–69. But see also David Lewis, "Counterfactual Dependence and Time's Arrow" in his *Philosophical Papers Vol. II* (Oxford: Oxford University Press, 1986). The counterfactuals that Plantinga discusses here are what Lewis calls "backtracking counterfactuals." Backtracking counterfactuals can be true, but only in extraordinary circumstances. Under the standard resolution of vagueness for counterfactuals, we assume that the past does not depend on what we do in the present or future. That the past remains unchanged is made an auxiliary assumption in determining which worlds are most similar to ours. So, under the standard resolution, backtracking counterfactuals come out false. The asymmetry between that past and the future that Plantinga discusses is, according to Lewis, the asymmetry of counterfactual dependence.

UA.  God can unrestrictedly actualize a morally perfect world iff necessarily, for some E-perfect world W and for every instantiation $E_n$
of any essence E, there is a state of affairs T such that,

(1)  T is the largest state of affairs that God strongly actualizes in W;
(2)  Necessarily, God strongly actualizes T of W only if $E_n$ always
freely goes right; and
(3)  God can strongly actualize T.

God cannot unrestrictedly actualize a morally perfect world only if (2) or
(3) is false. (2) is false just in case, possibly, for every morally perfect world
W and some instantiation $E_n$, God strongly actualizes the state of affairs T of
W and $E_n$ does not always freely go right. (3) is false just in case, possibly, for
every morally perfect world W, God cannot strongly actualize T of W.

## 4.4  Weak Essentialism and Strong Essentialism

Weak essentialism is the view that counterfactual suppositions incompossible with the essential properties of an object or being S are not in general
incompossible with the existence of S.

For instance, the supposition that Descartes is material and the supposition that he is
immaterial both are entertainable. Presumably, one supposition or the other is
contrary to Descartes' essence. Yet it makes sense to reason hypothetically about
what would be the case under either supposition, and the reasoning need not end
in contradiction. Further, even when an entertainable supposition is not itself
contrary to essence, still it may happen that what would be the case given that
supposition is contrary to essence . . .
    If all creatures were material, Descartes would be material
    If material things couldn't think, Descartes would be immaterial.
Presumably one consequent or the other is contrary to Descartes' essence; yet both
counterfactuals seem non-vacuously true, and neither antecedent is contrary to
essence.[10]

According to (2) it is a necessary truth that God strongly actualizes T of
W only if $E_n$ always freely goes right. The reason is that the state of affairs
T includes God's predicting that E's instantiation $E_n$ will go right with
respect to every morally significantly action. Since God is essentially a

---

[10]  See David Lewis, "Evil for Freedom's Sake" in his *Papers in Ethics and Social Philosophy
Vol. III* (Cambridge: Cambridge University Press, 2000) p. 123 ff.

perfect predictor, it follows that, necessarily, God predicts $E_n$ goes right with respect to every morally significant action it faces only if $E_n$ goes right with respect to every morally significant action.

The weak essentialist might deny (2) in UA. The fact that God is essentially a perfect predictor does not entail that there are no worlds in which he makes an inaccurate prediction. Suppositions contrary to essence are entertainable because essence is itself a flexible matter. On weak essentialism God might, for instance, suffer one lapse from omniscience without ceasing to be God. It is not essentially mistaken to assert that a glass is empty though it contains one remaining drop of beer. Only a strong form of essentialism—some might say an overly rigid form—makes it impossible to assert without contradiction that a glass containing one drop of beer is nonetheless empty.

The evidence for weak essentialism is found in the apparent inconstancy of representation de re. There sometimes seem to be no right answers, independent of context, for many questions about modality de re.

Your problem is that the right way of representing is determined . . . by context. . . . That is how it is in general with dependence on complex features of context. There is a rule of accommodation: what you say makes itself true, if at all possible, by creating a context that selects the relevant features so as to make it true. Say that France is hexagonal, and you thereby set the standards of precision low, and you speak the truth; say that France is not hexagonal (preferably on some other occasion) and you set the standards high, and again you speak the truth. In parallel fashion, I suggest that those philosophers who preach that origins are essential are absolutely right—in the context of their own preaching. . . . Their preaching constitutes a context in which de re modality is governed by a way of representing . . . that requires match of origins. But, if I ask how things would be if Saul Kripke had come from no sperm and egg but had been brought by a stork, that makes equally good sense. I create a context that makes my question make sense, and to do so it has to be a context that makes origins not be essential.[11]

But moderate Anselmians reject the notion that God is world-bound. All possible worlds overlap with respect to God, so the very same God exists in every possible world. Since there is no flexibility with respect to which beings might count as counterparts of God—the salient features of similarity are not a contextual matter—there is no possibility of inconstancy in representing God. And since there is no possibility of inconstancy in representing God, there is no flexibility in God's essential properties. Of

---

[11] See David Lewis, *On the Plurality of Worlds* (Oxford: Blackwell, 1986) p. 252 ff.

course, the lack of flexibility does not entail a lack of indecision about which properties are essential or a lack of knowledge about which properties are essential.

Strong essentialism is the view that counterfactual suppositions incompossible with the essential properties of an object or being S are in general incompossible with the existence of S. But strong essentialism and moderate Anselmianism can accommodate the intuition that counterfactual suppositions incompossible with the essential properties of God are not in general incompossible with the existence of that God.

It is not always possible to know apriori which modal suppositions are metaphysically entertainable and which are merely *epistemically entertainable*.[12] Counterfactual suppositions that are epistemically entertainable might not be metaphysically entertainable. The supposition, for instance, that God might be less than omniscient is not apriori impossible, so there is a least an epistemically possible world in which God lacks that essential property. The apriori possibility that God is less than omniscient invites the conclusion that suppositions contrary to essence are metaphysically entertainable. It invites the generous distinction that a being who suffers a lapse in omniscience might be loosely speaking God though not strictly speaking God. But the distinction is mistaken. It is apriori possible that God might suffer a lapse in omniscience, but that provides no more than the illusion that a less than omniscient God is a genuine possibility. Anything that might be identical to God must meet the inflexible standards in God's nature. But according to the moderate Anselmian, the nature of God is a matter of aposteriori necessity.

## 4.5  Prevolitional Counterfactuals

According to traditional Molinism, each possible world includes a set of contingent, prevolitional, counterfactuals of creaturely freedom. Counterfactuals of creaturely freedom (CCFs) have a specific form which includes an antecedent describing a *complete* state of affairs. The antecedent of a CCF is a proposition which describes a largest (or a maximally large) state of affairs T that God can strongly actualize or cause to obtain. The consequent of a CCF describes some or all of the states of affairs F which includes every undetermined state of affairs that would obtain were God to strongly actualize T.

---

[12]  Compare Chapter 1, Section 1.1 above.

Included in T of course are all the contingent states of affairs that God can cause to obtain. The states of affairs in T depend on God's creation of objects, people, planets, angels, demons, supernovas, flora, fauna, stars, leptons, quarks, photons, light waves, and so on. The states of affairs in T also depend on the circumstances in which he creates those objects and the properties he causes them to have. There are many states of affairs that God cannot cause to obtain. These are states of affairs that are essentially causally undetermined. On traditional Molinism, essentially causally un-determined states of affairs are not included in T.

On traditional Molinism, CCFs are prevolitional in the sense that their truth or falsity does not depend on what God freely does. It is a nice heuristic to think of God discovering or coming to learn that certain CCFs are true before he chooses to actualize a world. God knows what free and undetermined events would occur or what undetermined states of affairs would obtain for each possible maximal state of affairs T he might strongly actualize. The profile of true, contingent CCFs typically constrain or limit the worlds that God can weakly actualize.

There are prevolitional contingent truths in every possible world, in-cluding of course worlds in which God has created nothing. Not every contingent truth places any limits on the worlds God might create. Among the contingent truths in each world is the set of true CCFs. The set of true CCFs is exhaustive in the sense that, for each instantiation $E_n$ of creaturely essence E and each circumstance T, if $E_n$ is free with respect to A in T, then either T $\square\rightarrow$ A or T $\square\rightarrow$ ~A. This follows from the Molinist assumption of conditional excluded middle for counterfactuals of creaturely freedom.[13]

Counterfactuals of conditional freedom extend to non-free, *chancy* events as well, where chances are genuine, objective probabilities. These include chancy micro-events such as the random decay of uranium atoms and chancy macro-events such as rolling sixes with fair die. God knows, for instance, that were a particular atom of radon created yesterday, in a certain set of circumstances, its half-life would be exactly 0.001 seconds. And God knows that were a particular plate dropped toward the floor today, in otherwise normal circumstances, chance would it have fly off sideways instead of hitting the floor.

---

[13] Thomas Flint, *Divine Providence: The Molinist Account* (Ithaca, NY: Cornell University Press, 1998) 49.

At each world W there are infinitely many maximal states of affairs $T_0$, $T_1$, $T_2 \ldots T_n$ that God might have to strongly actualize. And for each W and $T_n$ pair, $<W, T_n>$, there corresponds the state of affairs $F_n$ that includes every undetermined state of affairs $F_n$ that would have obtained, had $T_n$ been strongly actualized at W. Call the set $S_C$ of all true CCFs at a world W be the *creaturely world-type* of W. And call the set of all worlds $S_{WC}$ at which all of the members of $S_C$ are true the *galaxy* of $S_C$.[14]

The galaxy $S_{WC}$ is just the set of feasible worlds relative to W as determined by the true CCFs in $S_C$. Suppose $W_0$ is in $S_{WC}$. It is true at $W_0$ that God can actualize any other world in $S_{WC}$ and that God cannot actualize any world that is not in $S_{WC}$. God's choice among worlds to actualize is limited to the set of feasible worlds in the galaxy. The set of feasible worlds is not coextensive with the set of all possible worlds, but it is coextensive with the set of all actualizable worlds.

To reconsider a familiar example, Alvin Plantinga urged that there is a possible world $W_1$ such that for every world $W_n$ in the galaxy $S_{W1C}$ in which some creaturely essence is instantiated, $W_n$ is a morally imperfect world. That is to say that every T that God might have strongly actualized at $W_1$ is such that had God actualized T then the individual essences instantiated in T would have gone wrong with respect to some morally significant action. Since God can actualize any world in $S_{W1C}$ and God cannot actualize any world outside of $S_{W1C}$, it follows that, as a matter of contingent fact, God actualizes a world with significantly free moral agents only if God actualizes a morally imperfect world.

At each world W, God knows the maximal states of affairs $T_0$, $T_1$, $T_2 \ldots T_n$ that he might have to strongly actualize. And for each maximal state of affairs $T_0$, $T_1$, $T_2 \ldots T_n$ he knows what possible world in $S_{WC}$ would have obtained had he strongly actualized that maximal state of affairs. He knows, for instance, that $W_0$ would have obtained had he actualized $T_0$ and he knows that $W_1$ would have obtained had he actualized $T_1$ and so on. Knowledge of these counterfactuals of creaturely freedom form part of God's *middle knowledge*. And it is on the basis of God's middle knowledge that God decides which maximal state of affairs to strongly actualize.

According to traditional Molinism, God *strongly* actualizes a maximal state of affairs $T_n$ and God *weakly* actualizes the state of affairs $F_n$ where

[14] These terms were introduced in Flint, *Divine Providence: The Molinist Account*, op. cit. p. 51 ff.

$T_n + F_n = W_n$. As we move from one world to the next the set of strongly actualizable states of affairs is constant, but the set $S_C$ of true CCFs—the creaturely world-type—and the galaxy of worlds $S_{WC}$ varies. The variance in $S_C$ and $S_{WC}$ across worlds is explained in part by variance in undetermined states of affairs in $F_n$. At world $W_0$ it might be true that, were God to strongly actualize $T_1$, the instantiated essence $E_n$ would perform A. But in some world $W_1$ not included in $S_{W0C}$ it might be true that were God to strongly actualize $T_1$, the instantiated essence $E_n$ would perform B. The set of true CCFs in $S_C$ places limitations on the essentially uncaused states of affairs in $F_n$ that God can weakly actualize.

But there are also constraints on the maximal states of affairs T that God can strongly actualize. We noted that in addition to strong actualization and weak actualization there is also *restricted actualization* and *unrestricted actualization*. Recall that God can unrestrictedly actualize a maximal state of affairs T just in case B3 is true.

> B3. Necessarily God can strongly actualize a state of affairs T including the instantiation $E_n$ of essence E such that (i) necessarily, God strongly actualizes T only if $E_n$ performs action A and (ii) God does not cause the state of affairs of $E_n$ performing A.

Among the maximal states of affairs that God can unrestrictedly actualize are states of affairs T that include the state of affairs of God's having predicted or prophesied, prior to the strong actualization of any other state of affairs, that every instantiated essence $E_n$ in T will always go right. Clause (i) of B3 is true since, necessarily, God predicts that every instantiated essence $E_n$ in T always goes right only if every instantiated essence $E_n$ in T always goes right. Clause (ii) of B3 is true since, predicting that every instantiated essence $E_n$ in T will always go right does not cause every instantiated essence $E_n$ in T always to go right. The state of affairs of every instantiated essence always going right counterfactually depends on God's prediction that they will always go right, but it does not causally depend on God's prediction that they will always go right. And God can actualize T in every possible world unrestrictedly.

The intersection of the sets $S_C$ of true CCFs in each possible world is the set $S_U$ of CCFs whose antecedents God can unrestrictedly actualize. The set of CCFs in $S_U$ is the set of all counterfactuals of creaturely freedom $T_n \square\!\!\rightarrow F_n$ such that God can actualize $T_n$ in every possible world and

$\Box(T_n \supset F_n)$. Since every member of $S_U$ is a CCF, there is no member $T_n$ $\Box\rightarrow F_n$ of $S_U$ such that $F_n$ causally depends on $T_n$. Of course there are lots of other counterfactuals $T_n \Box\rightarrow D_n$ true in every possible world where the states of affairs in $D_n$ depend causally on $T_n$. In deterministic worlds, for instance, $D_n$ depends causally on $T_n$. There are other counterfactuals true in every possible world where $D_n$ depends fatalistically on $T_n$ and so on. But the set of counterfactuals in $S_U$ are CCFs.

We might expect that there is no such thing as the best actualizable world simpliciter. The best actualizable world varies depending upon the CCF's in $S_C$ that are true. The best actualizable world will include certain essentially undetermined states of affairs—the actions of free agents, for instance, and the occurrences of undetermined events—that, necessarily, God cannot strongly actualize. Rather, the best actualizable world is the best world God can weakly actualize and the set of weakly actualizable worlds varies across possible worlds.

But since the set $S_U$ of CCFs whose antecedents God can strongly actualize is true in every possible world, we know there are undetermined states of affairs that God can unrestrictedly actualize. There are undetermined states of affairs $F_n$ such that $\Box(T_n \supset F_n)$ and necessarily God can strongly actualize $T_n$. Most importantly, God can unrestrictedly actualize a state of affairs in which every instantiated essence always goes right.

Since Molinists maintain that CCFs are prevolitional, it might be objected that this generates a problem for the thesis that God can unrestrictedly actualize a morally perfect world. God cannot make any counterfactuals of creaturely freedom true, so he cannot make it the case that the counterfactuals in $S_U$ are true. Suppose it is true that Smith will perform a morally wrong action A were Smith placed in circumstances T. It is then *prevolitionally true* that T $\Box\rightarrow$ A. And suppose it is true that God strongly actualized T. Since the set $S_U$ includes the CCFs whose antecedents God can strongly actualize, we know there are undetermined states of affairs that God can unrestrictedly actualize. In particular, we know that God can unrestrictedly actualize a state of affairs in which Smith always goes right. God simply has to utter the prediction or prophesy that Smith will always go right. But this entails no genuine problem for the thesis that CCFs are prevolitionally true. It remains prevolitionally true that T $\Box\rightarrow$ A. That is consistent with the fact that all of the counterfactuals in the set $S_U$ are true in every world. God does not make them true in any world. It is necessarily true that God can actualize a morally perfect world, but that does not entail that it is necessarily true that he does. In fact God actualized T. But God might have actualized $T_n$ and brought about a world in which Smith always goes right.

Consider, on the other hand, a morally ideal world $W_n$ at which it is true that God strongly actualized the state of affairs of God's predicting that every instantiated essence will always go right. The counterfactual that $T_n$ $\square \to W_n$ will of course be prevolitional. But suppose that God might not have strongly actualized the state of affairs of his predicting that every instantiated essence will always go right. The complete creative act God might have performed is $T_m$ and the resulting world is $W_m$ in which we can assume some instantiated essences go wrong. Clearly $T_m \neq T_n$, since $T_n$ includes God strongly actualizing the state of affairs of his predicting that every instantiated essence will always go right and $T_m$ does not. It is true that $T_n \square \to W_n$, but of course that is consistent with it also being true that $T_m \square \to W_m$. The argument generalizes to any possible world $W$ at which God strongly actualizes some maximal state of affairs $T$. It is true at $W$ that God did actualize $T$ and it is true there that $T_n \square \to W_n$. But it is also true at $W$ that God could have performed the complete creative act $T_m$ and $T_m \square \to W_m$. So the fact that CCF's are prevolitional gives us no reason to believe it is not necessarily true that God can actualize a morally perfect world. Indeed it gives us no reason to believe that God cannot unrestrictedly actualize a morally perfect world.

It is true that the set $S_U$ includes counterfactuals of creaturely freedom that are true in every world. The true counterfactuals in $S_U$ ensure that there is a set of worlds $S_W$ such that necessarily God can actualize a world in $S_W$. And the worlds in $S_W$ include the morally perfect worlds. Since, necessarily, God can actualize a morally perfect world, we know that the thesis of universal transworld depravity is false. And so are the weaker theses of multiworld depravity and intraworld depravity.

## 4.6  Fatalism and Significant Freedom

Suppose $T$ is the largest state of affairs that God strongly actualizes in a world $W$. We have assumed that the general conditions of significant freedom in $W$ are given in S1.[15]

---

[15]  Certainly there will have to be restrictions on S1 to make it plausible. These are discussed in what follows. We will have to ignore some cases of restricted actualization, for instance.

S1. S has significant freedom in doing A at t if and only if (i) A is morally significant for S at t and (ii) $\sim\Box$(God actualizes T $\supset$ S does A at t) & $\sim\Box$(God actualizes T $\supset$ S does $\sim$A at t).

The second clause in S1 specifies the necessary conditions on libertarian free action. According to (ii) no action A that is logically entailed by the states of affairs in T is free.

Let's reconsider whether God can unrestrictedly actualize a morally perfect world. In morally perfect worlds it is true that every instantiated essence always freely goes right. God can unrestrictedly actualize a morally perfect world if and only if God can strongly actualize some states of affairs T such that, necessarily, God strongly actualizes T only if every instantiated essence $E_n$ will always freely go right.

Consider the following objection to the claim that there is a T such that, necessarily, God can strongly actualize T and, necessarily, God strongly actualizes T only if every essence that God instantiates will always freely go right. Let the maximal state of affairs T include the state of affairs of God having predicted that every significantly free essence that he instantiates will always go right. The argument assumes that $T_0$ follows from S1.

$T_0$.  $\Box$(Every significantly free essence that God instantiates will always freely go right $\supset$ God does not predict that every significantly free essence that he instantiates will always go right.

Suppose that God does predict that every significantly free essence that he instantiates will always go right. That prediction entails that every significantly free essence that he instantiates will always go right. But then by clause (ii) in S1 no significantly free essence that he instantiates will always *freely* go right. But then God does not actualize a morally perfect world in predicting that every significantly free essence that he instantiates will always go right. Instead, according to S1, God actualizes a world in which every instantiated essence will always go right, but no instantiated essence will freely go right. We should conclude that God cannot unrestrictedly actualize a morally perfect world.

There is very good reason not to accede to this conclusion. There are, of course, trivial and non-trivial violations of S1. Every action and state of affairs is necessitated by some action or state of affairs, but that does not entail that no action is libertarian free.[16] So God might strongly actualize a state of affairs that entails that he freely performs some action A at t yet remain free to do A at t. Consider $T_1$, for instance, which is also entailed by S1.

$T_1$.   $\Box$(God does A at t $\supset$ God does not freely do A at t)

The antecedent in $T_1$ includes a state of affairs that God strongly actualizes: viz. God's doing A at t. Of course, that logically entails God's doing A at t. So according to S1, it is false that God freely does A at t. But it's obvious in this case that the violation of S1 offers no reason to believe that God does not have significant freedom with respect to A at t. This exception to S1 is not a counterexample to the analysis of freedom, since it is obvious that God is free not to do A at t. So, God's strongly actualizing the state of affairs of having freely done A at t does not determine in any non-trivial way what God does at t.[17]

But there are some important non-trivial violations of S1 as well. Consider, for instance, $T_2$.

$T_2$.   $\Box$(God knows at t − 2 that S will do A at t $\supset$ S does A at t)

God's foreknowledge that S will do A at t entails that S does A at t, and so it is not possible that God foreknows that S will do A at t and S fails to do A at t. Since God is omniscient, he necessarily knows every future contingent proposition, including chancy future contingents. God's knowing that S does A at t is in the largest strongly actualized state of affairs T. So we have a non-trivial violation of clause (ii) in S1. And of course some have concluded from this that S does not freely do A at t.

---

[16]  Where no confusion threatens, I speak loosely of entailments between states of affairs and actions. Strictly entailment relations hold only between propositions.

[17]  Compare William Rowe, "In Defense of 'The Free Will Defense'" *International Journal for Philosophy of Religion* 44 (1998) 115–20. Rowe's discussion provides some reason to believe that if S1 is too weak as an analysis of significant freedom, there might be cases in which the free actions of some agents determine the actions of other agents. William Rowe provides the following supposition: $\Box$(Gandhi freely chooses depravity $\supset$ Capone chooses non-depravity). Rowe has us suppose that there is no possible world in which every agent is depraved and that there are just two agents, Gandhi and Capone. If Gandhi freely chooses depravity then Capone cannot. Since Gandhi chooses depravity, Capone is not free to choose non-depravity. But according to S1, Capone is free to choose non-depravity, since Gandhi's free actions are not included in the largest strongly actualized state of affairs T.

But there are familiar and important arguments that God's foreknow-ledge is consistent with significant freedom despite the fact that $T_2$ is not consistent with the most natural reading of clause (ii) in S1. Perhaps the most familiar argument is based on the Ockhamist distinction between soft facts and hard facts. Certainly no proposed analysis of the distinction is definitive, but there is no doubt an intuitive distinction between a hard fact and a soft fact. The intuition is that a soft fact or 'soft proposition' is one whose truth-value at some time t depends on states of affairs that obtain or fail to obtain at some time after t and a hard fact is one whose truth-value at t does not depend on states of affairs that obtain or fail to obtain after t.

The proposition <Smith believes truly at t that it will rain at t +1> is a soft fact, since the proposition is true at t if and only if the state of affairs of its raining obtains at t + 1. 'John had tea for lunch' uttered in the afternoon does not express a soft fact, since the truth-value of the proposition expressed by that utterance does not depend on any states of affairs that obtain any time in the future. Consider, then, the soft fact in the antecedent of $T_3$.

$T_3$. □(It is true at 6 a.m. that John will have a cup of tea at 12 p.m. ⊃ John has a cup of tea at 12 p.m.)

The truth of the proposition in the antecedent of $T_3$ depends on the state of affairs of John's having a cup of tea at 12 p.m. The soft fact in the antecedent of $T_3$ necessitates John's having a cup of tea at 12 p.m. So, if the antecedent is true then John will have a cup of tea at 12 p.m.

There is nothing John can do to alter the future with respect to his having tea at 12 p.m. We cannot change the future any more than we can change the past. But only the most implausible form of fatalism would conclude from this fact that John does not freely have a cup of tea at 12 p.m.[18] John's freely having a cup of tea at 12 p.m. does not entail John's being able to alter the future with respect to having tea at 12 p.m. It is useful to compare William Hasker's description of the relation between the propositions in the antecedent and consequent of $T_3$.

---

[18] For a well-known argument of this sort for fatalism, see Richard Taylor, *Metaphysics* (Englewood Cliffs: Prentice Hall, 1992) 54 ff.

No doubt, (10) "John had a cup of tea for lunch" spoken at some time after lunch, would be beyond our control. . . . On the other hand [the antecedent of $T_3$] spoken at 6:01 of that same morning, does not seem to be beyond our control in the way indicated: assuming it is true, there may be still quite a number of people who have it in their power to bring it about that it is false, by preventing the cup of tea from being drunk.[19]

Hasker describes the relationship in unfortunate terms of *controlling* and *having power* over the truth-values of propositions. But if the proposition in the antecedent of $T_3$ is true then no one, not even God, can make that proposition false. God can make a blue ball into a red ball or a green lawn into a brown lawn, since it is possible that a ball is blue at one time and red at another and it is possible that a lawn is green at one time and brown at another. But the proposition that it is true at 6 a.m. that John will have a cup of tea at 12 p.m. cannot be true at one time and false at another. So neither John nor God nor anyone else has the power to make the proposition that it is true at 6 a.m. that John will have a cup of tea at 12 p.m. true at one time and false at another. If the proposition is true, it is immutably true.[20]

Of course there is an extended sense in which we have power or control over the future that does not include having the power to alter the future. It is helpful to consider Plantinga's description of an important symmetry between the past and the future.

The interesting asymmetry between past and future, therefore, does not consist in the fact that the past is unalterable in a way that the future is not; nonetheless this asymmetry remains. Now, before 9:21, it is within Paul's power to make it false that he walks out at 9:21; after he walks out at 9:21 he will no longer have that power. In the same way in 1995 BC God could have brought it about that Adam did not exist in 1995 BC; now that is no longer within his power.[21]

---

[19]  See William Hasker, *God, Time and Knowledge* (Ithaca: Cornell University Press, 1989) 78 ff.

[20]  See Plantinga, "On Ockham's Way Out," op. cit. Plantinga makes a similar point with respect to our power to alter the future.

". . . so then Paul has power to alter the future." But the conclusion displays confusion; Paul's not walking out then were it to occur would effect no alteration at all in the future. To alter the future, Paul must do something like this: he must perform some action A at a time t before 9:21 such that prior to t it is true that Paul will walk out at 9:21, but after t (after he performs A) false that he will. Neither Paul nor anyone—not even God—can do something like that. So the future is no more alterable than the past.

[21]  Ibid. p. 245.

But it should be underscored that Paul does not have the power to make the proposition that he walks out at 9:21 false in the sense of causing it to be true rather than causing it to be false. What Paul can do is act in such a way that, were he to do so, it would always have been the case that the proposition <Paul walks out at 9:21> is false. But in worlds where that proposition has always been false Paul clearly does not *make* that proposition false. There is no time in that world at which it isn't already false and so no time at which Paul makes it false. In worlds where that proposition has always been false, it is false in 1995 BC, long before Paul has the power to do anything.

Paul can also act in such a way that, were he to do so, it would always have been the case that the proposition <Paul walks out at 9:21> is true. But in worlds where that proposition has always been true Paul clearly does not make that proposition true. There is no time in that world at which it isn't already true and so no time at which Paul makes it true. In worlds where that proposition has always been true, it is true in 1995 BC, long before Paul has the power to do anything.

So Paul can neither make that proposition true nor make that proposition false in the sense of causing it to be true or causing it to be false. Neither walking outside nor remaining inside involves bringing about the semantic properties of the proposition <Paul walks out at 9:21>.

Our "power" over future contingent propositions, such as it is, is no different in kind from our power over past contingent propositions. Before 9:21 Paul is able—Paul can or has the power—to act in such a way that, were he to do so, his walking out of the door at 9:21 would always have been true. But after 9:21, Paul might still have the power to act in such a way that, were he to do so, his walking out of the door would always have been false. Recall that Plantinga makes this point.

It is possible (though no doubt unlikely) that there is something you can do such that, if you were to do it, then Abraham would never have existed.[44]

Our power over future contingent propositions is no different in kind from our power over past contingent propositions, so our power over soft facts it is not different in kind from our power over hard facts. But our power over future contingent propositions is certainly far more expansive than our power over past contingent propositions. Our power over past

---

[22] Ibid. p. 257. See also Lewis, "Counterfactual Dependence and Time's Arrow," op. cit.

contingent propositions depends in many cases on rare circumstances in which backtracking counterfactuals are true.[23]

Let's describe the extended sense in which we have power over the truth-values of propositions. An agent S has power over the truth-value of a proposition p just in case the conditions in $P_0$ are satisfied.

> $P_0$. S has power over the truth-value of proposition p iff p is true (false) at t and there is an action A such that (i) S can perform A at t or later and (ii) if S were to perform A then it would always have been the case that $\sim$p.

According to $P_0$, John has power over the truth-value of the proposition that it is true at 6 a.m. that John will have a cup of tea at 12 p.m. John can perform an action at 12 p.m. which is such that, were he to perform it, then it would always have been false that at 6 a.m. John will have a cup of tea at 12 p.m. But then $T_3$ and S1 do not entail that John does not freely have his cup of tea at 12 p.m.

But consider whether $T_2$ and God's knowledge entails that S does not freely do A at t. According to $P_0$, S has power over the truth-value of the proposition <God knows at t − n that S will do A at t>. There is some action that S can perform which is such that, were he to perform it, it would always have been false that God knows at t − n that S will do A at t. But then $T_2$ together with God's knowledge does not entail that S will not freely do A at t. $T_2$ and God's knowledge constitute a violation of the conditions in S1, so those conditions certainly require some modification.

But then consider $T_0$ and whether God can unrestrictedly actualize a morally perfect world. Necessarily, God can predict that every significantly free essence that he instantiates will always go right. Necessarily, if God does predict that every significantly free essence that he instantiates will always go right, then every significantly free essence that he instantiates will always go right. But certainly there is something that instantiated

---

[23] Compare William Hasker, *God, Time and Knowledge*, op. cit. p. 103, commenting on Plantinga's observation on acting in such a way that, were one to do so, Abraham would not exist.

So the scope of our power over the past is, potentially at least, very extensive. Yet this will be counterfactual power over the past, rather than power to bring about the past.

This is plainly false. Our power over the past is not extensive. It is limited to those rare contexts in which backtracking counterfactuals are true.

essences can do such that, if they were to do it, it would always have been false that God uttered the prediction that every instantiated essence will always go right. Consider $T_4$.

> $T_4$.  $\Box$(God predicts at t that every significantly free essence that he instantiates will always go right $\supset$ every significantly free essence that he instantiates will always go right).

The situation is the substantially same for $T_4$ as it is for $T_2$. According to $P_0$, each instantiated essence has power over the truth-value of the proposition that God predicts at t that every significantly free essence that he instantiates will always go right. There is some action that each instantiated essence can perform which is such that, were he to perform it, it would always have been false that God predicts at t that every essence that he instantiates will always go right. But then $T_4$ together with God's prediction do not entail that no instantiated essence will freely go right.

### 4.6.1 A Non-Ockhamist Response to Theological Fatalism

The fact that God can predict that every instantiated essence always goes right generates a powerful argument for fatalism.[24]

> (1) Jones has no choice about: <God's predicting that Jones goes right at t> was true fifteen billion years ago.
> (2) Necessarily, <God predicts that Jones goes right at t> was true fifteen billion years ago only if Jones goes right at time t.

Therefore,

> (3) Jones has no choice about: Jones's going right at time t.

But if Jones has no choice about his going right at t, then Jones does not freely go right at t.

Premise (1) in the argument claims that Jones has no choice about the truth of the proposition <God's predicting that Jones goes right at t>. And, as we have argued, there is a sense in which this is true. Jones cannot cause the proposition <God's predicting that Jones goes right at t> to change its truth-value. If that proposition was true fifteen billion years ago or if that proposition is true fifteen billion years from now, then Jones

---

[24] See Trenton Merrick's, "Truth and Freedom" *Philosophical Review*, 118/1 (2009) 29–57. The forthcoming argument is based on the Merrick's "main argument."

cannot alter its truth-value and neither can God. So, in that sense, Jones
has no choice about the truth-value of that proposition. Propositions do
not change their truth-values over time; they are either always true or
always false.[25]

But there is also a sense in which premise (1) is false. Recall that an agent
S has power over the truth-value of a proposition p just in case the
conditions in $P_0$ are satisfied.

> $P_0$.   S has power over the truth-value of proposition p if and only if p is
> true (false) at t and there is an action A such that (i) S can perform
> A at t or later and (ii) if S were to perform A then it would always
> have been the case that $\sim$p is true (false).

In Jones' particular case, $P_0$ takes the following instantiation.

> $P_{01}$.   Jones has power over the truth-value of the proposition <God
> predicts that Jones goes right at t> if and only if <God predicts
> that Jones goes right at t> is true fifteen billion years ago and there
> is an action A such that (i) S can perform A at t or later and (ii) if
> S were to perform A then it would always have been the case that
> <God does not predict that Jones goes right at t>.

Recall the symmetry of the past and future with respect to our power to
change or alter them. We can no more alter or change the future than we
can alter or change the past. It is confused to think that our power, such as
it is, over the truth-value of future contingent propositions is or entails a
power to change or alter the future and it no less confused to think that our
power, such as it is, over the truth-value of past propositions is or entails a
power to change or alter the past. We have no such power to change or
alter the past or the future.

Despite the fact that we cannot change or alter the future, we clearly do
have power in the sense of $P_0$ over the truth-value of future propositions.
Compare the following instantiation of $P_0$.

---

[25] Some hold that propositions have different truth-values at different times. See, for
instance, Trenton Merricks, "Truth and Freedom," op. cit. pp. 34–5; Thomas M. Crisp,
"Presentism" in Michael J. Loux and Dean Zimmerman (eds.) *The Oxford Handbook of
Metaphysics* (Oxford: Oxford University Press, 2003) 211–45; and Mark Hinchliff, "The
Puzzle of Change" in James E. Tomberlin (ed.) *Philosophical Perspectives*, Vol. 10, *Metaphysics*.
(Oxford: Blackwell, 1996) 119–36.

$P_{02}$. Jones has power over the truth-value of the proposition <God retrodicts that Jones goes right at t> iff <God retrodicts that Jones goes right at t> is true *fifteen billion years from now* and there is an action A such that (i) S can perform A at t or later and (ii) if S were to perform A then it would always have been the case that <God does not retrodict that Jones goes right at t>.

We can say two things about the instantiation in $P_{02}$.[26] First, it is true that Jones cannot change the future and so Jones cannot alter the truth-value of the true proposition <God retrodicts that Jones goes right at t>. Second, it is true that Jones can do something such that, if he does it, the proposition <God retrodicts that Jones goes right at t> would never have been true. The proposition would not have undergone a change or alteration in truth-value and neither would any other feature of the future. But instead it would always have been false that God retrodicts that Jones goes right at t. What Jones can do at t is fail to go right. And were he to do that, then it would always have been false that God retrodicts that Jones goes right at t.

Of course, the very action shows that Jones has power over the truth-value of <God predicts that Jones goes right at t>. It is true that Jones cannot change or alter the past in any way and he cannot alter or change the truth-value of <God predicts that Jones goes right at t>. But Jones can do something such that, were he to do it, it would never have been true that God predicts that Jones goes right at t. And it should be noted that nothing in the argument assumes that there is a distinction between hard facts and soft facts or that such a distinction is relevant to the discussion of fatalism.

### 4.6.2 Fatalism and Modal Contextualism

David Lewis urges that the argument in (4.6) that no instantiated essences will freely go right is a bit of fatalist trickery. Lewis observes,

Fatalists . . . are philosophers who take facts we count as irrelevant in saying what someone can do, disguise them somehow as facts of a different sort that we count as relevant, and thereby argue that we can do less than we think—indeed that there is nothing at all that we don't but can do. I am not going to vote Republican next fall. The fatalist argues that, strange to say, I not only won't but can't; for my voting

---

[26] Compare the parodic argument in Trenton Merricks, "Truth and Freedom," op. cit. p. 35 ff.

Republican is not compossible with the fact that it was true already in the year 1548 that I was not going to vote Republican 428 years later. My rejoinder is that this is a fact, sure enough; however it is an irrelevant fact about the future masquerading as a relevant fact about the past, and so should be left out of account in saying what, in any ordinary sense, I can do. We are unlikely to be fooled by the fatalist's methods in this or other ordinary cases. But in cases of time travel, precognition or the like, we are on less familiar ground, so it may take less of a disguise to fool us.[27]

Lewis, as is well-known, is a contextualist about *de re* modal attributions. It is compatible with Lewis's view, for instance, that we can consistently say the essentially omniscient being could not make a faulty prediction and the essentially omnipotent being could make a faulty prediction, even if both descriptions denote God. The definite descriptions invoke different counterpart relations that determine distinct modal properties each of which we refer to by the same phrase "could make a faulty prediction."[28]

Contextualism about de re modality is an interesting position that comports with much of commonsense modal discussion, but the argument against the fatalist does not depend on the assumption of modal contextualism. Suppose we are *realists* about modality.[29] We maintain that God exists in every world—the very same being and not merely a representation of the same being—and there is no world in which God is not omniscient. We reject the proposal that counterpart relations are relevant to the modal properties we should attribute to God and so we deny that the omnipotent being might make a faulty prediction.

God predicts at t that every significantly free essence that he instantiates will always go right. But there is some action that each instantiated essence can perform which is such that, were he to perform it, it would always have been false that God predicts at t that every essence that he instantiates will always go right. It would not be true that God made a faulty prediction. It would be true that he never predicted that every significantly free essence he instantiates will always go right.

[27] See David Lewis, "The Paradoxes of Time Travel" in his *Philosophical Papers Vol. II* (Oxford: Oxford University Press, 1986).

[28] See Ross Cameron, "What's Metaphysical About Metaphysical Necessity?" *Philosophy and Phenomenological Research* (2009) 1–16.

[29] "Realist" might be misleading, since there is nothing anti-realist about the contextualist view. It is only meant to convey a more robust notion of de re modality.

What are the alternatives? One alternative is to maintain that, if each instantiated essence goes wrong, then God makes a faulty prediction and God cannot make a faulty prediction. This alternative is to maintain that the closest worlds in which each instantiated essence goes wrong are worlds in which a contradiction is true. But certainly that's false. Worlds in which God does not make the prediction that every instantiated essence will go right and none go right obviously involves much less of a departure from our world than worlds in which a contradiction is true and none go right.

Another alternative is to maintain that in worlds where one or more instantiated essences sometimes goes wrong, God *could not* have predicted that every instantiated essence always goes right. But if there is anything an omnipotent being can do it is to utter a simple prediction—that is, to strongly actualize the state of affairs of having made a prediction prior to instantiating any essences and prior to creating anything at all.

## 4.7 Problems from Power over the Past

There is another illuminating argument that God believes at $t_1$ that Smith will do $\sim A$ at $t_2$ only if Smith does not freely do $\sim A$ at $t_2$. There is an equally illuminating argument that God predicts that every significantly free essence that he instantiates will always go right only if no significantly free essence that he instantiates freely goes right. Each of these arguments is unsound and each makes the same mistake.

### 4.7.1 Bringing About God's Beliefs

1. God believes at $t_1$ that Smith will do $\sim A$ at $t_2$. Assumption
2. It is within Smith's power to perform an action A at $t_2$. Assumption
3. $/\therefore$ It is within Smith's power to bring it about that God believes at $t_1$ that Smith will do A at $t_2$. From (1), (2)
4. It is not within Smith's power to bring it about that God believes at $t_1$ that Smith will do A at $t_2$. Contradiction (3), (4)
5. $/\therefore$ It is not within Smith's power to perform an action A at a time $t_2$.

The argument is designed to show that divine foreknowledge is not compatible with significant freedom. The most difficult and interesting inference is from premises (1) and (2) to (3). The kind of principle that is supposed to license the inference from (1) and (2) to (3) is the so-called "power entailment principle." Consider the power entailment principle in P1.

P1. If (a) it is within S's power to bring it about that p is true, (b) it is within S's power to bring it about that p is false, and (c) p entails q and not-p entails not-q, then it is also within S's power to bring it about that q is true.[30]

The principle in P1 is restricted to cases where the propositions in p and q are logically equivalent. Concerning the plausibility of P1 William Hasker avers,

About this principle Talbott says that it "seems not only true but obviously true. Where p and q are logically equivalent, it could hardly be up to me whether or not p is true unless it were also up to me whether or not q is true." It seems to me that this is absolutely correct.[31]

If we suppose that P1 is true, we still have the question of whether P1 licenses the inference from (1) and (2) to (3). The inference is supposed to proceed as follows.

1. God believes at $t_1$ that Smith will do $\sim A$ at $t_2$.

2. It is within Smith's power to perform an action A at $t_2$.

2.1. It is within Smith's power to bring it about that the proposition <Smith does A at $t_2$> is true. (2)

2.2. $\Box$(Smith does A at $t_2$ ≡ God believes at $t_1$ that Smith does A at $t_2$)

3. /∴ It is within Smith's power to bring it about that God believes at $t_1$ that Smith will do A at $t_2$. From (2), (2.1), (2.2), P1

The problem of course is that (2.1) does not follow from (2). It follows from (1) that the proposition <Smith will do A at $t_2$> is false. But if the proposition <Smith will do A at $t_2$> is false, then no one, not even God, can bring it about that the proposition is true. No one can cause a false proposition to be true. As we have noted, Smith's power with regard to the truth-value of the proposition <Smith does A at $t_2$> is specified in $P_0$. Smith can perform A at $t_2$ and if Smith were to perform A at $t_2$ then it would always have been the case that the proposition <Smith does A at $t_2$> is true. In worlds where Smith performs A at $t_2$ it is false that Smith

[30] See Thomas Talbott, "On Divine Foreknowledge and Bringing About the Past" *Philosophy and Phenomenological Research* (1986) 455–69. Talbott denies premise (4) in this argument and believes that Smith does have the power to bring it about that God believes at t1 that Smith will do A at t2.

[31] William Hasker, *God, Time and Knowledge*, op. cit. p. 109.

causes the proposition that Smith performs A at $t_2$ to be true. That proposition was always true in that world; it was true in 1995 BC, long before Smith could cause or bring about anything.

Smith has no more than $P_0$ power over the truth-value of the proposition <Smith does A at $t_2$>. But then (3) does not follow from (1), (2), (2.1), (2.2), and P1. There is however a valid inference in the vicinity.

1. God believes at $t_1$ that Smith will do $\sim$A at $t_2$.

2. It is within Smith's power to perform an action A at $t_2$.

2.1'. Smith has $P_0$ power over the truth-value of the proposition <Smith does A at $t_2$> is true. (2)

2.2'. $\Box$(Smith does A at $t_2 \equiv$ God believes at $t_1$ that Smith does A at $t_2$).

3. $/\therefore$ Smith has $P_0$ power over the proposition <God believes at $t_1$ that Smith will do A at $t_2$>. (2), (2.1'), (2.2').

The conclusion in (3) follows from (2), (2.1'), (2.2') and the valid counterfactual rule that A $\Box\rightarrow$ B and $\Box$(B $\equiv$ C) entails A $\Box\rightarrow$ C.

### 4.7.2 Bringing About God's Predictions

Similar arguments aim to show that Smith has the power to bring it about that God does not predict that Smith does A at $t_2$. These arguments encounter the same difficulties.

1. God predicts at $t_1$ that Smith will do $\sim$A at $t_2$.

2. It is within Smith's power to perform an action A at $t_2$.

2.1. It is within Smith's power to bring it about that the proposition <Smith does A at $t_2$> is true. (2)

2.2. $\Box$(Smith does A at $t_2 \supset$ God does not predict at $t_1$ that Smith does A at $t_2$)

3. $/\therefore$ It is within Smith's power to bring it about that God does not predict at $t_1$ that Smith will do A at $t_2$. From (2), (2.1), (2.2)

4. It is not within Smith's power to bring it about that God does not predict at $t_1$ that Smith will do A at $t_2$. Contradiction (3), (4)

5. $/\therefore$ It is not within Smith's power to perform an action A at a time $t_2$.

The argument is designed to show that God's predictions are not compatible with significant freedom. The most difficult and interesting inference is from premises (1), (2), (2.1), and (2.2) to (3). Once again the kind of principle that is supposed to license the inference is called a power entailment principle. Consider the power entailment principle in P2.

> P2. If (a) it is within S's power to bring it about that p is true, (b) p entails q, and (c) q is not a necessary condition of S's having the power to bring it about that p is true, then it is also within S's power to bring it about that q is true.[32]

Principle P2 is designed for situations in which the propositions p and q are not logically equivalent. And certainly there are cases in which we would want to say that p and q are not logically equivalent, but if S has power over the truth-value of p then S has power over the truth-value of q. Talbott argues for P2 as follows.

One might prefer, therefore, a principle that would, in a more general way, distinguish between those cases where the power to bring it about that p is true entails the power to bring it about that q is true and those where, though p entails q, the power to bring it about that p is true does not entail the power to bring it about that q is true. And fortunately there does seem to be such a principle. For if p entails q and yet one's having the power to bring it about that p is true does not entail the power to bring it about that q is true, there seems to be but one alternative left: q must be a necessary condition not only of p but also of one's having the power to bring it about that p is true.[33]

It is a necessary condition of Armstrong walking on the moon that there is a moon. But we don't want to say that, since Armstrong has power over the truth-value of the proposition that Armstrong walks on the moon he also has power over the truth-value of the proposition that there is a moon. Such cases are supposed to be ruled out in clause (c) of P2, since there being a moon is a necessary condition of having the power to walk on it.

The argument proceeds that (2), (2.1), (2.2), entail (3) given the power entailment principle in P2. But even if P2 is true, the inference is invalid. As we have noted Smith's power with regard to the truth-value of the proposition <Smith does A at $t_2$> is specified in $P_0$. Smith can perform A at $t_2$ and if Smith were to perform A at $t_2$ then it would always have been

---

[32] Thomas Talbott, "On Divine Foreknowledge and Bringing About the Past," op. cit. p. 460.
[33] Ibid. p. 459.

the case that Smith does A at $t_2$. That proposition was true in 1995 BC, long before Smith could cause or bring about anything.[34]

Smith has no more than $P_0$ power over the truth-value of the proposition <Smith does A at $t_2$> But then (3) does not follow from (1), (2), (2.1), (2.2), P1. There is however a valid inference in the vicinity.

1. God predicts at $t_1$ that Smith will do $\sim$A at $t_2$.

2. It is within Smith's power to perform an action A at $t_2$.

2.1'. Smith has $P_0$ power over the truth-value of the proposition <Smith does A at $t_2$>. From 2

2.2'. $\square$(God predicts at $t_1$ that Smith does A at $t_2 \supset$ Smith does A at $t_2$)

3. $/\therefore$ Smith has $P_0$ power over the proposition <God believes at $t_1$ that Smith will do A at $t_2$>. (2), (2.1'), (2.2')

The conclusion in (3) follows from (2), (2.1'), (2.2') and the valid counterfactual rule that A $\square\rightarrow$ B and $\square$(B $\supset$ C) entails A $\square\rightarrow$ C.

## 4.8 Consequences for the Free Will Defense

The counterexample to the thesis of universal transworld depravity assumed that, before God instantiates any significantly free individual essences, he makes the following prediction: I predict that every significantly free essence that I instantiate will always go right. If God then instantiates essences that are significantly free, then since God's predictions are always correct, it follows that every essence instantiated always goes right. That is, since it is a necessary truth that God predicts that p will obtain only if p will obtain it follows that were God to predict that p will obtain then it would be the case that p will obtain.

In Section (4.3) we considered whether God has the power to strongly actualize a state of affairs such that, were he to do so, it would always have been true that every essence he instantiates always freely goes right.

---

[34] There is also good reason to reject P2. If God creates Jones in world $w_{100}$, then it is necessarily true that God creates Jones in world $w_{100}$. It follows that a necessary condition of Smith's singing the star spangled banner is the fact that God creates Jones in world $w_{100}$. But obviously, it is not a necessary condition of Smith singing the star spangled banner that God creates Jones in world $w_{100}$.

Indeed, God does have that power and he has it necessarily. It is the power specified in $P_0$.

Since, necessarily, God *can* strongly actualize such a state of affairs there is no correct analysis of transworld depravity. It is true in no possible world that God does not have the power to actualize a morally perfect world. And since, necessarily, God can strongly actualize such a state of affairs it follows that, necessarily, God can actualize a morally perfect world. We are forced to the conclusion that necessarily the thesis of universal transworld depravity is false and so are the weaker depravity theses available to the free will defense. But then the free will defense cannot resolve the logical problem of evil.

# 5

# The Logical Problem of Evil Redux

## 5.0 Introduction

John Mackie argued that God's perfect goodness is incompatible with his failing to actualize the best world that he can actualize. And God's omnipotence is incompatible with his being unable to actualize a morally perfect world. As Mackie put it:

If God has made men such that in their free choices they sometimes prefer what is good and sometimes what is evil, why could he not have made men such that they always freely choose the good? If there is no logical impossibility in his freely choosing the good on one or several occasions, there cannot be a logical impossibility in his freely choosing the good on every occasion. God was not, then, faced with a choice between making innocent automata and making beings who, in acting freely, would sometimes go wrong; there was open to him the obviously better possibility of making beings who would act freely but always go right. Clearly his failure to avail himself of this possibility is inconsistent with his being omnipotent and wholly good.[1]

The argument in Chapter 4 suggests that Mackie was entirely right. It is true that, necessarily, it is within God's power to predict that every significantly free essence that he instantiates will always go right in that world. God's omnipotence and omniscience ensure that he can predict that every instantiated essence always goes right and that his predictions are necessarily accurate. So God predicts that every significantly free essence always goes right only if every significantly free essence always freely goes

[1] See John Mackie, "Evil and Omnipotent" in Michael Rea and Louis Pojman (eds.) *Philosophy of Religion: An Anthology, Fifth Edition* (Belmont: Wadsworth, 2008).

right. But then Mackie's conclusion follows; necessarily, God can actualize a morally perfect world.

So the logical problem of evil re-emerges in a much more serious form. If, necessarily, God can actualize a morally perfect world, then, necessarily, God can actualize a world that includes no evil states of affairs at all. St Augustine famously argued that all natural evil is a species of moral evil. And Plantinga famously urged that, possibly, the Augustinian view is correct.[2]

But perhaps the atheologian can regroup once more. What about natural evil? Evil that cannot be ascribed to the free actions of human beings? Suffering due to earthquakes, disease and the like? Is the existence of evil of this sort compatible with [an omnipotent, omniscient, wholly good being]?... Perhaps some natural evils and some persons are so related that the persons would have produced less moral good if the evils had been absent. But another and more traditional line of thought is pursued by St. Augustine, who attributes much of the evil we find to Satan, or to Satan and his cohorts.[3] Satan, so the traditional doctrine goes, is a mighty non-human spirit who, along with many other angels, was created long before God created man. Unlike most of his colleagues, Satan rebelled against God and has since been wreaking whatever havoc he can. The result is natural evil. So the natural evil we find is due to free actions of non-human spirits.[4]

If the traditional Augustinian view is mistaken, then God can strongly actualize a world that includes no naturally evil states of affairs. But suppose that the Augustinian view is right. If Augustine is right, then God can actualize a morally perfect world only if God can actualize a world that includes no evil states of affairs at all. It does not matter to the soundness of logical problem of evil redux whether the Augustinian view is necessarily true, necessarily false, or contingently true or false.

We can provide a proof that (1) and (2) are broadly, logically inconsistent. And the inconsistency cannot be resolved by rejecting the thesis that, necessarily, God can actualize a morally perfect world.

1. God is omnipotent, omniscient, and wholly good.
2. Evil exists.

---

[2] But we should keep in mind that Augustine was offering a theodicy and Plantinga is offering a defense.

[3] St Augustine, *Confessions and Enchiridion*, Albert Outler (ed.) (tr.) (Philadelphia: Westminster John Knox Press, 2006) 341 ff.

[4] See Alvin Plantinga, *The Nature of Necessity* (Oxford: Oxford University Press, 1974) 191–2.

Since, necessarily, it is within God's power to predict that every significantly free essence that he instantiates will always go right, it follows that
(3) is true.

> 3. Necessarily, God can actualize a morally perfect world that includes
>    no evil states of affairs.

As we noted, either the Augustinian view of natural evil is true or false. If it
is true, then God can unrestrictedly actualize a morally perfect world only
if God can *unrestrictedly actualize* a world that includes no evil states of affairs
at all. If the Augustinian view is false, then God can *strongly actualize* a
naturally perfect world and unrestrictedly actualize a morally perfect
world. In either case (3) is true.

Mackie's observation is that God's omnipotence and perfect goodness
are inconsistent with his failing to avail himself of the possibility of
actualizing a morally perfect world.

> 4. Necessarily, God can actualize a morally perfect world that includes
>    no evil states of affairs only if God does actualize a morally perfect
>    world that includes no evil states of affairs.

Since (5) follows from (3) and (4), we have derived a contradiction. (5) and
(2) cannot both be true: there are no evil states of affairs in the morally perfect
worlds that an omnipotent, omniscient, wholly good being actualizes.

> 5. Necessarily God actualizes a morally perfect world that includes no
>    evil states of affairs.

The logical problem of evil redux provides the sought-after proof of
Mackie's atheological conclusion. It is not possible that God is omnipotent, omniscience, and wholly good and that evil exists. Obviously the
problem cannot be resolved by appeal to the possibility of God's limited
power to actualize a morally perfect world that includes no evil states of
affairs. It is necessarily true that God can actualize a morally perfect world
that includes no evil states of affairs. Just as obviously the problem cannot
be resolved by appeal to God's limited goodness in actualizing possible
worlds. It is necessarily true that God is essentially perfectly good. Any
solution to the logical problem of evil redux must be consistent with God's
perfect power to actualize a morally perfect world that includes no evil
states of affairs and God's perfect goodness in actualizing a possible world.

# 5.1  God's Power and Morally Perfect Worlds

The only premises in the logical argument from evil redux that are open to critical assessment are premises (3) and (4). But there is a strong argument for (3) based on God's power to predict that every significantly free essence that he instantiates will always go right. We have shown that an omnipotent being would have the power to make such a prediction in every world in which it exists. Since God exists in every possible world, premise (3) follows quickly.

But consider premise (4) that, necessarily, God *can* actualize a morally perfect world that includes no evil states of affairs only if God *does* actualize a morally perfect world that includes no evil states of affairs. Premise (3) and premise (4) together entail that one of the theses in (3.3)–(3.5) is true.[5]

> 3.3  Necessarily, an omnipotent, omniscient, wholly good being brings about *the best possible world* and the best possible world includes no evil states of affairs at all.

> 3.4  Necessarily, an omnipotent, omniscient, wholly good being brings about *the best actualizable world* and the best actualizable world includes no evil states of affairs.

> 3.5  Necessarily, an omnipotent, omniscient, wholly good being brings about *a good enough world* and a good enough actualizable world includes no evil states of affairs.

Premises (3.3)–(3.5) exhaust the sorts of possible worlds that might be morally perfect and that include no evil states of affairs. And of course many have believed that one or more of these is true.

Nonetheless Nelson Pike urged that (3.3)–(3.5) might all be false. Pike's suggestion is that the best possible worlds might include some morally evil states of affairs.

A world containing instances of suffering as necessary components might be the best of all possible worlds. And if a world containing instances of suffering as necessary components is the best of all possible worlds, an omnipotent and omniscient being would have a morally sufficient reason for permitting instances of suffering.[6]

---

[5]  The thesis in (3.3)–(3.5) was presented in Chapter 2, p. 59 ff.

[6]  See Nelson Pike, "Hume on Evil" in Marilyn McCord Adams and Robert Merrihew Adams (eds.) *The Problem of Evil* (Oxford: Oxford University Press, 1990) 38–52.

Pike's intuition is that (4) is not necessary, and that (3.3)–(3.5) are all false. God might actualize the best possible world and, possibly, the best possible world includes instances of suffering. That is, the best possible world is not a morally perfect world that includes no evil states of affairs. But if the best possible world might include instances of suffering there is little reason to believe (4) is necessary and no reason to believe that (3.3)–(3.5) are true.

John Wisdom adduced some interesting reasons to believe that a best possible world might include at least some evil states of affairs. According to Wisdom, the addition of evil states of affairs might increase the overall value of a world.

[Suppose] I believe (rightly or wrongly) that you are in pain and become unhappy as a result of that belief. The resulting complex [state of affairs] would appear to be better than it would have been had I believed you to be in pain [and became happy].[7]

Suppose that in the best possible world you are *not* in pain, but I nonetheless believe that you are. Feelings of unhappiness are intrinsically bad. But the complex state of affairs of my believing that you are in pain and my feeling unhappy about it is intuitively better than the complex state of affairs of my believing that you are in pain and my feeling happy or indifferent about it. If the best possible world might include states of affairs such as my believing that you are in pain, then it would be better if it also included evil states of affairs such as my feeling unhappy. But then there is at least some reason to believe that (4) is not true.

The suggestions in Pike and Wisdom provide some reason to doubt (4) and (3.3)–(3.5), but those suggestions certainly do not settle the matter. We can do better. It is true that, necessarily, God can actualize a morally perfect world. But we can show that it is not possible that, necessarily, God does actualize a morally perfect world. If the impossibility argument in (5.2) is sound, then premises (4) and (5) above are necessarily false and so are (3.3)–(3.5). We will conclude that the logical argument redux is unsound.

## 5.2  An Impossibility Argument

The aim is to prove that premise (5) in the logical problem of evil is necessarily false. The proof directly shows that it is *impossible* that,

---

[7] John Wisdom, "God and Evil" *Mind* New Series 44, 173 (1935) 1–20. Wisdom is quoted in Nelson Pike, "Hume on Evil," op. cit. p. 48.

necessarily, God actualizes a morally perfect world. It follows that, possibly, God does not actualize a morally perfect world and therefore possibly God does not actualize a morally perfect world that includes no moral evil. Therefore premise (5) is false and, indeed, necessarily false.

It also follows that premise (4) is necessarily false. The impossibility argument shows that it is impossible that, necessarily, God can actualize a morally perfect world that includes no evil states of affairs only if God does actualize a morally perfect world that includes no evil states of affairs. The logical problem of evil redux is therefore necessarily unsound.

Let's say that W is a morally perfect world if and only if (i) the largest state of affairs T that God strongly actualizes in W includes the instantiation of significantly free individual essences, (ii) there are some actions that are morally significant for each instantiated essence and (iii) every essence that God instantiates in T always goes morally right in W. The first premise in the impossibility proof is that there are, of course, morally perfect worlds.

1.   There exist morally perfect worlds.

We have shown in Chapter 4 that God can unrestrictedly actualize a morally perfect world. It follows that, necessarily, God *can* actualize a morally perfect world. So (2) is also true.

2.   Necessarily, God can actualize a morally perfect world.

According to Leibniz, Mackie, Rowe, and a host of others, necessarily, if God can actualize a morally perfect world, then God does actualize a morally perfect world. Let's assume for reductio that (3) is true.

3.   Necessarily, God does actualize a morally perfect world.

Of course, morally perfect worlds include some significantly free instantiated essences performing morally significant actions. But surely morally perfect worlds vary in the amount of moral value they include. A morally perfect world $W_0$ in which every instantiated essence always goes morally right might include only a few instantiated essences each of whom performs only a few small acts of beneficence. $W_0$ might thereafter include no instantiated essences performing any morally significant acts. $W_0$ is a morally perfect world, but $W_0$ does not contain much moral value. Another morally perfect world $W_1$ might include every instantiated essence always going right with respect to many large acts of beneficence. $W_1$ is a morally perfect world that contains much more moral value than $W_0$.

But most of the moral value of morally perfect worlds is the result of instantiated essences observing *moral prohibitions* against the violation of individual rights or fulfilling the (typically negative) duties that form the fundamental requirements of justice. The demands of justice, even among consequentialists, are typically regarded as the weightiest or most important requirements of morality. Compare John Stuart Mill on justice.

It seems to me that this feature in the case—a right in some person, correlative to the moral obligation—constitutes the specific difference between justice, and generosity or beneficence. Justice implies something which it is not only right to do, and wrong not to do, but which some individual person *can claim from us as his moral right*. No one has a moral right to our generosity or beneficence, because we are not morally bound to practice those virtues towards any given individual. And it will be found with respect to this, as to every correct definition, that the instances which seem to conflict with it are those which most confirm it.[8]

Concerning the importance of the moral claim we have on others to observe the requirements of justice, and to refrain from harming us or violating our moral rights, Mill notes,

[T]he [moral] claim we have on our fellow-creatures to join in making safe for us the very groundwork of our existence, gathers feelings around it so much more intense than those concerned in any of the more common cases of utility that the difference in degree ... becomes a real difference in kind. ... The feelings concerned are so powerful, and we count so positively on finding a responsive feeling in others (all being alike interested), that ought and should grow into must, and recognized indispensability becomes a moral necessity, analogous to physical, and often not inferior to it in binding force exhorted.[9]

Of course, the view Mill expresses on the relative importance of the requirements of justice are forcefully expressed in moral thinkers as diverse as Kant, Rawls, Nozick, Hume, Gauthier, and Cohen.[10] The requirements of justice prohibit the violation of basic moral rights including, property rights, the right to life, rights to freedom, political rights, rights to security, and even extend to certain social and economic rights.

---

[8]  See Mary Warnock (ed.) John Stuart Mill, *Utilitarianism, One Liberty, Essay on Bentham* (New York; Penguin Books, 1974) 305 ff. Emphasis added.

[9]  Ibid. p. 310.

[10]  G. A. Cohen, *Rescuing Justice and Equality* (Cambridge, Mass.: Harvard University Press, 2008); John Rawls, *A Theory of Justice* (Cambridge, Mass.: Harvard University Press, 1975); Robert Nozick, *Anarchy, State and Utopia* (New York: Basic Books, 1975); David Gauthier, *Morals by Agreement* (Oxford: Oxford University Press, 1987).

Consider a morally perfect world $W_2$ in which every instantiated essence always goes morally right with respect to observing the requirements of justice. $W_2$ might include many instantiated essences none of whom violates the moral rights of others. The essences instantiated in $W_2$ constrain their behavior in ways that always observes property rights, the right to life, the right to security and social or economic rights. Since the requirements of justice are the most important moral requirements, $W_2$ is a morally perfect world that is extremely morally valuable.

4. God can actualize the most valuable morally perfect worlds in which every moral agent observes the requirements of justice and never violates a moral right.[11]

We assumed for reductio that, necessarily, God actualizes a morally perfect world. But if necessarily God actualizes a morally perfect world, then it follows immediately that, necessarily, there exist no possible worlds that include a single instance of moral evil. But how does that follow? If necessarily God actualizes a morally perfect world then, since God exists in every world, every possible world includes the state of affairs of its being morally perfect. But every possible world includes the state of affairs of its being morally perfect only if no possible world includes an instance of moral evil. In short, morally perfect worlds have the essential property of containing no moral evil.

5. If, necessarily, God actualizes a morally perfect world, then necessarily there are no possible worlds that include a single instance of moral evil.

Any possible world that includes an instance of moral evil is a morally imperfect world. And from (2) and (5) it follows that necessarily there are no possible worlds which include moral evil.

6. Necessarily, there exist no possible worlds that include a single instance of moral evil.

In particular, there exists no possible worlds in which any instantiated essence violates a principle of beneficence and there exists no possible world in which any instantiated essence violates a principle of justice. It

---

[11] It does not matter if there are no morally perfect worlds that are best. All we need assume is that God can actualize an extremely good morally perfect world in which moral rights are never violated.

follows from premise (6) that it is metaphysically impossible for any moral agent *not* to fulfill the requirements of beneficence and justice.

7. It is metaphysically impossible for any moral agent not to fulfill the requirements of beneficence and justice.

It is metaphysically possible for any moral agent not to fulfill the requirements of justice and beneficence, only if there are possible worlds which contain at least some instances of moral evil. But we know from premise (6) that there are no such worlds. But if it is metaphysically impossible for any moral agent not to fulfill the requirements of beneficence and justice, then it is metaphysically necessary that every moral agent fulfills the requirements of beneficence and justice.

8. It is metaphysically necessary that every moral agent fulfills the requirements of beneficence and justice.

Of course, (8) entails that no instantiated essence in any world exemplifies significant freedom with respect to any action. Significantly free moral agents—significantly free instantiated essences—are libertarian free essences. Recall that an instantiated essence $E_n$ is significantly free with respect to action A in maximal state of affairs T only if A is morally significant and it is possible that $E_n$ performs A in T and *possible that $E_n$ performs $\sim$A in T*.[12] That is, in general, an individual $E_n$ is significantly free with respect to morally significant actions only if $E_n$ can fail to do what is morally right. But if it is metaphysically necessary that every moral agent $E_n$ fulfills the requirements of justice and beneficence, then no moral agent in any world is significantly free.

9. If it is metaphysically necessary that every moral agent fulfills the requirements of beneficence and justice, then it is metaphysically necessary that no instantiated essence is significantly free.

But no moral agent is significantly free only if no action has moral value. As Plantinga observes,

Now God can create free creatures, but he cannot cause or determine them to do only what is right. For if he does so, then they are not significantly free after all; they do not do what is right freely. To create creatures capable of moral good,

---

[12] Recall the conditions on significant freedom specified in S1.

S1: S has significant freedom in doing A at t if and only if (i) A is morally significant for S at t and (ii) $\sim\Box$(God actualizes T $\supset$ S does A at t) & $\sim\Box$(God actualizes T $\supset$ S does $\sim$A at t).

therefore, he must create creatures capable of moral evil; and he cannot leave these free to perform moral evil and at the same time prevent them from doing so.[13]

Here's a useful example. Reconsider the world $W_2$. Suppose Smith observes the requirement not to violate the property rights of Jones. Suppose, for instance, that Smith refrains from stealing Jones' bicycle at t in $W_2$. The state of affairs of Smith's refraining from stealing Jones' bicycle at t in $W_2$ is morally valuable only if Smith freely refrained from stealing Jones' bicycle at t in $W_2$. But Smith freely refrains from stealing Jones' bicycle at t in $W_2$ only if there is a possible world $W_3$ in which Smith freely does not refrain from stealing Jones' bicycle at t. More exactly, Smith freely refrains from stealing Jones' bicycle at t in $W_2$ only if there is some world $W_3$ that shares the same past as $W_2$ until time t but diverges from $W_2$ at t and thereafter. At time t, we have one branch $W_2$ from the past in which Smith refrains from stealing Jones' bicycle and another branch $W_3$ from the same past in which Smith steals Jones' bicycle.[14]

But if there are no morally imperfect worlds as (8) and (9) entail, then there is no possible world in which Smith steals Jones' bicycle at t. But then $W_3$ describes a metaphysically impossible world. It is therefore metaphysically necessary that Smith refrains from stealing Jones' bicycle at t. But of course it is metaphysically necessary that Smith refrains from stealing Jones' bicycle at t only if Smith did not freely refrain from doing so. So, the state of affairs of Smith's refraining from stealing Jones' bicycle at t in $W_2$ has no moral value. The argument generalizes to every action of every moral agent.

> 10. If it is metaphysically necessary that no moral agent is significantly free, then it is metaphysically necessary that no action has moral value.

Of course if it is metaphysically necessary that no action has moral value, then it is impossible that God actualizes a morally perfect world.

> 11. It is impossible that God actualizes a morally perfect world.

The conclusion in (11) is not consistent with our assumption for reductio in (3) that necessarily God actualizes a morally perfect world. But then

---

[13] Plantinga, *The Nature of Necessity*, op. cit. pp. 166–7.
[14] Of course the past will vary with respect to "soft facts" (assuming there are soft facts) when branching respectively to W2 and W3. If Leibniz's Law of the indiscernibility of identicals applies to relational properties, then no two distinct worlds branch from a single past.

premise (3) is false, indeed, it is necessarily false. And we have reached the conclusion of the impossibility argument.

12.   It is impossible that, necessarily, God actualizes a morally perfect world.

Since it is impossible that, necessarily, God actualizes a morally perfect world, the logical problem of evil redux is necessarily unsound. There is no world in which premise (5) in that argument is true. But recall that premise (5) is a logical consequence of premises (3) and (4) in the logical problem of evil redux. In Chapter 4 we showed that premise (3) is true. Therefore premise (4) in the logical problem of evil redux is necessarily false.

### 5.2.1  The Logical Problem of Evil Redux and Consistency Proofs

An impossibility argument is a consistency proof. The argument shows that, possibly, God can actualize a morally perfect world and God does not actualize a morally perfect world. Therefore, it is consistent that an omnipotent, omniscient, wholly good God can prevent an instance of moral evil at no moral cost and he does not prevent that moral evil. The logical problem of evil redux is therefore unsound.

To prove the inconsistency of (1) and (2), the logical problem of evil redux asserts (3) and (4).

1. God is omnipotent, omniscient, and wholly good.
2. Evil exists.
3. Necessarily, God can actualize a morally perfect world that includes no evil states of affairs.
4. Necessarily, God can actualize a morally perfect world that includes no evil states of affairs only if God does actualize a morally perfect world that includes no evil states of affairs.

But the impossibility argument shows that (3) and (4) are themselves inconsistent. There is a world in which <God can actualize a morally perfect world that includes no evil states of affairs> and <God does not actualize a morally perfect world that includes no evil states of affairs> are both true. An impossibility argument therefore shows that (1) and (2) are consistent.

## 5.3  God's Bad Worlds

John Mackie observed that God's omnipotence and perfect goodness are inconsistent with his failing to avail himself of the possibility of actualizing a morally perfect world. But the impossibility argument shows that this observation is false. It is true in every possible world that God can actualize a morally perfect world, but it simply *could not* be necessary that God does actualize a morally perfect world. The first two consequences of the impossibility argument are in I1 and I2.

I1. It is impossible that, necessarily, God actualizes a morally perfect world.

I2. Necessarily, it is possible that God actualizes a morally perfect world only if it is possible that God actualizes a morally imperfect world.

But there is an even more intriguing implication of the impossibility argument. For any morally perfect world W, it is possible that every instantiated essence in W goes wrong with respect to every significantly free action in W. Let's say that W is a *morally bad* world if and only if the largest state of affairs T that God strongly actualizes in W includes the instantiation of significantly free individual essences and every essence that God instantiates in T always goes morally wrong in W. The impossibility argument entails that, necessarily, for any morally perfect world $W_P$, there is a corresponding *bad world* $W_B$ such that every significantly free instantiation in $W_P$ goes wrong with respect to every morally significant action in $W_B$.

I3. Necessarily, it is possible that God actualizes morally perfect world $W_P$ only if it is possible that God actualizes morally bad world $W_B$.

Every morally perfect world is such that every instantiated essence always goes right with respect to the requirements of beneficence and the requirements of justice. But for each action A and each instantiated essence $E_n$, $E_n$'s performing A has moral value only if it's possible that $E_n$ performs $\sim$A. Consider morally perfect worlds W and $W'$ which are indiscernible except for the following modal facts. In W it is possible that instantiated essence $E_1$ tortures $E_2$. In $W'$ it is not possible that $E_1$ tortures $E_2$. It is true in W that $E_1$'s refraining from torturing $E_2$ is morally significant and has moral value. But it is a modal fact in $W'$ that $E_1$ cannot torture $E_2$. Therefore $E_1$'s refraining from torturing $E_2$ in $W'$ has no moral value. In otherwise indiscernible possible worlds, the modal facts that obtain in those worlds determine the moral value of those worlds.

Consider a morally perfect world in which every instantiated essence always goes morally right with respect to observing the requirements of justice and the requirements of beneficence. The agents always freely go right with respect to every requirement of justice and beneficence only if it is possible that, for every action A that justice prohibits or beneficence prohibits, and for every instantiated essence $E_n$ for whom A is morally significant, it is possible that $E_n$ performs A. The essences instantiated in $W_P$ constrain their behavior in ways that always observes all moral rights. The essences instantiated in $W_P$ also constrain their behavior from both minor violations of the requirements of justice and beneficence and from the most grievous violations of the requirements of justice and beneficence. Let $W_B$ be a world in which every free instantiated essence in $W_P$ goes grievously wrong with respect to the requirements of beneficence and justice. The fourth consequence of the impossibility argument is I4.

I4. Necessarily, it is possible that God actualizes an extremely valuable morally perfect world $W_P$ that includes no evil states of affairs only if it is possible that God actualizes an extremely disvaluable world $W_B$ that includes many evil states of affairs.

It is true in every possible world that God can actualize a morally perfect world. But we know there are some worlds in which God can actualize a morally perfect world but does not. The fifth consequence of the impossibility argument is I5.

I5. Necessarily, there is some morally imperfect world W such that God actualizes W and it is true at W that God could have actualized a morally perfect world that includes no evil states of affairs.

The impossibility argument demonstrates that the logical problem of evil redux is necessarily unsound. And the impossibility argument does so without making any controversial metaphysical assumptions such as the possibility that every individual essence is transworld depraved or the possibility that every individual essence is transworld untrustworthy, etc.

The impossibility argument entails that (3.3)–(3.5) are all false, since their second conjunct is false. But the impossibility argument does *not* entail that the first conjuncts of (3.3)–(3.5) are false. It is consistent with the impossibility argument that necessarily God actualizes the best possible world. As we've noted, Gottfried Leibniz and Nelson Pike urged that the best possible world might be morally imperfect. More recently, Alvin Plantinga too has also argued that the best possible world might be imperfect.[15] It is false that, necessarily, God actualizes a morally perfect world. But that is perhaps consistent with it being true that, necessarily, God actualizes the best possible world or a good enough world.

## 5.4  An Impossibility Argument: Best Worlds

We have shown that counterfactuals of creaturely freedom place no restrictions on the possible worlds that God can actualize. Necessarily, the set of all actualizable worlds just is the set of all possible worlds. God can unrestrictedly actualize a morally perfect world and if there is a best possible world, then God can unrestrictedly actualize it.[16] Certainly the most famous defender of the view that God must actualize the best possible world is Gottfried Leibniz.

Now this supreme wisdom, united to a goodness that is no less infinite, cannot but have chosen the best. For as a lesser evil is a kind of good, even so a lesser good is a kind of evil if it stands in the way of a greater good; and there would be something to correct in the actions of God if it were possible to do better.... So it may ... be said in respect of perfect wisdom, ... that if there were not the best (optimum) among all possible worlds, God would not have produced any.[17]

Many contemporary philosophers too have arrived at the same conclusion. William Rowe and Phillip Quinn, for instance, have defended the same view. According to Rowe, if there is a best possible world, then it is impossible that a morally perfect and omnipotent being should fail to actualize it.

On the assumption that God (the supremely perfect being) exists and that there is a best, creatable world, we've reached the conclusion that God is neither free not to create a world nor free to create a world less than the best creatable world. Indeed, God would of necessity create the best of the creatable worlds, leaving us with no basis for thanking him, or praising him for creating the world he does. For given that God exists, and that there is a best world, God's nature as an omnipotent, omniscient, perfectly good being would require him to create that best world.

---

[15] See Alvin Plantinga, "Supralapsarianism, or 'O Felix Culpa'" in Peter van Inwagen (ed.) *Christian Faith and the Problem of Evil* (Grand Rapids: Wm. B. Eerdmans Publishing Company, 2004). Plantinga urges here that every very valuable world will include the atonement and resurrection, so every very valuable world will include moral evil.

[16] Since, necessarily, the set of possible worlds just is the set of actualizable worlds, an impossibility argument for best possible worlds just is an impossibility argument for best actualizable worlds. So I do not offer an impossibility argument for actualizable worlds, though it is not difficult to see how it would go.

[17] See Gottfried Leibniz, *Theodicy* Austin Farrer (ed.) (La Salle: Open Court, 1985).

Doing less than the best he can do—create the best creatable world—would be inconsistent with his being the perfect being he is.[18]

According to Rowe, it follows from the nature of God that he necessarily brings about the best possible world. Since God possesses the divine attributes in every possible world, Rowe's argument entails that, necessarily, God brings about the best possible world. Phillip Quinn similarly argues that a perfect being necessarily actualizes an unsurpassable world.

If an omnipotent and superlatively good moral agent were to actualize a possible world he would actualize some . . . world of unsurpassable moral goodness.[19]

There is therefore what we might call the *Logical Problem of the Best Possible World* according to which, necessarily, God actualizes the best possible world. The argument is not difficult to formulate.

1. God is omnipotent, omniscient, and wholly good.
2. There is a uniquely best possible world.
3. The actual world is not the best possible world.

Since, necessarily, it is within God's power to predict that every significantly free essence that he instantiates will always go right or always do what is best, it follows that (4) is true.

4. Necessarily, God can actualize the best possible world.

Leibniz's observation is that God's omnipotence and perfect goodness are inconsistent with his failing to avail himself of the possibility of actualizing the best possible world.

5. Necessarily, God can actualize the best possible world only if God does actualize the best possible world.

Since (6) follows from (4) and (5), we have derived a contradiction: (6) and (3) cannot both be true.

6. Necessarily God actualizes the best possible world.

---

[18] See William Rowe, "Can God Be Free?" *Faith and Philosophy* 19 (2002) 405–24.
[19] Phillip Quinn, "God, Moral Perfection and Possible Worlds" in Frederick Sontag and M. Darrol Bryant (eds.) *God: The Contemporary Discussion* (New York: Rose of Sharon Press, 1982) 212.

But we can show that it's false that, necessarily, God actualizes the best possible world. Recall the assumption in premise (2) that there is a uniquely best possible world W★.[20] The best possible world will contain the greatest possible amounts of moral and natural value. The claim to be proven is that it is impossible that God necessarily actualizes W★.

Suppose for reductio that God necessarily brings about the possible world W. And suppose that W is identical to the best possible world W★.

7. Necessarily, God brings about W and W = W★

If God necessarily brings about the possible world W, then there is some maximal state of affairs T such that necessarily God strongly actualizes T and some maximal state of affairs F which includes the occurring of undetermined events and the performing of morally significant actions. Necessarily, God unrestrictedly actualizes the possible world W.

8. Necessarily, God unrestrictedly actualizes possible world W.

The possible world W is the maximal state of affairs such that W = T & F. Since according to (8) God *necessarily* brings about the possible world W, we know it is metaphysically necessary that W obtains. There is no possible world that is not identical to the best possible world if God necessarily actualizes the best possible world.

9. It is metaphysically necessary that W obtains.

But, of course, it is necessary that W obtains only if W is the only possible world. And if W is the only possible world, then everything that occurs in W, necessarily occurs in W.

10. Everything that occurs in W necessarily occurs.

If everything that occurs in W necessarily occurs, then W is a necessitarian world.[21] Necessitarianism is the position that there is exactly one possible world. The thesis entails the equally implausible thesis known as fatalism.

---

[20] We could assume instead that there is a set of best possible worlds: a set of worlds such that no world is better than any world in that set. The argument would then show that God does not necessarily actualize a world in that set. See the argument below from good enough worlds.

[21] See Hud Hudson, *A Materialist Metaphysics of the Person* (Ithaca: Cornell University Press, 2001) 5–6. See also M. J. Almeida, *The Metaphysics of Perfect Beings* (London: Routledge, 2008) esp. ch. 8.

Fatalists maintain that everything that does occur unavoidably occurs. But it is consistent with fatalism that there should be many possible worlds which only a divine being could bring about. Necessitarianism is the far more austere thesis that not even God could bring it about that the most insignificant event is different.[22]

11. W is a necessitarian world.

In necessitarian worlds such as W it is impossible that any instantiated essence acts in a way that is even slightly different from the way it does act. Let p be a proposition stating that the instantiated essence Smith performs some morally wrong action. Let $\Box$ represent metaphysical necessity. Finally let Aw represent the proposition that God actualizes W. It is easy to show that if an instantiated essence performs a morally wrong action then it is metaphysically necessary that the instantiated essence performs a morally wrong action. The inference is a simple syllogism.[23]

(i)   $\Box(Aw \supset p)$
(ii)  $\Box Aw$
(iii) $/\therefore \Box p$

According to premise (i), necessarily, God actualizes the best possible world W only if Smith performs a morally right action. Premise (ii) states that necessarily God actualizes the best possible world W. But, then, (iii) follows straightforwardly. The conclusion states that necessarily Smith performs a morally wrong action. But it is necessary that Smith performs a morally wrong action only if Smith is not significantly free with respect to that action. The conclusion generalizes to every action of every essence instantiated in W. But then no instantiated essence in W is significantly free.

12. No instantiated essence in W is significantly free.

No agent in W is free only if W includes no moral value. And if W contains no moral value, then W is not the best possible world.

13. W is not the best possible world.

[22] See Hudson, *A Materialistic Metaphysics of the Human Person*, op. cit. pp. 5–6.
[23] The necessitarian problem generalizes to the case of multiverses. See Almeida, *The Metaphysics of Perfect Beings*, op. cit. pp. 152 ff; and M. J. Almeida, "O'Connor's Permissive Multiverse" *Philosophia Christi* 12/2 (2010) 297–308.

But if W is not the best world then W $\neq$ W$^\star$.

14. W is not identical to the best possible world W$^\star$.

Since (14) is inconsistent with (7), we conclude that it is not necessary that God actualizes the best possible world. The assumption that necessarily God actualizes the best possible world yields a contradiction. It follows as well that it is impossible that necessarily God actualizes the best possible world.[24]

According to the logical problem of the best possible world, there is a uniquely best possible world and God can actualize it. But we have shown that any world that God necessarily brings about is a necessitarian world. And obviously no best possible world is a necessitarian world. So it is possible that God actualizes the best possible world but it is impossible that God necessarily brings about the best possible world. We can strengthen this conclusion. Even if it is necessarily possible that God actualizes the best possible world, it is not possibly necessary that God actualizes the best possible world.

Certainly the most famous defender of the view that necessarily God actualizes the best possible world is Gottfried Leibniz. But contemporary philosophers have also defended that view, including William Rowe, Philip Quinn, and of course many others. The impossibility argument demonstrates that the view is necessarily false. The conclusion, it should be emphasized, does not entail that it is impossible for God to actualize the best possible world. We have assumed that there is a best possible world and that it is possible that God actualizes it. Indeed we have assumed that it is necessarily possible that God actualizes the best possible world. The impossibility argument shows only that it is not necessary that God actualizes the best possible world. God can actualize the best possible world only if he can actualize a less than best possible world.

### 5.4.1 The Logical Problem of the Best Possible World and Consistency Proofs

An impossibility argument: best world is a consistency proof. The argument shows that, possibly, God can actualize the best possible world and God does not actualize the best possible world. Therefore, it is consistent that an omnipotent, omniscient, wholly good God might have actualized the best possible world and an omnipotent, omniscient, wholly good God

---

[24] Premise (10) follows from (9) given the S5 theorem $\Diamond p \supset \Box \Diamond p$.

did not actualize the best possible world. So, the argument is to show that the logical problem of the best possible world is unsound.

To prove the inconsistency of (1) and (2), the logical problem of the best possible world asserts (3) and (4).

1. God is omnipotent, omniscient, and wholly good.
2. The actual world is not the best possible world.
3. Necessarily, God can actualize the best possible world.
4. Necessarily, God can actualize the best possible world only if God does actualize the best possible world.

But the impossibility argument shows that (3) and (4) are themselves inconsistent. There is a world in which God can actualize the best possible world and God does not actualize the best possible world. An impossibility argument therefore shows, in addition, that (1) and (2) are consistent.

## 5.5  An Impossibility Argument: Good Enough Worlds

It is reasonable to suppose that God must actualize some member of a set of worlds all of which have a positive overall value at least as high as some minimum positive value N.[25] Call the set of all worlds whose value is N or greater the set S of *Good Enough Worlds*. We make no other assumptions about the set S. S might be the set of best worlds where every member of S has an equal and unexceeded value N. S might be finite including every world whose overall value is N or greater. S might be infinitely large including infinitely many worlds whose overall value is N or greater. Finally, it could be that S is infinitely large and infinitely improving. In that case S includes infinitely many better and better worlds all of which is N or greater in overall value.

There is a *Logical Problem of Good Enough Worlds* according to which, necessarily, God actualizes a good enough possible world. The argument is not difficult to formulate.

1. God is omnipotent, omniscient, and wholly good.
2. Our world is not a good enough world.

---

[25] For a sustained argument that God must actualize a good enough world, see Bruce Langtry, *God, the Best, and Evil* (Oxford: Oxford University Press, 2008).

Since, necessarily, it is within God's power to predict that every signifi-cantly free essence that he instantiates will always go right, or that the significantly free essences that he instantiates will together produce a world whose moral value is N or greater, it follows that (3) is true.

3. Necessarily, God can actualize a good enough world.

God's omnipotence and perfect goodness do seem inconsistent with his failing to avail himself of the possibility of actualizing a good enough world.

4. Necessarily, God can actualize a good enough world only if God does actualize a good enough world.

Since (5) follows from (3) and (4), we have derived a contradiction. (5) and (2) cannot both be true.

5. Necessarily God actualizes a good enough world.

The aim of the impossibility argument for good enough worlds is to show that it is not necessary that God actualizes a member of the set S of good enough worlds. The conclusion in (5) is false, and so premise (4) is false. The impossibility argument shows that it is necessary that God actualizes a member of S only if there is some world W such that the overall value of W is less than N and W ∈ S. But that's impossible since any world W whose overall value is less than N is such that W ∉ S. The assumption that necessarily God actualizes some world in S entails a contradiction, so the assumption is false. Indeed, it is impossible that necessarily God actualizes a world in S. It is therefore impossible that necessarily God actualizes a good enough world.

Let $S^\star$ be the set of all possible worlds. Let the set $S \subset S^\star$ be the set of good enough worlds. The set of good enough worlds is a subset of the set of all possible worlds; it is the set of all worlds in $S^\star$ that are good enough for actualization. By hypothesis the set S includes every possible world whose overall value is N or greater, for some positive N. Assume that S includes all and only the worlds in $S^\star$ that have an overall value of N or greater for some positive N.

6. S includes all and only the worlds in $S^\star$ whose overall value is N or greater for some positive N.

Let $W_0$ be a world whose overall value is exactly N. $W_0$ contains the least value any world could contain among the good enough worlds in S. $W_0$ has a value of N, but it might not include any significantly free beings. Let's assume that $W_0$ is a just and beneficent world that includes significantly free beings and whose overall value is N. Let every significantly free being in $W_0$ generally refrain from violation of the prohibitions of justice and generally fulfill the requirements of beneficence.

7. The overall value of world $W_0$ is exactly N.

Since every instantiated essence in $W_0$ is significantly free it is possible that God strongly actualizes T in $W_0$ and every instantiated essence $E_n$ in $W_0$ always gravely violates the requirements of beneficence. We could make a weaker claim. Among the worlds whose overall value is N there are worlds that include significant free instantiated essences that go right with respect to some duties of beneficence. Of course among the worlds whose overall value is exactly N there are also worlds that contain only natural good. And among the worlds whose overall value is exactly N there are some that include natural good and moral good, assuming that natural good is not a species of moral good, and so on. Good enough worlds simply have to have an overall value of N or greater.

So it is possible in $W_0$ that with respect to all duties of beneficence, every significantly free instantiated essence goes wrong. But if all instantiated essences in $W_0$ were to go wrong with respect to every duty of beneficence, these essences would of course actualize a world $W_1$ that has less overall value than $W_0$. The violations of justice and beneficence in $W_1$ would make the overall value of $W_1$ is less than N. So (8) is true.

8. There is a possible world $W_1$ whose overall value is less than N.

So, the overall value of $W_0$ is N and the overall value of $W_1$ is less than N. Now assume for reductio that necessarily God actualizes some world in the set S of good enough worlds.

9. Necessarily God actualizes some world in S.

If necessarily God actualizes a world in S then every possible world is a member of S. So every possible world has an overall value of N or greater. The members of S exhaust the possible worlds that exist.

10. Every possible world is in S.

But if every possible world is in S then $W_1$ is in S. If every instantiated essence is significantly free in $W_0$, then it is possible in $W_0$ that every significantly free instantiated essence goes wrong and together actualize, $W_1$. So, if it is possible in $W_0$ that every instantiated essence goes wrong, then $W_1$ is possible. But $W_1$ is possible only if $W_1 \in S$.

11. $W_1 \in S$

But of course it follows from premise (8) that $W_1$ is not in S.

12. $W_1 \notin S$

Premises (11) and (12) are inconsistent. Therefore our assumption for reductio in (9) is false. It is false that, necessarily, God actualizes some world in S. And it follows that it is impossible that, necessarily, God actualizes some world in S. More generally it is impossible that, necessarily God actualizes some world whose overall value is N or greater for some positive N.

### 5.5.1 The Value Added Argument

Let's reconsider the modal facts about world $W_0$. We know that $W_0$ has an overall value of N and that in $W_0$ every significantly free instantiated essence $E_n$ might have gone wrong with respect to every duty of justice or beneficence. It is a modal fact in $W_0$ that had every significantly free instantiated essence gone wrong with respect to every duty of justice in $W_0$, then the world $W_1$ would be actual and $W_1$ is morally worse than $W_0$. But then some world whose moral value is less than N would be among the good enough worlds and that's not possible.

But it might be argued that the modal facts obtaining in $W_0$ are not those we have attributed to it. If $W_0$ is in the set of good enough worlds, and every metaphysically possible world is among the good enough worlds, then $W_1$ is not a possible world. Had every significantly free instantiated essence "gone wrong" with respect to his duties of justice in $W_0$, then it is *not* the case that world $W_1$ would have been actual. Rather, another possible world $W_2$ whose moral value is N or greater would have been actual.

According to the value added argument, the world $W_1$ would not have been actual, but rather another world $W_2$ would have been actual whose moral value is N or greater. Perhaps God would have added value to $W_0$ or perhaps God would have instantiated other individual essences that would have added value to $W_0$ to compensate for the lost value. But if it is true that $W_2$ is no less valuable than $W_0$ then it is not true that any free being in $W_0$ can perform any action that has moral disvalue. No significantly free being can do anything in $W_0$ that lessens the overall moral value of $W_0$, either in terms of beneficence or in terms of justice. But then there are no actions A in $W_0$ which are such that performing A makes the world morally worse either in terms of justice or in terms of beneficence.

But that is in violation of our hypothesis that $W_0$ includes significantly free beings performing morally significant actions.

Assume some broadly axiological or consequentialist moral view is correct. The rightness or wrongness of actions depends exclusively on the value of the consequences of those actions. If there are no actions A in $W_0$ such that were a significantly free being to perform A it would be overall worse either in terms of justice or in terms of beneficence, then there are no morally wrong actions in $W_0$. So, on axiological or consequentialist moral theories, it is false that free beings face morally significant actions. But that is contrary to our hypothesis about $W_0$.

Suppose some broadly deontological theory is correct. Deontological theories advance the view that the rightness or wrongness of actions does not depend exclusively on the value of the consequences of those actions. That certainly does not mean that any deontological view maintains that a possible world is not morally worsened—that is, not worsened in terms of justice or beneficence—if every significantly free agent chooses to act contrary to the requirements of justice and beneficence. The world might be worsened by the violations of certain individual moral rights, for instance. But the violations of certain moral rights are not justified by the observation of other equally important moral rights. If some broadly deontological theory is right then it is false that adding value—or adding more just actions or adding more people observing individual rights—to $W_0$ will justify any violation of justice that occurs in $W_0$. But that is contrary to the *Value Added Argument*.

Here is another way to see what is wrong with the value added argument. The logical problem of good enough worlds begins with the assumption that God did not actualize a good enough world. This observation is supposed to generate an atheological argument. The impossibility argument therefore begins with the shared assumption that, for each positive value N, the sequence of all possible worlds S includes worlds that are good enough and also includes worlds that are not good enough

relative to N. The question is whether, for some preferred positive value
N, God could have actualized all and only those worlds that have value
N or greater. The impossibility argument returns the answer that, for any
preferred positive value N, God could not have actualized just those
worlds whose value is N or greater. The reason God cannot actualize
just those worlds whose value is N or greater is that there exists, for each
possible positive N, a world W whose value is N and such that W has value
N only if W′ has a value less than N. Therefore there is some world W′ not
in the series S for any proposed series of good enough worlds.[26]

So the value added argument rests on the false assumption that, for any
good enough world of value N, there exist no worlds whose value is N in
part because there exist worlds whose value is less than N. In fact, there are
worlds W whose value is N because the significantly free instantiated
essences in W are acting in ways that prevent the actualization of a morally
worse world W′. Such worlds would have to be included in any set
of worlds good enough for God to actualize. But worlds such as W′
cannot be included in the set of worlds good enough for God to actualize.
So there is no set of worlds such that all of those worlds have value N or
greater and only those worlds are possible.

There is yet another way to see the problem with the value added
argument. Consider any sequence of worlds S = $W_0$, $W_1$, $W_2$,...,$W_n$
whose value begins at N and increases as we move up the numbered
sequence, perhaps infinitely. No matter where we begin the sequence S,
there will be some worlds in the sequence whose moral value is derived in
part from significantly free instantiated essences refraining from actualizing
worlds outside of S. There will be some worlds W in S, for instance, whose
moral value is derived in part from significantly free instantiated essences
refraining from actualizing worlds W′ outside the sequence in which some
of the gravest violations of justice and beneficence occur. The modal fact
about W that the significantly free instantiated essences in W can actualize
W′ but, in fulfilling the requirements of justice and beneficence, freely
refrain from actualizing W′ is part of what makes W such a morally
valuable world. The existence of world W in the sequence S depends on

---

[26]  It is conceded that when we imagine a sequence of worlds all of which have a value of
N or greater, we are imagining a counterpossible. Of course, it is the logical problem of good
enough worlds which proposes that some such counterpossible sequence would have obtained had God existed.

the existence of world $W'$ that is not in sequence S. The central problem for the added value argument is the assumption that for some sequence S of worlds whose value is N or greater, there is no member W of S whose moral value depends on the existence of worlds that are not in S. That assumption is false.[27]

### 5.5.2 Conclusions about Good Enough Worlds

We have arrived at an interesting conclusion. It is not necessary that God actualizes a good enough world. It is in fact impossible that, necessarily, God actualizes a good enough world. The conclusion in the logical problem of good enough worlds is necessarily false. There is therefore a world in which it is true that God can actualize a good enough world and God does not actualize a good enough world.

Some explanation is in order. Certainly there's a set of worlds that have an overall value equal to or greater than N. Call the good enough worlds N-worlds. The impossibility argument shows that the set of good enough worlds includes at least some N-worlds such that, necessarily those N-worlds are possible only if a non-N-world is possible. The N-world discussed in the argument above is $W_0$. $W_0$ includes instantiated essences that are significantly free and always observe the requirements of justice and beneficence. Since the essences in $W_0$ are significantly free, it is possible that every instantiated essence in $W_0$ always goes gravely wrong with respect to the requirements of justice and beneficence. Since it is possible for every instantiated essence in $W_0$ always to go gravely wrong with respect to the requirements of justice and beneficence, some world $W_1$ at which every instantiated essence does go gravely wrong with respect to the requirements of justice and beneficence and whose value is less than N. So $W_1$ is a non-N-world. The impossibility argument shows that the set of good enough worlds includes an N-world W such that, necessarily W is possible only if a non-N-world is possible. Non-N-worlds are not good enough worlds. But then it is false that necessarily God actualizes a good enough world.

---

[27]  This is not to say that there is no sequence that (i) includes some of the worlds that have value N or better and (ii) includes no world whose value depends on the existence of worlds outside of S. It is not difficult to form such a sequence. Take any sequence of worlds S that includes every possible world whose value is N or greater. Remove every world in S whose value depends in part on worlds not in S.

### 5.5.3 The Logical Problem of Good Enough Worlds and Consistency Proofs

The impossibility argument for good enough worlds is a consistency proof. The argument shows that, possibly, God can actualize a good enough world and God does not actualize a good enough world. Therefore, it is consistent that an omnipotent, omniscient, wholly good God might have actualized a good enough world and an omnipotent, omniscient, wholly good God did not actualize a good enough world. So the *Logical Problem of Good Enough Worlds* is unsound.

The consistency proof in the impossibility argument shows that the premises in *The Logical Problem of Good Enough Worlds* are not consistent. To prove the inconsistency of (1) and (2), the logical problem of good enough worlds asserts (3) and (4).

1. God is omnipotent, omniscient, and wholly good.
2. Our world is not a good enough world.
3. Necessarily, God can actualize a good enough world.
4. Necessarily, God can actualize a good enough world only if God does actualize a good enough world.

But the impossibility argument shows that (3) and (4) are themselves inconsistent. There is a world in which <God can actualize a good enough world> and <God does not actualize a good enough world> are both true. The impossibility argument therefore shows, in addition, that propositions (1) and (2) are consistent.

## 5.6  A Word on Natural Evils

Natural evils include states of affairs such as the pain and suffering due to deadly diseases, earthquakes, famines, pestilence, hurricanes, drought, and the like. There is nothing intrinsically evil about these natural events, it is simply a contingent fact that these events often cause pain and suffering. As a matter of fact, they are often instrumentally disvaluable. But just as often these events are environmentally or ecologically valuable. Broadly speaking whole species have evolved in ways that benefit from such natural evils. Droughts, for instance, are valuable to species distribution among plant life, and infectious bacteria play a very important ecological role despite causing death and disease.

It is perhaps a taxonomical error to categorize any evil as natural evil. What is called natural evil is in many cases evil that significantly free being $E_n$ might have prevented. It's true in many cases that had significantly free beings acted otherwise, the evil that results from natural disasters would have been avoided. The natural evil that most of us suffer is the result of a calculated risk that most of us take in pursuit of other values. To take one example, the pain and suffering due to drought or hurricanes is often due to choices to live—or to continue to live—in drought-prone and hurricane-prone areas. No doubt these decisions are often difficult to avoid, and are largely not proper objects of blame. But this is not the question we are asking. We are asking whether there is any natural evil that does not result in part from the choices of significantly free beings, whether those choices are appraisable or not.

Similar decisions determine the extent of natural evil due to famine and earthquakes. Since natural evil is largely the result of decisions to live in areas prone to natural disaster—granting that these decisions are certainly made under epistemic and economic limitations and social and cultural pressure—much or all of what we call natural evil might easily be assimilated to moral evil.

Natural evil is standardly understood to be evil that results from or is caused by natural events and not evil that is caused by significantly free beings. Worlds in which there are no sentient beings—no beings capable of suffering pains or enjoying pleasures, no beings capable of changes in well-being or, in other words, no beings possessing a welfare—are worlds where deadly diseases, earthquakes, famines, pestilence, hurricanes, drought, and the like cause no pain and suffering. There are no natural evils in such worlds.

We briefly noted in Section 5.0 that Alvin Plantinga famously—infamously, in some quarters—offered two responses to the specific problem of natural evil.[28] The traditional response advances the epistemically possible thesis that every purported instance of natural evil is the result of significantly free action. The traditional response that he endorses states the following.

What about natural evil? Evil that cannot be ascribed to the free actions of human beings? Suffering due to earthquakes, disease and the like? . . . Here two lines of

---

[28] Complaints about the Augustinian response can be found, among other places, in Richard Swinburne, *The Existence of God* (Oxford: Oxford University Press, 2004) 202 ff; and John Mackie, *The Miracle of Theism* (Oxford: Clarendon Press, 1982) 162 ff.

thought suggest themselves. . . . [The] more traditional line of thought is pursued by St. Augustine, who attributes much if the evil we find to *Satan*, or to Satan and his cohorts. . . . We have noted the possibility that God could not have actualized a world with a better balance of moral good over moral evil than this one displays. Something similar holds here; possibly natural evil is due to the free activity of a set of non-human persons, and perhaps it was not within God's power to create a set of such persons whose free actions produced a greater balance of good over evil.[29]

On the Augustinian line, God actualizes a world in which the suffering and pain attributed to natural evils is in fact the result of significantly free action. Natural evil is a species of moral evil. The suggestion is that, possibly, God actualizes a world that contains natural evil, but he could not have actualized one that has a better overall balance of good over evil.

Plantinga's traditional response depends on the thesis of universal trans-world depravity. But we know that the thesis of universal transworld depravity is necessarily false. Necessarily, God can actualize a morally perfect world with a better overall balance of good over evil than the world Plantinga describes. Indeed, necessarily, God can actualize a morally perfect world that includes no evil states of affairs at all.

The less traditional line of argument emphasizes the value of our free *moral responses* to natural evil.

Some people deal creatively with certain kinds of hardship or suffering, so acting that on balance the whole state of affairs is valuable. Perhaps their responses would have been less impressive and the total situation less valuable without the evil. Perhaps some person and some evils are so related that the persons would have produced less moral good if the evils had been absent.[30]

But certainly among the best moral responses to natural evil is the prevention of natural evil altogether. Among the best worlds, the good enough worlds and the morally perfect worlds we should expect to find worlds in which significantly free beings satisfy the requirements of beneficence by preventing every state of affairs that includes the pain and suffering due to natural events. Call the worlds in which there is no suffering and pain due to natural events *naturally perfect worlds*.

There is a *Logical Problem of Naturally Perfect Worlds* according to which, necessarily, God actualizes a naturally perfect world.

[29] Plantinga, *The Nature of Necessity*, op. cit. pp. 191–2.
[30] Ibid.

1. God is omnipotent, omniscient, and wholly good.
2. Our world is not a naturally perfect world.

Since, necessarily, it is within God's power to predict that every significantly free essence that he instantiates will prevent all natural evil, it follows that (3) is true.

3. Necessarily, God can actualize a naturally perfect world.

But God's omnipotence and perfect goodness are inconsistent with his failing to avail himself of the possibility of actualizing a naturally perfect world.

4. Necessarily, God can actualize a naturally perfect world only if God does actualize a naturally perfect world.

Since (5) follows from (3) and (4), we have derived a contradiction. (5) and (2) cannot both be true.

5. Necessarily God actualizes a naturally perfect world.

But the premises in the logical problem of naturally perfect worlds are inconsistent. It is impossible that, necessarily, God actualizes a naturally perfect world.

Let S be the set of all naturally perfect possible worlds. The set S includes, among other worlds, the set of best possible worlds in which there is no natural evil and the set of morally perfect worlds in which there is no natural evil and the set of good enough worlds in which there is no natural evil. Also included in S is the morally perfect world W in which every significantly free instantiated essence in W satisfies some of the requirements of beneficence by preventing every state of affairs that includes the pain and suffering due to natural events. $W_0$ includes no states of affairs that are morally evil, since W is a morally perfect world, and W includes no state of affairs that is naturally evil, since W is naturally perfect. Significantly free instantiated essences in W take every measure necessary to prevent all of the pain and suffering from diseases, earthquakes, hurricanes, wildfires, famines, pestilence, hurricanes, drought, and the like. Of course, there are also worlds $W_1$ in S such that every significantly free instantiated essence together with God freely prevents every state of affairs that includes the pain and suffering due to natural events. And there are many other morally perfect and naturally perfect worlds in S.

Necessarily, God can actualize a naturally perfect world, since God can unrestrictedly actualize a morally perfect and naturally perfect world. Assume for reductio that, necessarily, God does actualize a naturally perfect world.

6.  Necessarily, God actualizes a naturally perfect world.

The assumption (6) entails that every possible world is naturally perfect and every possible world is in S.

7.  Every possible world is in S. (6)

The state of affairs of there being pain and suffering due to disease, earthquakes, hurricanes, pestilence, wildfires, famine, drought, and the like obtains in no world in S. So, that state of affairs is impossible.

8.  There is no possible world $W_3$ in S such that the state of affairs of there being pain and suffering due to disease, earthquakes, hurricanes, pestilence, famine, drought, and the like obtains in $W_3$. (6), (7)

But if every possible world is in S, then W is in S. Recall that W is a morally perfect and naturally perfect world. W is such that every significantly free instantiated essence in W satisfies the requirements of beneficence by preventing every state of affairs that includes the pain and suffering due to natural events. But if W is in S, then $W_3$ is also in S. Significantly free instantiated essences in W do everything necessary to prevent the pain and suffering due to diseases, earthquakes, famines, pestilence, hurricanes, drought, and the like. But every significantly free instantiated essence fulfills some of the requirements of beneficence in preventing the pain and suffering due to natural events only if it is possible that every significantly free instantiated essence freely violates the requirements of beneficence in allowing the pain and suffering due to natural events. But then it is possible there is pain and suffering due to disease, pestilence, famine, hurricanes, drought, and the like. But then $W_3$ is a possible world. Since every possible world is in S, W is possible only if $W_3$ is in S.

9.  $W_3$ is in S.

But it follows from premise (8) above that $W_3$ is not in S.

10.  $W_3$ is not in S.

Premises (9) and (10) are obviously inconsistent. So our assumption for reductio is false. So, it is false that, necessarily, that God actualizes a world that includes no natural evil. And it follows that it is impossible that, necessarily, God actualizes a world that includes no natural evil.

Of course, it is possible that God actualizes a world in which the pain and suffering due to natural events is prevented. Indeed it is necessary that God can actualize a world in which the pain and suffering due to natural events is prevented. God can actualize a world in which there is no disease, pestilence, famine, hurricanes, drought, or the like. God can actualize worlds such as $W_0$ in which every instantiated essence freely prevents the pain and suffering caused by hurricanes, droughts, famine, or the like. But it is impossible that, necessarily, God actualizes a world without suffering due to natural events. Therefore there is some world in which God can prevent the pain and suffering due to natural events and God does not prevent the pain and suffering due to natural events.

### 5.6.1 The Logical Problem of Natural Evil and Consistency Proofs

*A Word on Natural Evil* provides a consistency proof. We have shown that, possibly, God can actualize a naturally perfect world and God does not actualize a naturally perfect world. Therefore, it is consistent that an omnipotent, omniscient, wholly good God can actualize a naturally perfect world and that God does not actualize a naturally perfect world. The *Logical Problem of Natural Evil* is unsound.

The consistency proof shows that the premises in the *Logical Problem of Natural Evil* are not consistent. To prove the inconsistency of (1) and (2), the logical problem of natural evil asserts (3) and (4).

1. God is omnipotent, omniscient, and wholly good.
2. Our world is not a naturally perfect world.
3. Necessarily, God can actualize a naturally perfect world.
4. Necessarily, God can actualize a naturally perfect world only if God does actualize a naturally perfect world.

But the impossibility argument shows that (3) and (4) are themselves inconsistent. There is a world in which <God can actualize a naturally perfect world> and <God does not actualize a naturally perfect world> are both true. The impossibility argument also shows, that propositions (1) and (2) are consistent.[31]

---

[31]  It is tempting to suggest the following revision to the logical argument from natural evil. Necessarily, God actualizes a world in which he prevents all natural evil. But that is

## 5.7  Some Striking Conclusions

Premise (3) and premise (4) in the *Logical Problem of Evil Redux* together entail that one of the theses in (3.3)–(3.5) is true.[32]

> 3.3  Necessarily, an omnipotent, omniscient, wholly good being brings about *the best possible world* and the best possible world includes no evil states of affairs at all.

> 3.4  Necessarily, an omnipotent, omniscient, wholly good being brings about *the best actualizable world* and the best actualizable world includes no evil states of affairs.

> 3.5  Necessarily, an omnipotent, omniscient, wholly good being brings about *a good enough world* and a good enough actualizable world includes no evil states of affairs.

Each of (3.3)–(3.5) entails that necessarily God actualizes a morally perfect world. But the impossibility argument in Section 5.2 shows that it is impossible that, necessarily, God actualizes a morally perfect world. Since we have been assuming that God is an essentially omnipotent, essentially omniscient, essentially perfectly good, and necessarily existing being, that conclusion is very surprising. The impossibility argument shows that it is impossible that, necessarily, an essentially omnipotent, essentially omniscient, essentially perfectly good, and necessarily existing being actualizes a morally perfect world. The thesis that an essentially perfect being fails to actualize a morally perfect world only if that being is not omnipotent or not omniscient or not perfectly good, is nothing more than philosophical dogma. It is perfectly possible that an essentially perfect being fails to actualize a morally perfect world. It follows that all of (3.3)–(3.5) are false and the *Logical Problem of Evil Redux* is necessarily unsound.

It is widely agreed that, possibly, an essentially omnipotent, essentially omniscient, essentially perfectly good, and necessarily existing being fails to actualize the best possible world only if either there is no best possible world or the best possible world is not actualizable. But the impossibility argument in (5.4) assumes both that there is a best possible world and that,

---

inconsistent with the existence of worlds in which significantly free creatures prevent natural evil. Certainly there is no atheological problem with the existence of worlds in which significantly free creatures prevent natural evil.

[32]  The thesis in (3.3)–(3.5) was presented in Chapter 2, p. 59 ff.

necessarily, God can actualize the best possible world. We found that it's impossible that, necessarily, an essentially omnipotent, essentially omniscient, essentially perfectly good, and necessarily existing being actualizes the best possible world. It's a necessary truth that there is some possible world in which God *can* actualize the best possible world and God *does not* actualize the best possible world.

We might have expected that, minimally, God must actualize some member of a set of good enough worlds. The set of good enough worlds is just the set S of worlds all of which have a positive overall value at least as high as some minimum value N. But the impossibility argument in (5.5) shows it's impossible that, necessarily, God actualizes some world in S. It is impossible that, necessarily, God actualizes a good enough world.

This conclusion is particularly interesting since we make no other assumptions about the set S other than that all of the possible worlds in S have an overall value of N or greater for some positive N. S might be the set of best worlds where every member of S has an equal and unexceeded value N. S might be finite and include every world whose overall value is N or greater. S might be infinitely large including infinitely many worlds whose value is N or greater. It could be that S includes infinitely many better and better worlds all of which is N or greater in overall value. It does not matter what members we select for S. It is impossible that, necessarily, God actualizes a world in S. It is therefore not necessary that God actualizes a good enough world.

The impossibility arguments show that (3.3)–(3.5) are all necessarily false. The *Logical Problem of Evil Redux* is therefore necessarily unsound and so is the *Logical Problem of the Best Possible World* and the *Logical Problem of Good Enough Worlds*. Let us state the main consequences of each impossibility argument explicitly in C1–C6.

*An Impossibility Argument*

   C1. It is impossible that, necessarily, God actualizes a morally perfect world.
   C2. It is a necessary truth that, possibly, God can actualize a morally perfect world and God does not actualize a morally perfect world.

*An Impossibility Argument: Best World*

   C3. It is impossible that, necessarily, God actualizes the best possible world.
   C4. It is a necessary truth that, possibly, God can actualize the best possible world and does not actualize the best possible world.

*An Impossibility Argument: Good Enough Worlds*
- C5. It is impossible that, necessarily, God actualizes a good enough world.
- C6. It is a necessary truth that, possibly, God can actualize a good enough world and does not actualize a good enough world.

## 5.8  The Moral of Impossibility Arguments

We observed in Section 5.5.2 that some explanation is in order for the results of the impossibility arguments. *An Impossibility Argument* assumes that there are morally perfect worlds and that necessarily God can actualize a morally perfect world. So the explanation for conclusion C1 obviously cannot be that there are no morally perfect worlds or that God cannot actualize a morally perfect world. Some other explanation is necessary.

The assumptions are perfectly analogous in every impossibility argument. The *Impossibility Argument: Best Worlds* assumes that there is a best possible world and that necessarily God can actualize the best world. And the *Impossibility Argument: Good Enough Worlds* assumes that there is a set of good enough worlds and that necessarily God can actualize a good enough world. We need an explanation for the conclusions in C1–C6 that does not appeal to the existence of those worlds or to God's power to actualize them.

Recall that the *Impossibility Argument: Good Enough Worlds* shows that the set S of good enough worlds includes at least some S-worlds, W, such that, necessarily W is possible only if a non-S-world, W′, is possible. The impossibility argument shows that the set S of good enough worlds includes an S-world, W, such that, necessarily W is possible only if S includes the non-S world, W′. If we assume that, necessarily, God actualizes an S-world, then every possible world is in S. But since W is possible we know that W′ is possible. But W′ is possible only if a non-S-world is an S-world. But that's impossible. It is therefore impossible that, necessarily, God actualizes a good enough world.

We find the same structure in *An Impossibility Argument*. There are morally perfect worlds W such that, necessarily W is possible only if the morally imperfect world W′ is possible. If we assume that, necessarily, God actualizes a morally perfect world, then every possible world is morally perfect. Since W′ is possible, the imperfect world W′ is morally perfect.

But of course that's impossible. It is therefore impossible that, necessarily, God actualizes a morally perfect world.

Consider the structure in the *Impossibility Argument: Best Worlds*. The best possible world W is such that, necessarily W is possible only if some less-than-best world W′ is possible. If we assume that, necessarily, God actualizes the best possible world, then the less-than-best world W′ is the best possible world. But of course that's impossible. It is therefore impossible that, necessarily, God actualizes the best possible world.

The structure of these arguments shows that it is impossible that, necessarily, God actualizes an acceptable world of kind K or an acceptable world in the class of worlds of kind K. It is true in general that the moral value of acceptable worlds of any kind entails the existence of free beings fulfilling the requirements of justice and beneficence. The moral value of acceptable worlds entails the existence of free beings that can violate the most important moral prohibitions and moral requirements. The existence of the most valuable acceptable worlds, or the most valuable acceptable class of worlds, entails the existence of unacceptable worlds in which every free being consistently elects to violate the most important moral prohibitions and moral requirements. It cannot be true that, necessarily, God actualizes a acceptable world of kind K since, necessarily, God actualizes a acceptable world of kind K only if some unacceptable non-K worlds are among the acceptable worlds. And that is, of course, impossible.

The moral of impossibility arguments is that there are no extremely good worlds unless there are extremely bad worlds. That might have been the motto of this chapter. God cannot actualize extremely good worlds unless he can actualize extremely bad worlds as well. It is no more than philosophical dogma that, necessarily, God actualizes a morally perfect world or that necessarily God actualizes the best possible world, or that necessarily God actualizes a good enough world. It is indeed impossible that, necessarily, God actualizes such worlds

# 6

# Four Important Objections

## 6.0  Taking Stock

The argument in Sections 4.2–4.7 shows that God's power extends to the *unrestricted actualization* of a morally perfect world. Necessarily, God can strongly actualize a maximal state of affairs that includes the state of affairs of God's having predicted or prophesied that an instantiated essence $E_n$ will always go right. But if it is true that, necessarily, God can predict that $E_n$ will always go right, then it is true in every world that God can bring it about that $E_n$ always goes right *without causing* $E_n$ always to go right. Therefore, necessarily, God can actualize a morally perfect world.

In Section 5.0 the logical problem of evil re-emerges in a much more serious form in the *Logical Problem of Evil Redux*. The logical problem of evil redux provides the sought-after proof of Mackie's atheological conclusion. It is impossible that God is omnipotent, omniscient, and wholly good, and that evil exists. The problem presented in the logical problem of evil redux cannot be resolved by appeal to limitations in God's power. It is necessarily true that God can actualize a morally perfect world. The problem cannot be resolved by appeal to limitations in God's goodness or knowledge. It is necessarily true that God is essentially perfectly good and essentially omniscient. Any solution to the logical problem of evil redux must be consistent with God's unlimited power to actualize a morally perfect world, God's essential perfect goodness, and God's essential omniscience.

*An Impossibility Argument* in Section 5.2 provides the critical solution to the problem presented in the logical problem of evil redux. The impossibility argument shows that the proposition < an omnipotent, omniscient, and wholly good being can actualize a morally perfect world> is consistent with the proposition <an omnipotent, omniscient, and wholly good being *does not* actualize a morally perfect world>. The argument falsifies the philosophical dogma that, necessarily, God can actualize a morally perfect world only if God does actualize a morally perfect world. Since it is impossible that, necessarily, God actualizes a morally perfect world, it follows that there is some world in which it is true that God can actualize a morally perfect world and does not. The impossibility argument in Section 5.2 is a consistency proof that entails that the logical problem of evil redux is necessarily unsound.

In Sections 5.4–5.6 additional consistency proofs are advanced. *An Impossibility Argument: Best Worlds* falsifies the philosophical dogma that, necessarily, God can actualize the best possible world only if God does actualize the best possible world. *An Impossibility Argument: Good Enough Worlds* falsifies the philosophical dogma that, necessarily, God can actualize a good enough world only if God does actualize a good enough world. These dogmas, and others, are the unfortunate bases of several logical problems of evil. Since each of these philosophical dogmas has been falsified, the corresponding logical problems of evil are unsound.

It is the aim of this chapter to observe and note additional implications of the consistency proofs. The consistency proofs provide the resources to resolve several other atheological problems. I consider in turn the problem of Heller's worst world, the problem of God existing alone, the problem of gratuitous evil, and the problem of horrendous evil.

## 6.1 Heller's Worst World

There is an ingenious atheological argument that there exists an essentially omnipotent, essentially omniscient, essentially morally perfect, and necessarily existing being only if the actual world is among the *worst possible worlds*.[1] Since it is evident that the actual is not among the worst possible worlds, we are moved to conclude that there is no essentially omnipotent, essentially omniscient, essentially morally perfect, and necessarily existing being. The argument raises three important questions. (1) can God exist alone, (2) can God exist in worlds that include gratuitous evil, and (3) must God actualize the best world he can actualize? We will find that the consistency proofs entail that there are worlds in which God is the only rational and free being. They also provide the resources to show that there are worlds in which God exists along with gratuitous evil and there are

[1] See Mark Heller, "The Worst of All Worlds" *Philosophia* 28/1–4 (2001) 255–68.

worlds in which it is true that God can actualize a better world and God does not actualize a better world.

### 6.1.1 The Worst World Argument

The initial assumption in the *Worst World Argument* is that God has the traditional Anselmian attributes. God is an essentially omnipotent, essentially omniscient, essentially morally perfect, and necessarily existing being. Since God has the traditional Anselmian attributes, (1) is true in every world.

1. For each possible world W we must (a) deny God's perfection at W or (b) hold that W is best or tied for best or (c) appeal to the Free Will Defense to explain how W's not being the best is compatible with God's perfection.

In defense of (1) Heller observes the following.

Premise [1] deserves a little clarification. In effect, it is a statement of the problem of evil. If a given world contains a perfect being, that being would want the world to be the best possible. If this desire is not fulfilled, it must be because of events that even a perfect being cannot control. Such events must be the outcomes of the free choices of other agents.... [I]n order to give a full answer to the problem of evil the defense must also show that God's existence at a particular world W is consistent with W's being as bad as it is. The free will defense must say that the features of W that make it less than best are the responsibility of non-divine free agents. What [1] is claiming is that any other explanation of the so called evil in W that seeks to avoid denying God's perfection in W will be an argument to the effect that the world would not have been any better if that supposed evil had been absent. Such an explanation would be a version of ([1]b).[2]

So, according to the *Worst World Argument*, any possible world W that is not a best possible world must include an evil state of affairs S that is strongly actualized by non-divine free beings. Otherwise, W is a best world that includes no evil states of affairs or W is a best world that includes non-gratuitous evil states of affairs.

Premise (2) makes the reasonable assertion that God might have been the only rational and free being.

2. God could have been the only free agent.

Call worlds in which God is the only free agent, "Solo-worlds." There is no moral value produced by non-divine free agents in any Solo-world. Premise (3) states that a perfect being exists in every possible world.

---

[2] Ibid. pp. 255–6.

3. God is an essentially omnipotent, essentially omniscient, essentially morally perfect, and necessarily existing being.

And from premises (1) and (3) we derive (4).

4. Every world is one of the best unless it is less than best because of the free actions of non-divine agents.

Since Solo-worlds contain no non-divine significantly free beings, it follows from (4) that each Solo-world is a best possible world.[3]

5. Solo-worlds are best possible worlds.

Since Solo-worlds are best possible worlds, there is no possible world that God would prefer to a Solo-world. Now assume for reductio ad absurdum that there is some possible world that is less than best because of the free actions of non-divine agents.

6. There is a world that is less than best because of the free actions of non-divine agents.

Call any world that is less than best because of the actions of non-divine, free agents, Nasty-worlds. If Nasty-worlds are less than the best, then of course Nasty-worlds are worse than Solo-worlds

7. Nasty-worlds are worse than Solo-worlds.

Of course, there must be some explanation for Nasty-world's being less than best. It cannot be premise (1b), since (1b) rejects the claim that Nasty-worlds are less than best. But it also cannot be premise (1c). According to (1c) the non-divine free beings in Nasty-worlds cause Nasty-worlds to be worse than Solo-worlds. But if the non-divine free beings in Nasty-worlds cause them to be worse than Solo-worlds, then God would have actualized only Solo-worlds. It is necessarily true that God can actualize a Solo-world and Solo-worlds are (at least among the) best worlds.

The only explanation available is premise (1a) that Nasty-worlds do not include a perfect God.

8. There is no perfect God at Nasty-worlds.

---

[3] Ibid. p. 257.

But premise (8) is not consistent with premise (3). So the assumption for reductio is false and we arrive at (9).

9.    There are no worlds that are less than best because of the free actions of non-divine agents.

But from premise (4) and premise (9) we derive (10).

10.    Every possible world is a best possible world.

But if every world is tied for best, then every world is tied for worst. And so the actual world is among the worst possible worlds.

11.    The actual world is a worst of all possible worlds.

A morally perfect being does not prefer the actual world to any other world. And, for that matter, a morally perfect being does not prefer any other worlds to the actual world. Further, there is nothing anyone could do to make the actual world any better than it is, and there is nothing anyone could do to make the actual world any worse.

Premise (11) is obviously untenable. It is certainly possible to make the actual world worse than it is, and it is certainly possible to make the actual world better than it is. The *Worst World Argument* must be unsound. According to the *Worst World Argument* the only candidate for rejection is premise (3). Therefore God is not an essentially omnipotent, essentially omniscient, essentially morally perfect, and necessarily existing being.

## 6.2  Let's Be Serious: There is Gratuitous Evil

According to the *Worst World Argument*, any possible world W that is not a best possible world must include an evil state of affairs S that is strongly actualized by non-divine free beings. Otherwise, W is a best world that includes no evil states of affairs S or W is a best world that includes some evil states of affairs S that is necessary to a greater good.[4]

---

[4]  We've argued that the free will defense fails. But it ought to be observed that the free will defense would not support premise (1) in the *Worst World Argument*. According to the free will defense there are less than best worlds that include no free non-divine agents at all. So, there are less than best worlds that are not less than best because of the free activity of non-divine agents. Recall that for each possible world W there is a galaxy $S_{WC}$ that is just the set of feasible worlds at W as determined by the set $S_C$ of true counterfactuals of creaturely freedom

Recall that the intersection of the sets $S_C$ of true CCFs in each possible world is the set $S_U$ of CCFs whose antecedents God can unrestrictedly actualize. The set of CCFs in $S_U$ is the set of all counterfactuals of creaturely freedom $T_n \; \square\!\!\rightarrow F_n$ such that God can actualize $T_n$ in every possible world and $\square(T_n \supset F_n)$. Since every member of $S_U$ is a CCF, there is no member $T_n \; \square\!\!\rightarrow F_n$ of $S_U$ such that $F_n$ causally depends on $T_n$.

Typically we would expect that the best actualizable world is the best world God can weakly actualize and the set of weakly actualizable worlds varies across possible worlds. But since the set $S_U$ of CCFs whose antecedents God can unrestrictedly actualize is true in every possible world, we know there are undetermined states of affairs that God can unrestrictedly actualize. There are undetermined states of affairs $F_n$ such that $\square(T_n \supset F_n)$ and necessarily God can strongly actualize $T_n$. God can, for instance, unrestrictedly actualize the state of affairs in which every instantiated essence always goes right. Indeed God can unrestrictedly actualize the best possible world, if there is one.[5]

The *Worst World Argument* assumes that there is a unique, best possible world W and that, necessarily, God can actualize the best world only if God does actualize the best world. But we know that's false. *An Impossibility Argument: Best World* shows that, possibly, God can actualize the best world and God does not actualize the best world. Indeed, the argument shows that, necessarily, there are worlds in which God might have prevented an evil state of affairs at no moral cost and God does not do so. Premise (1) in the *Worst World Argument* is false because the standard view on gratuitous evil is false.

For a typical formulation of the standard view on evil consider William Rowe's well-known version in the following.

---

at W. It is true at W that God can actualize any other world in $S_{WC}$ and that God cannot actualize any world that is not in $S_{WC}$. God's choice among worlds to actualize is constrained by the set of feasible worlds in the galaxy. According to the free will defense, the set of feasible worlds is not coextensive with the set of all possible worlds, but it is coextensive with the set of all actualizable worlds. So, consider a world $W_1$ such that for every world $W_n$ in the galaxy $S_{W1C}$ in which some creaturely essence is instantiated, $W_n$ is an on balance bad world. If every world $W_n$ in the galaxy $S_{W2C}$ in which some creaturely essence is instantiated is such that $W_n$ is an on balance bad, then God actualizes a world $W_2$ with no free creaturely essences. $W_2$ is the best actualizable world in $S_{W1C}$, but $W_2$ is not bad because of the free actions of non-divine agents. $W_2$ includes no non-divine agents. $W_2$ is simply the best *actualizable* world. Of course, $W_2$ might not be a very good world.

[5] For the argument, see *An Impossibility Argument: Best Worlds* in Section 5.5.

An omniscient, wholly good being would prevent the occurrence of any intense evil it could, unless it could not do so without thereby losing some greater good or permitting some evil equally bad or worse.[6]

According to the standard view expressed here, an omniscient and wholly good being may allow the occurrence of evil E in world W if such a being could not prevent that evil E without losing a greater good G or permitting a greater evil $E'$.

We discussed the difficulties with typical formulations of the standard view on evil in Chapter 2, Section 2.2. We noted in particular that in many cases where some evil E and good G is such that $\square(E \supset G)$ and $(G \& E) > (\sim G \& \sim E)$, it is nevertheless true that E is gratuitous. We noted that even if an evil state of affairs E is necessary to some greater good G, E might be unnecessary to an even greater good $G'$. The world in which Smith endures the pain and bears up well is a good world. But there might be an even better actualizable world in which Smith does not exist and therefore endures no pain at all. So, even in worlds where G and E obtain and it is true both that $\square(E \supset G)$ and that $(G \& E) > (\sim G \& \sim E)$, the evil E might be gratuitous. E is necessary to a greater good G, but E might not be necessary to a greater actualizable good $G'$. So the standard view on evil is mistaken.

It is a natural response to this problem to begin reformulating the standard view on evil in terms of largest states of affairs or worlds. Consider $G_0$, where $W' > W$ represents $W'$ is more valuable than W.

> $G_0$. The evil state of affairs E is gratuitous in W iff E obtains at W and it is true at W that there is some actualizable world $W'$ such that $W' > W$ and $W'$ does not include E.

The revised standard view $S_1$ would then tell us that, necessarily, God would prevent all of the gratuitous evil as specified in $G_0$.

> $S_1$. Necessarily, an omniscient, wholly good being would prevent the occurrence of every gratuitously evil state of affairs.

But while $G_0$ seems a more accurate analysis of gratuitous evil, we know that $S_1$ is false. Suppose there is a best possible world, as the *Worst World*

---

[6] See William Rowe, "The Problem of Evil and Some Varieties of Atheism" collected in Daniel Howard-Snyder (ed.) *The Evidential Argument from Evil* (Indianapolis: Indiana University Press, 1996) 1–11.

*Argument* assumes. The best possible world will include a great deal of moral good, but it is sufficient to assume it will include some moral good. God can unrestrictedly actualize the best world. So, necessarily, God *can* actualize the best world. But we know from *An Impossibility Argument: Best World* that it's possible that God does not actualize the best world. According-ing to the argument, there is a best possible world W only if there are worlds W′ in which every essence instantiated in W freely fails to satisfy the requirements of justice and beneficence in W. Since the *Worst World Argument* assumes there is a best world, we know there is a world W′ that includes gratuitous evil. So contrary to $S_1$, it is not necessary that an omniscient, wholly good being prevents the occurrence of all gratuitous evil.

It is an important consequence of the impossibility arguments that they show the logical consistency of the existence of God and the existence of gratuitous evil. The impossibility arguments afford a solution to the *Logical Problem of Evil Redux* but they also show that God can co-exist with gratuitous evil. Since God can co-exist with gratuitous evil, premise (1) in the *Worst World Argument* is false. There are possible worlds W such that God is perfect at W, W is not among the best worlds, and we do not appeal to the free will defense to explain how W's not being the best is compati-ble with God's perfection.

## 6.3 God Can Exist Alone: Catastrophic Worlds

The *Worst World Argument* assumes that there are worlds where God is the only rational and free being. These are worlds in which there are contingent states of affairs and there are contingent objects, but there are no rational and free beings except God. But the odd conclusion in the *Worst World Argument* is that worlds in which God is the only rational and free being are among the best possible worlds. Recall that the argument proceeds as follows.

4. Every world is one of the best unless it is less than best because of the free actions of non-divine agents.

Since Solo-worlds contain no non-divine significantly free beings, it follows from (4) that each Solo-world is a best possible world.

5. Solo-worlds are best possible worlds.

In fact there are worlds in which God is the only rational being possible and such worlds are not among the best possible worlds. There are extremely valuable worlds in which significantly free instantiated essences satisfy the requirements of justice and beneficence in avoiding the terrible outcome of catastrophic universal self-destruction. It is of course a morally appalling outcome on which instantiated essences can brink. But there are also worlds in which significantly free instantiated essences freely violate the requirements of justice and beneficence and actualize the catastrophic outcome.

*An Impossibility Argument: Good Enough Worlds* shows that God can actualize extremely valuable worlds in which significantly free instantiated essences satisfy the requirements of justice and beneficence in avoiding the terrible outcome of catastrophic universal self-destruction. Certainly such worlds are among the good enough worlds. But those extremely valuable worlds are among the good enough worlds only if there are worlds in which significantly free instantiated essences freely violate the requirements of justice and beneficence and actualize the catastrophic outcome. There are worlds in which God is the only rational and free agent, but at least some of these are worlds in which non-divine significantly free instantiated essences have actualized the catastrophic outcome. And as we might expect these are not among the best possible worlds.

## 6.4  Is the Actual World a Worst World?

The *Worst World Argument* entails that the actual world is among the worst worlds. But the *Worst World Argument* is unsound. As many have observed, the actual world is not the best possible world. There are many states of affairs such that, had they obtained, the world would have been better. But the actual world is not among the worst worlds, either, assuming there are worst worlds. There are many states of affairs such that, had they obtained, the actual world would have been much worse.

The *Worst World Argument* correctly assumes that there are worlds in which God is the only rational and free being. But the argument is wrong in assuming that worlds in which God is the only rational and free being must be among the best possible worlds. Indeed, at least some worlds in which God is the only rational and free beings are catastrophic worlds. These are worlds in which non-divine significantly free instantiated essences have actualized the outcome of catastrophic universal self-destruction. So at least some worlds in which God is the only rational and free being are not among the best possible worlds.

The *Worst World Argument* assumes that there are no worlds in which God exists and there are gratuitously evil states of affairs. But it's a consequence of the impossibility arguments that the proposition <God exists> and the proposition <there exist gratuitously evil states of affairs> are broadly logically consistent. The impossibility arguments show that God can co-exist with gratuitous evil. Contrary to the *Worst World Argument* there are possible worlds W such that God is perfect at W, W is not among the best worlds, and we need not appeal to the free will defense to explain how W's not being the best is compatible with God's perfection.

## 6.5  The Problem of Horrendous Evils

According to Marilyn McCord Adams there is a problem of evil that has been neither resolved nor addressed in the otherwise vast literature on the problem of evil. Here is Adams.

... the problem of horrendous evils is largely skirted by standard treatments for the good reason that they are intractable by them. After showing why, I will draw on other Christian materials to sketch ways of meeting this, the deepest of religious problems.[7]

Horrendous evils are understood as evils so bad that a person who suffers or performs such evils has prima facie reason to doubt that his life could be a great good to him on the whole.

Horrendous evils seem prima facie, not only to balance off but to engulf the positive value of a participant's life. Nevertheless, that very horrendous proportion, by which they threaten to rob a person's life of positive meaning, cries out not only to be engulfed, but to be made meaningful through positive and decisive defeat.[8]

Adams lists among the paradigmatic horrendous evils the rape of a woman and axing off of her arms, psychophysical torture whose ultimate goal is the disintegration of personality, betrayal of one's deepest loyalties,

---

[7]  Marilyn McCord Adams, "Horrendous Evils and Goodness of God" in M. Adams and R. Adams (eds.) *The Problem of Evil* (Oxford: Oxford University Press, 1990) 211. See also Marilyn McCord Adams, *Horrendous Evils and Goodness of God* (Ithaca: Cornell University Press, 1999).

[8]  Adams, "Horrendous Evils and Goodness of God," op. cit. p. 211.

cannibalizing one's own off-spring, child abuse of the sort described by Ivan Karamazov, child pornography, parental incest, slow death by starvation, participation in the Nazi death camps, the explosion of nuclear bombs over populated areas, having to choose which of one's children shall live and which be executed by terrorists, being the accidental and/or unwitting agent of the disfigurement or death of those one loves best.[9]

Adams's central negative thesis is that horrendous evils cannot be justified by global goods. The fact that the world would be on balance better were I to participate in a horrendous evil does not justify God in permitting me to suffer that evil.

> ...such an exercise fails to give satisfaction. Suppose for the sake of argument that horrendous evil could be included in maximally perfect world orders; its being partially constitutive of such an order would assign it that generic and global positive meaning. But would knowledge of such a fact, defeat for a mother the prima facie reason provided by her cannibalism of her own infant, to wish that she had never been born? Again, the aim of perfect retributive balance confers meaning on evils imposed. But would knowledge that the torturer was being tortured give the victim who broke down and turned traitor under pressure, any more reason to think his/her life worthwhile?[10]

Adam's rejects the standard analysis of non-gratuitous evil. The fact that W is a best possible world and W includes a horrendously evil state of affairs E does not entail that E is justified. Not only do maximally good states of affairs fail to justify horrendous evils, it is difficult to imagine what sorts of reasons God might have to allow them. As Adam's observes, Plantinga concedes the difficulty of conceiving of an epistemic defense against horrendous evils.

> As Plantinga points out, where horrendous evils are concerned, not only do we not know God's actual reason for permitting them; we cannot even conceive of any plausible candidate sort of reason consistent with worthwhile lives for human participants in them.[11]

But Adam's does not deny that there are reasons why horrendous evils are allowed to occur. She believes that there are such reasons why, but that we are cognitively, emotionally, and spiritually too immature to fathom them.

---

[9]  Adams, "Horrendous Evils and Goodness of God," op. cit. pp. 212–13.
[10]  Ibid. p. 214.
[11]  Ibid. p. 215. See also "Self-Profile" in James E. Tomberlin and Peter van Inwagen (eds.) *Profiles: Alvin Plantinga* (Dordrecht: Holland, D. Reidel, 1985) 36–55.

Though we cannot know why they are allowed, Adam's shows how horrendous evils might be defeated.

Divine respect for and commitment to created personhood would drive God to make all those sufferings which threaten to destroy the positive meaning of a person's life meaningful through positive defeat. How could God do it? So far as I can see, only by integrating participation in horrendous evils into a person's relationship with God.[12]

Adam's suggests that the dimensions of integration are charted by Christian soteriology. God in Christ participated in horrendous evil through his passion and death, human experience of horrors can be a means of identifying with Christ, either through sympathetic identification or through mystical identification. Integration may be the result of a creature's experience of divine gratitude after death, which will bring full and unending joy. Another source of integration identifies temporal suffering with a vision into the inner life of God. Perhaps God is not impassable, but has matched capacities for joy and for suffering. Perhaps, God responds to human sin and the sufferings of Christ with an agony beyond conception.

Adam's suggestion then is that horrendous evils can be integrated into a person's relationship with God and such integration can confer meaning and positive value even on horrendous suffering. The result, according to Adams, coheres with basic Christian intuition: that the powers of darkness are stronger than humans, but they are no match for God.[13]

### 6.5.1. Horrendous Evil and Defeating Evil

Adams follows Plantinga in affirming that we cannot so much as conceive of a candidate for the reason God has for permitting horrendous evils. Nonetheless Adam's affirms that there exist reasons why God allows such evil.

But Adam's seems mistaken on this score. In fact, the only credible position is that things are just as they seem to be with regard to horrendous evils There might be no reasons for horrendously evil states of affairs that serve to justify God in permitting those states of affairs. It is a bit of philosophical dogma that there is no world in which God exists and unjustified horrendous evil exists. There are no doubt superb possible worlds in which every significantly free instantiated essence satisfies the requirements of justice and beneficence. It is true in those worlds that

---

[12] Ibid. p. 218 ff.    [13] Ibid. p. 220.

significantly free essences can, but do not, actualize a world in which, for instance, the profound horrors of the Nazi holocaust occur. It is part of the moral value of superb worlds that significantly free beings observe the deepest moral requirements prohibiting such horrendous action. But the impossibility arguments show that it simply could not be true that *necessarily* God actualizes such superb worlds. It is broadly logically impossible that there are only such superb worlds. Indeed it is necessarily true that there are superb worlds only if there are possible worlds in which significantly free instantiated essences all violate the most serious and profound moral prohibitions. But those possible worlds in which significantly free essences all violate the most profound moral prohibitions are worlds in which there are horrendous evils. In those worlds God can prevent those horrendous evils and it would be morally better if God did prevent the horrendous evils. Nonetheless these are worlds in which God does not prevent those horrendous evils.

As Adam's notes it is possible that horrendous evil is defeated. Worlds in which horrendous evil is defeated are worlds in which instantiated essences freely respond to evil in ways that integrate participation in horrendous evils into one's relationship with God. But there are also worlds in which instantiated essences defeat evil through their positive moral responses to evil. These are not merely the soul-making responses that are displayed in the development of certain virtues and sensibilities.

These are responses that make positive concrete changes in institutions of justice, for instance, that protect basic rights and liberties and provide opportunities. These are responses that make positive concrete changes in institutions of beneficence, for instance, in making charitable organizations more efficient and effective instruments in the relief of pain and suffering. So, as Adam's notes, there are ways of defeating horrendous evils and making them increasingly meaningful. And it is no doubt true that we should act in ways that aim to defeat horrendous evil. But it should be underscored that God does not permit horrendous evils *in order to* provide the opportunity for soul-making or *in order to* provide the opportunity to respond in morally significant ways. There are superb worlds such that, necessarily God can actualize them. But, it is a matter of metaphysical necessity that there are superb possible worlds only if there are possible worlds in which horrendous evils occur. So, it is a matter of metaphysical necessity that there are worlds in which horrendous evil occurs.

# 7

# Four More Objections

## 7.0  The Problem of Divine Freedom

There are two important questions that generate the *Problem of Divine Freedom*: (1) Was God free to refrain from creating any possible world at all? (2) Was God free to create worlds other than the world he did create?[1]

As usual, possible worlds are understood as maximal states of affairs. We will say that W is a maximal state of affairs if and only if, for each possible state of affairs S, either M includes S or M includes ~S.[2] Speaking strictly, of course, God does not create possible worlds. God creates or causes to exist contingent objects, and creates or causes to obtain contingent states of affairs. God weakly actualizes and strongly actualizes possible worlds, but he can also restrictedly actualize and unrestrictedly actualize possible worlds.[3]

Let's consider the second question. We assume that possible worlds can be ranked or partially ordered according to their overall value.[4] Suppose God chooses to display his power and goodness in actualizing a possible world. Suppose further, with Gottfried Leibniz and Samuel Clarke, that there is a uniquely best possible world in the ordering of worlds. It does

---

[1]  See William Rowe, "Can God be Free?" *Faith and Philosophy* (2002) 405–24; and his *Can God Be Free?* (Oxford: Oxford University Press, 2004).

[2]  The assumption is that each possible world is a maximal state of affairs: an abstract simple object. Treatments of possible worlds as maximal *sets* of propositions, or maximal sets of states of affairs run into serious and well-known obstacles analogous to Russell's Paradox. See Alvin Plantinga and Patrick Grimm, "Truth, Omniscience and Cantorian Arguments: An Exchange," *Philosophical Studies* (1993) 267–306; Patrick Grim, "Logic and the Limits of Knowledge and Truth" *Noûs* (1988) 341–67; and his "The Being that Knew Too Much" *International Journal for Philosophy of Religion* (2000) 141–54.

[3]  See Chapter 4, above.

[4]  Partially ordered sets have the properties (i) $a \leq a$ (reflexivity) (ii) if $a \leq b$ and $b \leq a$ then $a = b$ (antisymmetry) and (iii) if $a \leq b$ and $b \leq c$ then $a \leq c$ (transitivity). Partial orderings do not guarantee that possible worlds are comparable with respect to overall value. It might be true for some worlds $a$ and $b$ that $\sim(a \leq b$ or $b \leq a)$.

seem intuitive that God's choice among possible worlds to actualize would not be to actualize an overall disvaluable or bad world. It seems intuitive to some that God could not actualize an overall bad world.

Again, it seems obvious that he would create the very best world, the best of all possible worlds. As Leibniz points out: since "to do less good than one could is to be lacking in wisdom or in goodness", the most perfect understanding "cannot fail to act in the most perfect way, and consequently to choose the best".[5]

The most perfect being must actualize the best possible world, according to this view, whether or not it is a moral obligation to actualize the best possible world. Actualizing the best possible world might be both the best possible action and also a supererogatory action, for instance. Here again is Rowe.

And it appears to be inconceivable that a supremely perfect being would act to bring about less good than he can. On the assumption that God (the supremely perfect being) exists and that there is a best, creatable world, we've reached the conclusion that God is neither free not to create a world nor free to create a world less than the best creatable world. Indeed, God *would of necessity* create the best of the creatable worlds, leaving us with no basis for thanking him, or praising him for creating the world he does. For given that God exists, and that there is a best world, God's nature as an omnipotent, omniscient, perfectly good being would require him to create that best world. Doing less than the best he can do—create the best creatable world—would be inconsistent with his being the perfect being he is.[6]

Rowe urges that it follows from the nature of God that, necessarily, if he can actualize the best possible world then he does actualize the best possible world. Since God possesses the divine attributes in every possible world, Rowe's argument entails that God brings about the best possible world in every possible world. So, there is no world that is not identical to the best possible world. Call that *Rowe's Argument I*. Slightly more formally, the familiar argument runs as follows.

1. Necessarily, God can actualize the best possible world only if God does actualize the best possible world.

2. Necessarily God can actualize the best possible world.

3. /∴ Necessarily God does actualize the best possible world.

[5] See William Rowe, "Can God Be Free?," op. cit. pp. 409–10. See also Leibniz's *Theodicy*, Austin Farrer (ed.) (LaSalle, Ill.: Open Court, 1985), sect. 201.
[6] Ibid. p. 410.

4. Necessarily, God necessarily actualizes the best possible world only if God does not freely actualize the best possible world.

5. /∴. Necessarily God does not freely actualize the best possible world.

The *Problem of Divine Freedom* concludes that, if there is a best possible world, then God has no freedom at all. Necessarily God actualizes the best possible world and that exhausts the exercise of divine power.

The restriction on divine power is intrinsically problematic. One way to avoid the conclusion is to reject premise (4), perhaps on the grounds that God might be *compatibilist free*, but not libertarian free. But the appeal to compatibilist freedom provides no genuine reason to reject (4). According to premise (4), it is metaphysically necessary that God actualizes the best possible world only if God is not free in any sense, compatibilist, libertarian, or otherwise. An agent is compatibilist free with respect to action A only if it is (at least) metaphysically possible that the agent does ~A.[7]

The standard defense of compatibilism aims to show that agents could have done other than what they were causally determined to do. The locus classicus for the defense of strong compatibilism is David Lewis.

I have just put my hand down on my desk. That, let me claim, was a free but predetermined act. I was able to act otherwise, for instance to raise my hand. But there is a true historical proposition H about the intrinsic state of the world long ago, and there is a true proposition L specifying the laws of nature that govern our world, such that H and L jointly determine what I did. . . . They jointly contradict the proposition that I raised my hand. Yet I was free; I was able to raise my hand. The way in which I was determined not to was not the sort of way that counts as inability.[8]

But the compatibilist defense is ineffective against premise (4). If it is metaphysically necessary that you do not raise your hand, then raising your hand entails a contradiction.

What if I had raised my hand? Then at least one of three things would have been true. Contradictions would have been true together; or the historical proposition H would not have been true; or the law proposition L would not have been true. Which? . . . Of our three alternatives we may dismiss the first; for if I had raised my hand, there would still have been no true contradictions. Likewise we may discuss

---

[7] This is true on strong compatibilism and on any credible form of weak compatibilism. The supposition that actions that are metaphysically necessary might be free is the view that logical fatalism is compatible with free will. I know of no one who takes that position.

[8] See David Lewis, "Are We Free to Break Laws?" in *Philosophical Papers II* (Oxford: Oxford University Press, 1984).

186 FREEDOM, GOD, AND WORLDS

the second; for if I had raised my hand, the intrinsic state of the world long ago would have been no different. That leaves the third alternative. If I had raised my hand, the law proposition L would not have been true.[9]

Contrary to Lewis's reasoning, we cannot dismiss the first alternative. If it is metaphysically necessary that you do not raise your hand, then raising your hand occurs in no possible world. You raise your hand only if a contradiction is true. But that is just to say that the act of raising your hand is impossible. Similarly, the actualization of the best possible world is not free, it is metaphysically necessary that God actualizes the best possible world; it is impossible that he fails to do so.

But of course we have conclusive reason to reject premise (1) in *Rowe's Argument I*. In Chapter 5, Section 5.4, we provided *An Impossibility Argument: Best Worlds*. The argument shows that premise (1) is false. Suppose that there is a best possible world and that necessarily God can actualize the best possible world. The impossibility argument shows that it is false (indeed, impossible) that necessarily God actualizes the best possible world. There are possible worlds at which it is true that God can actualize the best possible world and God does not actualize the best possible world. So *Rowe's Argument I* is necessarily unsound. But then the intrinsically problematic conclusion is false. It is not the case that, necessarily, God does not freely actualize the best possible world. And the answer to the second question is yes, God was free to create other possible worlds instead of the possible world he did in fact create. Indeed, *Rowe's Argument I* reaches no interesting conclusions about God's freedom in the actualization of worlds. The impossibility arguments provide a straightforward solution to the problem of divine freedom.

## 7.1  The Problem of No Best World

William Rowe has argued that a perfectly good being is maximally excellent in every action. A perfectly good being fulfills every moral requirement and never does an action that is less good than another he could do instead. And so according to Rowe it is necessarily true that a perfectly good creator does not actualize a world that is less good than another world he could actualize. Rowe's *Principle B* expresses this moral restriction on perfectly good creators.

<hr/>

[9] Ibid. p. 292.

B. Necessarily if an omniscient and omnipotent being actualizes a world when there is a better world that it could have actualized, then that omniscient and omnipotent being is *not* essentially perfectly good.[10]

There is a more intuitive expression of *Principle B*. B★ follows from exportation and contraposition on B.

B★ Necessarily, if an omniscient, omnipotent and essentially perfectly good being actualizes a world, then there is no better world that it could have actualized instead.

Since Rowe maintains that all perfectly good beings are maximally excellent, the moral restriction in B requires that no essentially perfectly good being actualizes a world that is less good than another world it could actualize instead.[11] Rowe observes that if there is some best possible world then B will commit theists to the position that ours is the best.[12] Indeed, if there is a best possible world, then B will commit theists to the position that, necessarily, God actualized the best possible world. But few theists are prepared to defend the Leibnizian position that our world is as good as any world God might have actualized. The more common and defensible conclusion is that there is no best possible world.

But what reason do we have to accept principle B? Rowe suggests that the principle is self-evident, but he does offer an argument.

So the issue now before us is whether this principle . . . is indeed true. My own view is that the principle in question will appear to many to be plausible, if not self-evident. For if an omniscient being creates a world when it could have created a better world, then that being has done something less good than it could do (create a better world). But any being who knowingly does something (all things considered) less good than it could do falls short of being the best possible being.

---

[10] Rowe often presents B without explicitly stating that it is a necessary truth about all possible omniscient and omnipotent beings. But he does hold that it is necessary. See his "Can God Be Free?," op. cit. p. 416.

[11] There are other moral arguments against Principle B that are beyond the scope of the current discussion. See Daniel and Frances Howard-Snyder, "How an Unsurpassable Being Might Create a Surpassable World" *Faith and Philosophy* (1994); their "The Real Problem of No Best World" *Faith and Philosophy* (1996) 422–5; and William Wainwright, *Philosophy of Religion* (Belmont, Calif.: Wadsworth Publishing Company, 1988) 90 ff.

[12] Rowe, "Can God Be Free?," op. cit. p. 410. Given that God exists and there is a best creatable world, God's nature as an omnipotent, omniscient, perfectly good being would require him to create that best world. Doing less than the best he can do—create the best creatable world—would be inconsistent with his being the perfect being he is.

So, unless we find some reason to reject the principle stated above, or a reason to reject the line of argument supporting it, we are at the very least within our rights to accept it and use it as a principle in our reasoning. But the result of using this principle in our reasoning about God and the world is just this: if the actual world is not the best world that an omniscient, omnipotent being could create, God does not exist.[13]

But of course we have found good reason to reject principle B. The principle entails a necessary falsehood and so is itself necessarily false. As we noted, Rowe observes that if there is some best possible world then B will commit theists to the position that ours is the best.[14] Indeed, if there is a best possible world, then B will commit theists to the position that, necessarily, God actualized the best possible world.

Assume then that there is a best possible world and that necessarily God can actualize the best world.

1. Necessarily, God can actualize the best possible world. Assume
2. Necessarily, if an omniscient, omnipotent and essentially perfectly good being actualizes a world, then there is no better world that it could have actualized instead. B★
3. /∴ Necessarily, God actualizes the best possible world. 1, 2

We know that the conclusion in (3) is necessarily false. *An Impossibility Argument: Best World* shows that (3) is false. But then Rowe's assertion above is false.

But the result of using this principle in our reasoning about God and the world is just this: if the actual world is not the best world that an omniscient, omnipotent being could create, God does not exist.[15]

It can be true both that our world is not the best possible world God could actualize and that God exists. Either God can actualize a best possible world or B★ is false. Indeed, either God can actualize some good enough worlds or B★ is false.

But suppose there is no best possible world. Rowe urges that it is metaphysically impossible that God exists and that there is no best possible world.

But what if there is no best world? What if, as Aquinas thought to be true, for each creatable world there is a better world that God can create instead? In short, there is

---

[13] Ibid. p. 411     [14] Ibid. p. 410.     [15] Ibid. p. 410.

no best world. Here, I believe, in supposing that God exists and creates a world when for every creatable world there is a better creatable world, we are supposing a state of affairs that is simply impossible. . . . I am suggesting that there is an impossibility in the idea both that God exists and creates a world and that for every creatable world there is a better creatable world. For whatever world God would create he would be doing less good than he can do. And it is impossible for God to do less good than he can.[16]

According to Rowe, we can derive a contradiction from the assumption that God exists and the assumption that there is no best possible world. It is not easy to clearly formulate the problem of no best world.[17] But Rowe aims to generate a contradiction from principle B and what he calls *Kretzmann's Principle*. The final assumption in Rowe's no best world argument is attributed to Norman Kretzmann. Kretzmann argues that God was not free to choose whether to create a world.

The question I raise . . . is why God, the absolutely perfect being, would create anything at all . . . I summarize my own position by saying that God's goodness requires things other than itself as a manifestation of itself, and that God therefore necessarily (though freely) wills the creation of something or other, and that the free choice involved in creation is confined to the selection of which possibilities to actualize for the purpose of manifesting goodness. . . . So, although I disagree with Aquinas's claim that God is free to choose *whether* to create, I'm inclined to agree with him about God's being free to choose *what* to create."[18]

And according to Kretzmann, Aquinas is further committed to the view that there is no best possible world.

According to my attempted explanation here of Aquinas's claim that God could create a better world than this one, it is also *impossible* that God create something than which he could not create something better. My conclusion in the preceding essay and my explanation in this one taken together entail that a perfectly good (omniscient, omnipotent) God *must* create a world less good . . . than one he could create.[19]

Kretzmann's conclusion does not entail that God exists or that God creates anything at all. The conclusion is rather that if God exists, he must create

[16] Ibid. p. 410.
[17] See M. J. Almeida, *The Metaphysics of Perfect Beings* (London: Routledge, 2008) esp. ch. 1, Rowe's Argument from Improvability.
[18] See Norman Kretzmann, "A Particular Problem of Creation: Why Would God Create This World?" in Scott MacDonald (ed.) *Being and Goodness: The Concept of the Good in Metaphysics and Philosophical Theology* (Ithaca: Cornell University Press, 1991) 229–30.
[19] Ibid. p. 238.

some world in the infinite sequence. So the final assumption of Rowe's argument is K.

> K. Necessarily an omniscient, omnipotent, essentially perfectly good being must actualize some world in the sequence.

But it follows from principle B and the assumption that there is no best world that, necessarily, God actualizes no world in the infinite sequence, C.

> C. Necessarily no omniscient, omnipotent, essentially perfectly good being actualizes a world in the sequence.

It follows from C and K that, if God exists, then God both actualizes a world in the sequence and does not actualize a world in the sequence. That is of course impossible. Rowe concludes that therefore God does not exist.

But we know that the no best world argument is unsound, since K is necessarily false. Rowe imagines God deciding to actualize a possible world in the sequence.

Suppose then that God chooses to display his goodness and power in creating a world. We can imagine God, as it were, surveying all these worlds and deciding which one to create. He considers all of the bad worlds, the neutral worlds (neither good nor bad) and all the good worlds. . . . Faced with choosing from among these two series [the good worlds and the bad worlds] the world he shall create it is obvious that an infinitely good being would not, indeed could not, create one of the bad worlds. Which good world would he then create? . . . [20]

If there is an infinite series of improving worlds, then, necessarily, God must actualize some world that is among the good worlds. So Kretzmann's principle entails that, necessarily, God actualizes a good enough world. But we know that it's impossible that, necessarily, God actualizes a good enough world. *An Improvability Argument: Good Enough Worlds* shows that it's impossible that, necessarily, God actualizes a good enough world. Kretzmann's Principle is false. Indeed, it is necessarily false. And the no best world argument is unsound.

The *Problem of No Best World* depends on Rowe's Principle B and Kretzmann's Principle K. But both B and K are false. Indeed, both B and K are necessarily false. The problem of no best world presents no serious problem for Anselmian theists.

---

[20] See Rowe, "Can God Be Free?," op. cit. p. 409.

## 7.2 The Evidential Argument from Evil

The most famous formulation of the evidential argument from evil is William Rowe's well-known syllogism.

1. There exist instances of intense suffering which an omnipotent, omniscient being could have prevented without thereby losing some greater good or permitting some evil equally bad or worse.

2. An omniscient, wholly good being would prevent the occurrence of any intense suffering it could, unless it could not do so without thereby losing some greater good or permitting some evil equally bad or worse.

3. /∴ There does not exist an omnipotent, omniscient, wholly good being.[21]

The argument is clearly valid. The open question is whether the premises are true. Rowe urges that premise (2) is widely believed and uncontroversial.

So stated, (2) seems to express a belief that accords with our basic moral principles, principles shared by both theists and non-theists. If we are to fault the argument for atheism, therefore, it seems we must find some fault with its first premise.[22]

Indeed Rowe does find fault with the argument for premise (1), but he offers an excellent example of evil that satisfies the description in premise (1).[23] It is a purported instance of pointless or gratuitous evil.

Suppose in some distant forest lightening strikes a dead tree, resulting in a forest fire. In the fire a fawn is trapped, horribly burned and lies in terrible agony for several days before death relieves its suffering. So far as we can see, the fawn's intense suffering is pointless. For there does not appear to be any greater good such that the prevention of the fawn's suffering would require either the loss of that good or the occurrence of an evil equally bad or worse. Nor does there seem to be an equally bad or worse evil so connected to the fawn's suffering that it would have had to occur had the fawn's suffering been prevented.[24]

---

[21] See William Rowe, "The Problem of Evil and Some Varieties of Atheism" in Daniel Howard-Snyder (ed.) *The Evidential Argument from Evil* (Bloomington: Indiana University Press, 1996).

[22] Ibid. p. 4.

[23] See, for instance, William Rowe, "The Evidential Argument from Evil: A Second Look" in Daniel Howard-Snyder (ed.) *The Evidential Argument from Evil* (Bloomington: Indiana University Press, 1996).

[24] See Rowe, "The Problem of Evil and Some Varieties of Atheism," op. cit. p. 4.

It seems clear, further, that an omnipotent, omniscient being could have easily prevented the fawn from being burned or could have spared the fawn some of the terrible suffering it endured. So, it certainly appears that premise (1) is true. But as Rowe acknowledges, it is not certain that (1) is true. To show that it is rational to believe that atheism is true, Rowe urges that it is sufficient to establish that it is rational to believe that (1) is true.

One standard and controversial response to the evidential argument from evil is the epistemological response of skeptical theism. The defenders of skeptical theism maintain that, were theism true, we would not be in a position to know which goods might be connected with such evil states of affairs as the suffering of the fawn and we would not be in a position to know the metaphysical or logical relations holding between the goods and evils that obtain.[25] Skeptical theists aim to show that our cognitive limitations make it unlikely that we can establish premise (1) in Rowe's argument. We are simply not in an epistemic position to make it rational to believe (1).

But the impossibility arguments show that the main problem with Rowe's evidential argument from evil is premise (2). According to premise (2), God would prevent the occurrence of any intense suffering it could, unless it could not do so without thereby losing some greater good or permitting some evil equally bad or worse. But we know that that's false. *An Impossibility Argument*, for instance, shows that, necessarily, there are worlds in which God can actualize a morally perfect world and God does not actualize a morally perfect world. In those worlds there are evil states of affairs that God could prevent without thereby losing some greater good or permitting some evil equally bad or worse. It is also true that, necessarily, there are worlds in which God can actualize a naturally perfect world and does not. Necessarily, there are worlds in which naturally evil

[25]  The literature on skeptical theism is vast. See Michael Bergmann, "Skeptical Theism and Rowe's New Evidential Argument from Evil" *Noûs* (2001) 278–96; William L. Rowe "Friendly Atheism, Skeptical Theism, and the Problem of Evil" *International Journal for Philosophy of Religion* (2006) 2; William Rowe "Skeptical Theism: A Response to Bergmann" *Noûs* 35 (2001) 297–303; M. J. Almeida and Graham Oppy, "Sceptical Theism and Evidential Arguments From Evil" *Australasian Journal of Philosophy* 81 (2003) 496–516; Jim Stone, "CORNEA, Skepticism and Evil" *Australasian Journal of Philosophy* (2009) 1–12; Jeff Jordan, "Does Skeptical Theism Lead to Moral Skepticism?" *Philosophy and Phenomenological Research* 72 (2006) 403–17; Stephen Wykstra, "The Humean Obstacle to Evidential Arguments from Suffering: On Avoiding the Evils of 'Appearance'" *International Journal for Philosophy of Religion* (1984) 73–93; Stephen Wykstra, "Rowe's Noseeum Arguments from Evil" in Daniel Howard-Snyder (ed.) *The Evidential Argument from Evil* (Bloomington: Indiana University Press, 1996).

states of affairs obtain such that God could prevent them without thereby losing some greater good or permitting some evil equally bad or worse. So premise (2) in Rowe's evidential argument from evil is false.

The impossibility arguments show that the existence of God is consistent with the existence of gratuitous evil. As we have seen, it is necessarily true that there are worlds in which God exists along with gratuitously evil states of affairs. The evidential argument from evil is therefore unsound. But it should be noted that the controversial position of skeptical theism is also obviated. Theists are not saddled with the untenable position of defending a quarantined skepticism.

## 7.3 Evil and Non-Human Animals: The Darwinian Problem of Evil

Perhaps the most serious and difficult problem of evil is the problem of animal suffering. Richard Dawkins is eloquent on this point.

If Nature were kind, she would at least make the minor concession of anesthetizing caterpillars before they are eaten alive from within. But nature is neither kind nor unkind. . . . It is easy to imagine a gene that, say, tranquilizes gazelles when they are about to suffer a killing bite. Would such a gene be favored by natural selection? Not unless the act of tranquillizing a gazelle improved the gene's chances of being propagated into future generations. It is hard to see why this should be so, and we may therefore guess that gazelles suffer horrible pain and fear when they are pursued to death—as most of them eventually are. The total amount of suffering per year in the natural world is beyond all decent contemplation. During the minute it takes me to compose this sentence, thousands of animals are being eaten alive, others are running for their lives, whimpering with fear; others are being slowly devoured from within by rasping parasites; thousands of all kinds are dying of starvation, thirst and disease. . . . Theologians worry away at the problem of evil and a related problem of suffering. . . . The British newspapers all carried a terrible story about a bus filled with children from a Roman Catholic school that crashed for no obvious reason, with wholesale loss of life. . . . "How can you believe in a loving, all powerful God who allows such a tragedy?" . . . To quote one priest's reply: "The simple answer is that we do not know why there should be a God who let's these awful things happen". But the horror of the crash, to a Christian, confirms the fact that we live in a world of real values. . . . If the universe was just electrons, there would be no problem of evil and suffering. On the contrary, if the universe were just electrons and selfish genes, meaningless tragedies like the crashing of this bus are exactly what we should expect, along with equally meaningless good fortune.[26]

---

[26] See Richard Dawkins, *River out of Eden* (New York: HarperCollins, 1996).

Philip Kitcher puts the worry more succinctly. The problem of animal suffering is aptly described as the Darwinian problem of evil. The earth has existed for about 4.5 billion years. The Darwinian problem of evil consists in the vast amount of animal suffering resulting from evolutionary mechanisms that have been culling animals and organisms, often very painfully, for about three billion years.

[Were we to imagine] a human analogue peering down over . . . [his creation], it's hard to equip the fact with a kindly expression. Conversely, it's natural to adapt Alphonso X's famous remark about the convolutions of Ptolemaic astronomy: had a benevolent creator proposed to use evolution under natural selection as a means for attaining his purposes, we could have given him useful advice.[27]

It is of course an extraordinarily difficult task to try to show that each instance of suffering over three billion years of evolutionary carnage is necessary to some greater good.[28] It cannot be done, since it isn't true. But the question that concerns us is the consistency of the proposition <God exists> and the proposition <the actual indeterministic mechanisms of evolution have brought about extensive non-human animal suffering over, at least, millions of years>.

Consider the metaphysical atheological argument from animal suffering, *The Darwinian Problem of Evil*.

1. God is omnipotent, omniscient, and wholly good.
2. The evil of extensive animal suffering exists.

Necessarily, it is within God's power to predict that the mechanisms of evolution maximize non-human animal well-being and minimize non-human animal suffering. Call such worlds "evolutionarily perfect worlds." It follows that (3) is true.

3. Necessarily, God can actualize an evolutionarily perfect world.

But God's omnipotence and perfect goodness are inconsistent with his failing to avail himself of the possibility of actualizing an evolutionarily perfect world.

---

[27] See Philip Kitcher, "The Many-Sided Conflict Between Science and Religion" in William Mann (ed.) *Blackwell Guide to Philosophy of Religion* (Malden: Blackwell Publishers, 2005).

[28] For a valiant attempt to approximate a theodicy in a *causa dei* (an argument in defense of God or CD), see Michael Murray, *Nature Red in Tooth and Claw: Theism and the Problem of Animal Suffering* (Oxford: Oxford University Press, 2008).

4. Necessarily, God can actualize an evolutionarily perfect world only if God does actualize an evolutionarily perfect world.

Since (5) follows from (3) and (4), we have derived a contradiction. (5) and (2) cannot both be true.

5. Necessarily God actualizes an evolutionarily perfect world.

God actualizes an evolutionarily perfect world if and only if he actualizes a world in which the well-being of sentient beings is maximized and the suffering of sentient beings is minimized. Richard Dawkins, recall, considers the possibility that our indeterministic world is one in which the suffering of non-human animals is minimized.

It is easy to imagine a gene that, say, tranquilizes gazelles when they are about to suffer a killing bite. Would such a gene be favored by natural selection? Not unless the act of tranquillizing a gazelle improved the gene's chances of being propagated into future generations. It is hard to see why this should be so, and we may therefore guess that gazelles suffer horrible pain and fear when they are pursued to death—as most of them eventually are.[29]

Suppose it is discovered that the actual world is an indeterministic world in which non-human animal genes evolved that tranquilize gazelles and other sentient beings when they are about to suffer a killing bite. If God could actualize such a world, then there at least appears to be no Darwinian problem of evil. But we are assuming in this case that God contingently actualizes an evolutionarily perfect world. And, if it is so discovered, then certainly there are other possible worlds in which God exists and genes do not evolve that tranquilize gazelles when they are about to suffer a killing bite. If God could actualize a world like ours in which genes evolve that tranquilize gazelles when they are about to suffer a killing bite, then it is possible that God actualizes a world in which genes do not evolve that tranquilize gazelles when they are about to suffer a killing bite. But then (5) is false. It is false that, necessarily, God actualizes an evolutionarily perfect world.

Suppose it is discovered instead that the actual world is a deterministic world in which deterministic processes result in genes that tranquilize gazelles and other sentient beings before they suffer. We are again assuming that God contingently actualizes an evolutionarily perfect world. If God could actualize such a world, then there at least appears to be no Darwinian

---

[29] Dawkins, *River out of Eden*, op. cit. p. 132.

problem of evil. In deterministic worlds there is a true historical proposition H about the intrinsic state of the world long ago and a true proposition L stating the laws of nature in that world such that H and L together determine each event in the evolutionary process. But H and L together do not determine each event E in the evolutionary process in a way that precludes the metaphysical possibility of ~E occurring. Even if H and L together determine E, there is another world in which ~E occurs. It is at least metaphysically possible that ~E. So, if ~E had occurred, there would have been no true contradictions. Likewise if ~E had occurred, the intrinsic state of the world long ago would have been no different. Rather if ~E had occurred, the law proposition L would not have been true.[30]

So, if God could contingently actualize a deterministic world in which genes evolve that tranquilize gazelles and other sentient beings when they are about to suffer a killing bite, then it is possible that God actualizes a world in which genes do not evolve that tranquilize gazelles and other sentient beings when they are about to suffer a killing bite. There are worlds in which the laws of nature do not ensure that such genes evolve. But then (5) is false. It is false that, necessarily, God actualizes an evolutionarily perfect world.

However, if (5) is true, then necessarily God actualizes an evolutionary perfect world. If, necessarily, God actualizes an evolutionarily perfect world then it is metaphysically impossible that non-human animals suffer pain. There is no possible world in which animal suffering occurs. But if it is metaphysically impossible for non-human animals to suffer, then either non-human animals are essentially not phenomenally conscious beings or non-human animals are phenomenally conscious beings and their disposition to suffer pain is necessarily finked. Consider, first, the possibility that God necessarily actualizes a Cartesian or neo-Cartesian world.

### 7.3.1 Neo-Cartesian Worlds

It is the standard interpretation of Descartes that he took non-human animals to be ontologically incapable of suffering pain or enjoying pleasure. Non-human animals on this picture are unconscious automata. As a view about what non-human animals do and can experience, it has been subject to numerous objections. It is simply not consistent with neuroanatomical similarities among species and other evolutionary facts.

---

[30]  Cf. Lewis, "Are We Free to Break Laws?," op. cit. p. 292.

But there are more sophisticated neo-Cartesian views according to which non-human animals have first-order sensory experiences but lack higher-order cognitive capacities.[31] Animals therefore lack any reflective awareness of their sensory states. If reflective awareness on first-order mental states is necessary to those states having the property of being pleasurable or painful, then non-human animals might be incapable of having first-order states that are painful or pleasurable.

There are several ways to precisify the neo-Cartesian view in ways that make non-human animals incapable of *experiencing* pain or incapable of *suffering* pain. If it is possible that non-human animals do not experience pain or that they do not suffer pain, then the creation of non-human animals in a neo-Cartesian world would present no moral objection at all. Consider a neo-Cartesian proposal based on higher-order theories (HOT) of consciousness.

For a mental state to be a conscious state (phenomenally) requires an accompanying higher-order mental state (HOT) that has that state as its intentional object. This HOT must be a thought that one is, oneself, in that first-order state.[32]

Now suppose that the neo-Cartesian maintains that only human beings have the requisite higher-order mental states. Since non-human animals lack those higher-order mental states they never have any phenomenal consciousness of pain. Non-human animals are not merely incapable of suffering pain, they are incapable of experiencing pain. The existence of pain states depends on a relational property of a first-order mental state that non-human animals do not instantiate.

Suppose it is insufficiently good that God contingently actualizes a deterministic or an indeterministic world in which genes evolved that tranquilize gazelles and other sentient beings when they are about to suffer a killing bite or any other pain. God could not contingently actualize such a world, since such worlds entail the existence of evolutionarily imperfect worlds in which God exists and genes do not evolve that tranquilize gazelles and other sentience beings when they are about to suffer a killing bite.

Suppose rather that, necessarily, God actualizes a neo-Cartesian world in which every non-human animal lacks phenomenal consciousness. The

---

[31] Cf. Murray, *Nature Red in Tooth and Claw*, op. cit. 50 ff. Murray urges that the more sophisticated view might well have been Descartes' later position.

[32] Ibid. p. 55 ff. Michael Murray formulates four distinct positions available to the neo-Cartesian.

first-order mental states that result in pain behavior are not in fact painful. There is indeed, necessarily nothing it is like to be in pain for non-human animals since it is metaphysically impossible for non-human animals to experience pain.

But premise (5) is nonetheless not true. Necessarily, God actualizes an evolutionarily perfect world if and only if necessarily, the mechanisms of evolution maximize non-human animal well-being and minimize non-human animal suffering. The mechanisms of evolution minimize non-human animal suffering, but they certainly do not maximize non-human animal well-being. Since non-human animals have no phenomenal consciousness at all, they enjoy exactly no pleasurable or desirable mental states. The level of well-being among non-human animals makes their lives barely worth living.

There are alternative neo-Cartesian proposals. Suppose we reject the idea that phenomenal consciousness is an extrinsic property of first-order mental states. We instead take phenomenal consciousness in humans and non-human animals to be an intrinsic property of first-order mental states.

Some non-human creatures have states that have intrinsic phenomenal qualities analogous to those possessed by humans when they are in states of pain. These creatures lack, however, any higher-order states of being aware of themselves as being in first-order states. They have no access to the fact that they are having a particular feeling, though they are indeed having it. Since phenomenal properties of states of pain and other sensory states are intrinsic to the states themselves, there is no difference on this score between humans and other creatures.[33]

In these neo-Cartesian worlds non-human animals have phenomenal consciousness and do experience pain. But no non-human animals have higher-order access to these first-order states and so they cannot represent themselves as being in a state of pain. Since they cannot represent themselves as being in pain, non-human animals are not capable of suffering the pain that they experience.

Suppose that, necessarily, God actualizes a neo-Cartesian world in which no non-human animal lacks phenomenal consciousness, but every non-human animal lacks higher-order access to their phenomenal states. The first-order mental states that result in pain behavior are painful. There is, necessarily something it is like to be in pain for non-human

---

[33] Ibid. p. 56.

animals since non-human animals experience pain. But necessarily non-human animals are incapable of suffering the pain that they experience.

There are two important responses to the possibility of neo-Cartesian worlds of this sort. The first is to reject the proposal that non-human animals do not suffer in neo-Cartesian worlds. If there is phenomenal consciousness of pain, then there is something it feels like to be in pain in those worlds. But if there is something it feels like to be in pain in those worlds, then there is suffering in those worlds. And there is non-human animal suffering in these neo-Cartesian worlds only if it is false that, necessarily, God actualizes such worlds.

Michael Murray argues for the suitability of such a proposal in fending off the Darwinian problem of evil.

[D]efenders of this . . . proposal . . . can plausibly respond that, so long as an animal lacks higher-order access, so long as it cannot represent itself as being in a state of pain, there is nothing about its situation that is of intrinsic moral disvalue.[34]

But the response does not seem plausible at all. On the one hand it is insisted that the non-human animal has the phenomenal consciousness of pain states—there is something it is like to be in pain for these animals—and on the other hand it is asserted that those pain states do not matter morally since no animal can represent itself as being in pain. But what makes the pain state matter morally is the already conceded phenomenal consciousness of the pain, whether or not non-human animals are in an epistemic position to know or believe that the phenomenal consciousness is their own.

But suppose we concede that the phenomenal consciousness of pain is necessary but not sufficient for non-human animals to *suffer* pain. The phenomenal consciousness of pain in these neo-Cartesian worlds is not morally bad. If, necessarily, God actualizes such a neo-Cartesian world, then premise (5) is not true. Necessarily, God actualizes an evolutionarily perfect world if and only if necessarily, the mechanisms of evolution maximize non-human animal well-being and minimize non-human animal suffering. The mechanisms of evolution minimize non-human animal suffering, but they do not maximize non-human animal well being. Since the phenomenal consciousness of pain does not entail the suffering of pain, the phenomenal consciousness of pleasure does not entail the enjoyment of pleasure. Non-human animals enjoy exactly no pleasurable or desirable

---

[34] Ibid. p. 56.

mental states. The level of well-being among non-human animals makes their lives barely worth living.

### 7.3.2 An Impossibility Argument: Evolutionarily Perfect Worlds

Let's suppose for reductio that, necessarily, God actualizes an evolutionarily perfect world.

1. Necessarily, God actualizes an evolutionarily perfect world.

Necessarily, God actualizes an evolutionarily perfect world only if, necessarily, the mechanisms of evolution maximize non-human animal well-being and minimize non-human animal suffering. So in evolutionarily perfect worlds every non-human animal enjoys the most pleasurable mental states and no non-human animals suffer any painful mental states. Every non-human animal in an evolutionarily perfect world has phenomenal consciousness of its first-order mental states.

2. Necessarily, God actualizes an evolutionarily perfect world only if, necessarily, God actualizes a world in which every non-human animal has phenomenal consciousness of his first-order mental states.[35]

So, every non-human animal has phenomenal consciousness of his first-order mental states of pleasure, satisfaction, and happiness, and his first-order mental states are accessible to him. They have phenomenally conscious pleasurable states and they are in an epistemic position to enjoy those conscious pleasurable mental states. But since there is no suffering in any evolutionarily perfect world, no non-human animal even *possibly* manifests the disposition to suffer a painful mental state in any possible world.

3. Necessarily, God actualizes an evolutionarily perfect world only if, necessarily, it is not the case that a non-human animal possibly manifests the disposition to suffer painful mental states.

But if God actualizes a world in which every non-human animal has phenomenal consciousness of his first-order mental states, then every non-human animal in evolutionarily perfect worlds has the disposition to suffer painful mental states. That is, every non-human animal is such that, under specifiable ideal conditions, were it exposed to certain noxious

---

[35] The brackets indicate the scope of the modal operators in each sentence.

stimuli, it would have phenomenal consciousness of a painful first-order mental state. So God actualizes an evolutionarily perfect world only if God creates non-human animals that are phenomenally conscious and disposed to suffer painful mental states. Non-human animals do not suffer painful mental states in evolutionarily perfect worlds only if the disposition to suffer painful states is never manifested.

In an evolutionarily perfect world, we can suppose, God *finks* or *masks* the disposition shared among non-human animals to suffer painful mental states.[36] But God never finks the disposition to enjoy pleasurable mental states. God causes the disposition to suffer painful mental states never to be manifested and allows the disposition to enjoy pleasurable mental states always to be manifested. Consider David Lewis's extrinsic fink for fragility.

A sorcerer takes a liking to a fragile glass, one that is a perfect intrinsic duplicate of all the other fragile glasses off the same production line. He does nothing at all to change the dispositional character of his glass. He only watches and waits, resolved that if ever his glass is struck, then, quick as a flash, he will cast a spell that changes the glass, renders it no longer fragile, and thereby aborts the process of breaking. So his finkishly fragile glass would not break if struck—but no thanks to any protective disposition of the glass itself. Thanks, instead, to a disposition of the sorcerer.[37]

God, too, can extrinsically fink the disposition to suffer painful mental states without affecting the intrinsic disposition to enjoy pleasurable mental states. Indeed, God can fink the disposition to suffer painful mental states in every possible world. In evolutionarily perfect worlds, then, God finks the disposition among non-human animals to suffer painful mental states.

   4. Necessarily, God can fink the disposition to suffer painful mental states.

---

[36] "Fink" is C. B. Martin's name for a fact or action or event that, conditional on the occurrence of the stimulus, removes the causal basis of a disposition before the disposition can manifest. See C. B. Martin "Dispositions and conditionals" *The Philosophical Quarterly* (1994) 1–8. An "antidote" or "mask" works not by removing the causal basis of the disposition, but by interfering with the subsequent causal process by which the disposition would otherwise manifest itself. See for instance Toby Handfield, "Unfinkable Dispositions" *Synthese* (2008) 297–308.

A poison has the disposition to cause death if ingested. But it may be that, regarding a poisonous substance $x$, the sentence "if $x$ were ingested by $y$, $y$ would die" is false, because $y$ may have a ready supply of antidote. An antidote works not by removing the causal basis of the disposition, but rather by interfering with the subsequent causal process by which the disposition would otherwise manifest itself.

[37] David Lewis, "Finkish Dispositions" *The Philosophical Quarterly* (1997) 143–58.

The hypothesis for reductio is that, necessarily, God actualizes an evolutionarily perfect world. We know that God does so only if God *necessarily finks* the disposition among non-human animals to suffer painful mental states. But is it possible that God necessarily finks the disposition to suffer painful mental states? If there are some *possible* non-human animals that have the *essential property* of possibly manifesting the disposition to suffer painful mental states, then it is impossible that God necessarily finks the disposition to suffer painful mental states.

5. Necessarily, there is some possible world in which some phenomenally conscious non-human animals have the essential property of possibly manifesting the disposition to suffer some painful mental states only if, it is impossible that, necessarily, God actualizes an evolutionarily perfect world.

But theists will advance the thesis in (6) that some possible non-human animal has the essential property of possibly manifesting the disposition to suffer painful mental states.

6. There is some possible world in which some phenomenally conscious non-human animals have the essential property of possibly manifesting the disposition to suffer some pain.

The justification advanced for (6) will in fact provide good reason to believe the stronger thesis in (7).

7. There is some possible world in which most phenomenally conscious non-human animals have the essential property of possibly manifesting the disposition to suffer some pain.

Non-human animals perform intentional actions and bring about positive changes in the world. And according to Richard Swinburne, the intentional change that animals effect in the world constitutes a good.

... good actions may be good without being freely chosen. It is good that there be animals who show courage in the face of pain, to secure food and to find and rescue their mates and their young, and sympathetic concern for other animals. An animal life is of so much greater value for the heroism it shows.... Yet an animal cannot go on looking for a mate unless it is lost and the animal longs for it; nor decoy predators or explore despite risk of loss of life unless there are predators and there is a risk of loss of life. There will not be predators unless sometimes animals get caught.... And there will not be a risk of loss of life unless sometimes life is lost.

Nor can an animal intentionally avoid the danger of a forest fire or guide its offspring away from one unless the danger exists objectively. And that cannot be unless some animals get caught in forest fires. . . . The intentional act of rescuing, despite danger, simply cannot be done unless the danger exists and is believed to exist. The danger will not exist unless there is a significant natural probability of being caught in the fire . . . and to the extent that the world is indeterministic, that involves an inclination of nature to produce the effect unprevented by God.[38]

According to Swinburne, the actions of non-human animals are good insofar as they are intentional and bring about positive change. But whereas Swinburne regards the actions of non-human animals as unfree, it is certainly more accurate to characterize those actions as *not fully free* and those non-human animals as not fully responsible for those actions. But while non-human animals are not fully free and not fully responsible, they are not mere automatons, either.

Among the widely recognized conditions on moral responsibility there is an epistemic condition and a control condition. Roughly, the epistemic condition informs us that moral responsibility for the outcomes of one's actions requires knowledge or (at least) true belief about those consequences. Of course, many non-human animals have true beliefs about the consequences of their actions and in some cases have true beliefs about the permissibility of what they do. To take one obvious example, domesticated animals are often quite aware when they have violated household rules and they act in ways that display shame and remorse for having done so.

Feral animals also have true beliefs about the outcomes of their actions. They are certainly less aware of the permissibility of their actions, but they are not in general oblivious to permissibility of what they do. We find illustrations of non-instinctive moral behavior as far back as Darwin's discussion of the moral sense among non-human animals.

Many animals, however, certainly sympathize with each other's distress or danger. This is the case even with birds. Capt. Stansbury found on a salt lake in Utah an old and completely blind pelican, which was very fat, and must have been well fed for a long time by his companions. Mr. Blyth . . . saw Indian crows feeding two or three of their companions which were blind. . . . We may, if we choose, call these actions instinctive; but such cases are much too rare for the development of any special instinct. I have myself seen a dog, who never passed a cat who lay sick in a

[38] Richard Swinburne, *Providence and the Problem of Evil* (Oxford: Oxford University Press, 1998) 171–2.

basket, and was a great friend of his, without giving her a few licks with his tongue, the surest sign of kind feeling in a dog. . . . Besides love and sympathy, animals exhibit other qualities connected with the social instincts, which in us would be called moral; and I agree with Agassiz that dogs possess something very like a conscience.[39]

Of course, non-human animals also vary in the degree to which they meet the control condition on moral responsibility. Roughly, non-human animals meet the control condition to the extent that it is proper to blame and praise them for their actions. Again it is not in general true that blaming or praising non-human animals for what they do is inappropriate. The control that both human and non-human animals display varies over circumstances and individuals. But it is perhaps in general true that non-human animals are never fully responsible for their actions.

Non-human animals also display varying degrees of free will. Robert Kane urges that the main conceptions of free will include the alternate possibilities conception and the ultimate sourcehood conception.

We believe we have free will when we view ourselves as agents capable of influencing the world in various ways. Open alternatives, or alternative possibilities, seem to lie before us. We reason and deliberate among them and choose. We feel (1) it is "up to us" what we choose and how we act; and this means we could have chosen or acted otherwise. . . . This "up-to-us-ness" also suggests (2) the ultimate control of our actions lie in us and not outside us in factors beyond our control.[40]

Supposing that these conditions are equally important we might say that we are free in doing A only if we could have failed to do A and nothing outside of our choice to do A is the ultimate explanation for our doing A.[41] Non-human animals can of course positively and negatively affect the

---

[39] See Charles Darwin, "The Origin of the Moral Sense" in Peter Singer (ed.) *Ethics* (Oxford: Oxford University Press, 1994) 43–7. For some well-known recent discussions of moral agency among non-human animals, see Robert Trivers, "The Evolution of Reciprocal Altruism" *Quarterly Review of Biology* (1971) 35–57; Marc Bekoff and Jessica Pierce, *Wild Justice: The Moral Lives of Animals* (Chicago: University of Chicago Press, 2009); Frans De Waal, "Chimpanzee Justice" in Peter Singer (ed.) *Ethics* (Oxford: Oxford University Press, 1994) 67–9; and Jane Goodall, *The Chimpanzees of Gombe* (Cambridge, Mass.: Harvard University Press, 1986).

[40] See Robert Kane, *A Contemporary Introduction to Free Will* (New York: Oxford University Press, 2005) 6 ff.

[41] But Kevin Timpe usefully notes that many philosophers simply define free will as the freedom to do otherwise. See Kevin Timpe, *Free Will: Sourcehood and its Alternatives* (New York: Continuum Publishing, 2008). Among those who endorse this conception of free will, see Peter van Inwagen, *An Essay on Free Will* (Oxford: Oxford University Press, 1983); and Randolph Clarke, *Libertarian Accounts of Free Will* (New York: Oxford University Press, 2003).

world. We very likely inhabit an indeterministic world—or perhaps an indeterministic world with some deterministic enclaves—and so, for most of what we do, we have alternatives. We might have done otherwise. But both human and non-human animals vary in the degree to which the ultimate explanation for their behavior lies outside of them and so both humans and non-human animals vary in the degree to which they are free according to the ultimate sourcehood conception.

In evolutionary perfect worlds the mechanisms of evolution maximize well-being and minimize suffering. Some evolutionarily perfect worlds are morally perfect worlds that include significantly free humans and significantly free non-human animals. Of course, the fact that non-human animals are significantly free in those worlds does not entail that all non-human animals are fully free or fully responsible for their actions in those worlds. The significant freedom of non-human animals entails that many non-human animals enjoy some degree of freedom and some degree of moral responsibility. And the significant freedom of non-human animals contributes to the overall moral value of morally perfect worlds. In morally perfect worlds every significantly instantiated creature goes right with respect to every morally significant action.

But if there are evolutionarily perfect worlds in which every significantly instantiated creature goes right with respect to every morally significant action then the thesis in (7) is true. Recall that (7) states the following.

7. There is some possible world in which most phenomenally conscious non-human animals have the essential property of possibly manifesting the disposition to suffer some pain.

It is true in these evolutionarily perfect worlds that most phenomenally conscious non-human animals have the essential property of possibly manifesting the disposition to suffer some pain. Indeed, the value of these evolutionarily perfect worlds depends on the modal fact that possibly every significantly free human and non-human animal goes radically wrong with respect to most or all of its morally significant actions. Worlds in which every significantly free human and non-human animal goes radically wrong with respect to most of its morally significant actions are, in many cases, worlds in which there is tremendous pain and suffering. The value of evolutionarily perfect worlds consists in large measure in significantly free human and non-human animals satisfying the prohibitions of justice and beneficence. It consists in significantly free human and non-human animals constraining their behavior within bounds set by the requirements of justice and beneficence. There would be no such constraints were there no possible worlds in which the requirements of justice and beneficence were seriously violated.

Since (7) and (6) are true, our assumption for reductio is false. Recall that we assumed for reductio that, necessarily, God actualizes an evolutionarily perfect world. But clearly there are evolutionarily perfect worlds in which no sentient being suffers pain and every significantly free human and non-human animal goes right with respect to every morally significant action. The existence of evolutionarily perfect worlds of this sort entails the existence of worlds in which every significantly free human and non-human animal goes radically wrong with respect to most or all of its morally significant actions. But then it is false that, necessarily, God actualizes an evolutionarily perfect world. Indeed, it is impossible that, necessarily, God actualizes an evolutionarily perfect world. Our assumption for reductio is false.

### 7.3.3 An Atheological Rejoinder

It is central to the impossibility argument that it is an essential property of some possible non-human animals that they possibly manifest the disposition to suffer painful mental states.[42] There is some world in which non-human animals have the essential property of possibly manifesting the disposition to suffer painful mental states. As we have noted, the thesis in (6) is evinced by the fact that, as both non-Cartesian theists and atheists agree, actual non-human animals have the essential property of possibly manifesting the disposition to suffer painful mental states. Non-human animals do have the property of possibly manifesting the disposition to suffer painful mental states only if they have that property essentially. If non-human animals have that property in any world, then they have that property in every world in which they exist.[43] But non-human animals

---

[42] The development of this argument owes much to discussion with Jonathan Schaffer and Stephen Yablo. I should add, however, that neither reported being convinced.

[43] This follows from the S5 theorems that $\Diamond p \supset \Box \Diamond p$ and $\Diamond\Diamond p \supset \Diamond p$. In English, whatever is possible is necessarily possible and whatever is possibly possible is possible. If it is possible that a non-human animal possibly manifests the disposition D to suffer pain, then it is possible that a non-human animal manifests D. And if it is possible that a non-human animal manifests D, then it is necessarily possible that it manifests D. And if it is necessarily possible that a non-human animal manifests D, then it is an essential property of that non-human animal that it possibly manifests D.

manifest the disposition to suffer pain in the actual world, so they have the essential property of manifesting that disposition in some world.

It is important to note that having an essential property of possibly manifesting the disposition to suffer painful mental states is consistent with it being a contingent property of every animal in any world that it suffers pain. It might be an essential property of William Rowe's Bambi that he suffers pain in some world, but a contingent property of Bambi that he suffers pain in any world in which he does. The pain that Bambi suffers might then be gratuitous and finkable in every world in which it occurs. But since it is essential to Bambi that it is *possible* that he suffers pain, it is impossible that God necessarily finks the pain that Bambi suffers.

There is an interesting and important line of argument open to the atheologian that is consistent with the fact that it is an essential property of some possible non-human animals to possibly manifest the disposition to suffer painful mental states. The atheologian might argue that it is inconsistent with the existence of God that any non-human animal, in any world, possibly manifest the disposition to suffer painful mental states. It is therefore inconsistent with the existence of God that any non-human animal, in any world, have the essential property of possibly manifesting the disposition to suffer pain.

It is a very interesting claim that the essential properties of non-human animals might have been different. But this is the atheological claim being advanced. The atheological claim is that the conditional in C0 is true.[44]

C0.  Were it true that God existed, then it would be true that no non-human animal in any possible world suffers any painful mental states.

If the antecedent of C0 is true, then the degenerate "counterfactual" is false. The closest world to ours in which God exists is our world, and there is a vast amount of animal suffering in our world. So C0 cannot be a degenerate counterfactual.

But then C0 is either a genuine (disguised) counterfactual or a counter-possible. God either necessarily exists or necessarily fails to exist. If C0 is

---

[44] On the possibility of non-trivially true counterpossibles see, for instance, Berit Brogaard and Joe Salerno, "Why Counterpossibles are Non-Trivial" *The Reasoner* 1/1 (2007). Against the view that they might be non-trivially true see Timothy Williamson, *The Philosophy of Philosophy* (Oxford: Blackwell, 2008); and David Lewis, *Counterfactuals* (Oxford: Blackwell, 1973).

advanced as a trivially true counterpossible, then it simply begs the question. It just assumes the antecedent in C0 is necessarily false, so that God necessarily fails to exist.

But suppose C0 is proposed as a non-trivial counterpossible. Now consider the closest worlds to the actual world in which the God exists. In those worlds God has the essential property of necessarily existing, since it is metaphysically necessary that God has the essential property of necessarily existing. So, as a matter of necessity, God exists in some world only if he exists in every world. But then the closest world to ours in which God exists would be our world. In evaluating the counterpossible we keep unchanged the vast amount of animal suffering and accommodate the existence of God with the stipulation that the vast amount of suffering must be serving some larger purpose. But under this evaluation, the counterpossible is non-trivially false.

The counterpossible in C0 entails the counterpossible in C1, since the consequent in C0 entails the consequent in C1.

> C1.  Were it true that God existed, then it would be true that no non-human animal in any possible world has the essential property of manifesting the disposition to suffer painful mental states in some world.

But, if these counterpossibles are genuinely non-trivial, then we have better reason to affirm C2 than to affirm C1.

> C2.  Were it true that God existed, then it would be true that some non-human animals in some possible worlds have the essential property of possibly manifesting the disposition to suffer painful mental states.

The consequents in C1 and C2 are both consistent with the existence of God. If some non-human animals in some possible worlds have the essential property of possibly manifesting the disposition to suffer painful mental states, then there is nothing God could do to alter that fact. It is therefore consistent with God's perfect goodness and omnipotence not to alter what it is impossible to alter. It might be suggested that God could simply fail to create such beings, which is of course true. But it is false that God might have failed to create such beings in every world in which he exists. Indeed, it is necessary that God creates such beings in some world or other. And if such beings have the essential property of possibly manifesting the disposition to suffer painful mental states, then there is a possible world in which God exists and they suffer painful mental states.

It would certainly take much less of a departure from the actual world to reach a possible world at which the consequent of C2 is true than to reach a world at which the consequent of C1 is true.[45] Indeed, the consequent of C2 is true in the actual world and no world is as close to the actual world as it is to itself. But if the conditional in C2 is non-trivially true, then the conditional in C0 is non-trivially false.

We can revise C0 to ensure that the counterpossible is non-trivially true. Consider the conditional in C3.

> C3. Were the Anselmian God to exist, then there would not be a vast amount of *pointless* animal suffering over billions years of evolutionary history.

But if C3 is non-trivially true, then it is false that there is a vast amount of pointless animal suffering over billions years of evolutionary history. We cannot entertain a world in which the God exists but does not necessarily exist. So the probability of C3 increases only if the probability decreases that there is a vast amount of pointless animal suffering over billions of years of evolutionary history . And the probability that they are both true is zero.

But consider a Kripkean reductive approach to "counterpossibles," according to which they are genuine (though disguised) counterfactuals. We let the counterfactual connective in C3 operate on Fregean senses rather than on Russellian singular propositions. On this approach, when we think we are entertaining the antecedent of the counterpossible "were water not $H_2O$, then it would be XYZ," we are in fact entertaining the antecedent of the counterfactual "were the watery stuff not $H_2O$, then it would be XYZ." A reductive approach to counterpossibles would have C3 replaced with C4.

> C4. Were there a being playing the God role, then there would not be a vast amount of pointless animal suffering over billions of years of evolutionary history.

[45] There are lots of worries about the truth-conditions of counterpossibles. See Daniel Nolan, "Impossible Worlds: A Modest Approach" *Notre Dame Journal for Formal Logic* (1997) 325–527.

In evaluating C4 we consider the closest metaphysically possible worlds in which there is something playing the God role and determine whether in those worlds there is a vast amount of pointless animal suffering. The analogy is with considering worlds in which something other than water is playing the water role and we ask whether that stuff is XYZ. If we assume that God does not exist in that, or any other, world, then the question is whether the being we are envisaging as playing the God role has the relevant divine properties. If the being playing the God role is not a necessarily existing being, then there is little reason for theists to be concerned with the truth or falsity of C4. But if the being playing the God role is a necessarily existing being, then C4 is false.

The theist and the atheist agree that some possible non-human animals have the essential property of possibly manifesting the disposition to suffer painful mental states. After all, actual non-human animals have that essential property. God's existence is compatible with there being non-human animals that have the essential property of possibly manifesting the disposition to suffer pain. If God exists and non-human animals have that essential property, then it is impossible that God *necessarily* finks the disposition to suffer painful mental states. God might fink the disposition in many worlds, but he cannot do so in every world. It is therefore an unreasonable expectation that he should do so.

*An Impossibility Argument: Evolutionarily Perfect Worlds* is a consistency proof. It aims to show that it's impossible that, necessarily, God actualizes an evolutionarily perfect world. The argument stipulates that, necessarily, God *can* actualize an evolutionarily perfect world. The argument maintains that it is an essential property of some (at least) possible, phenomenally conscious, non-human animals to possibly manifest the disposition to suffer painful mental states. If so then there are possible worlds at which the proposition <God can actualize an evolutionarily perfect world> and the proposition <God does not actualize an evolutionarily perfect world> are both true. But then the existence of an evolutionary imperfect world presents no serious challenge to the existence of God.

# 8

# Redeeming Worlds

## 8.0 Redeemable Evil and Gratuitous Evil

In Chapter 5, it was argued that, necessarily, there are worlds in which God could have actualized a morally perfect world and God did not do so. Necessarily, there are worlds in which God allows moral agents to bring about evils when in fact he might have prevented them from doing so. It was observed that in every morally perfect world every significantly free instantiated essence can go wrong and can go radically wrong. It was argued that there are morally perfect worlds only if there are also worlds in which God allows significantly free instantiated essences to go radically wrong.

It is a tenet of certain strands of Calvinism that God first decreed to save at least some of the fallen and then decreed to permit humanity to fall into sin. This is the order of God's decrees according to *Supralapsarianism*. The decree to allow the fall comes after the decree to save some of the fallen. But the argument we have been advancing might be taken as suggesting that *Infralapsarianism* is closer to the truth. According to infralapsarianism God first decrees to permit humanity to fall into sin and then decrees to save at least some of the fallen. According to the argument advanced so far, God allows significantly free instantiated essences to go radically wrong. There can exist no morally perfect worlds unless God allows significantly free beings to go radically wrong in some worlds. God allows significantly free beings to go radically wrong but he might then redeem every instance of gratuitous evil.[1] Importantly, on this view, God does not allow significantly free beings to go radically wrong *in order to* redeem them.

There are worlds in which God can actualize a morally perfect world and God does not do so. These are worlds in which God allows or permits

---

[1] Infralapsarianism actually maintains that God first decreed to permit humanity to fall into sin and then decreed to save at least some of the fallen.

gratuitous evil.[2] Recall that in Chapter 6 we offered the reformulation in $S_0$ of the standard analysis of gratuitous evil.

> $S_0$.  The evil state of affairs E is gratuitous in W iff E obtains at W and it is true at W that there is some actualizable world $W''$ such that $W'' > W$ and $W''$ does not include E.

But gratuitously evil states of affairs are not in general *irredeemably evil* states of affairs. Evil states of affairs are gratuitous and redeemable relative to worlds. Let's say that an evil state of affairs is redeemable in world W if and only if it satisfies the conditions in RE. Otherwise, the evil state of affairs is irredeemable in W.

> RE.  The state of affairs E is redeemable in W iff (i) E is a gratuitously evil state of affairs in W and (ii) there is an actualizable world $W'$ such that $W' > W$ and $W'$ includes the state of affairs E and a state of affairs G and (iii) the state of affairs G atones for E in $W'$, and (iv) there is no world $W'$ that includes the state of affairs G and does not include the state of affairs E.

According to RE and $S_0$ evil states of affairs that are redeemed *might* nonetheless be gratuitous evils. A world $W'$ in which G atones for E might be such that, for some actualizable world $W''$, $W''$ does not include E and $W'' > W'$. Call worlds where every evil is redeemed, *Redeemed Worlds*. Redeemed worlds might not be as good, overall, as (at least some) worlds including no gratuitous evil at all. Still, in redeemed worlds, there are no instances of unredeemed evil. On the other hand, some redeemed worlds might be better than worlds containing no gratuitous evil. It might be better that the gratuitous evil in W is redeemed than that the gratuitous evil in W eliminated or prevented altogether.[3]

According to RE, God can actualize a redeemed world without preventing a single instance of gratuitous evil. In redeemed worlds there are evil states of affairs E and states of affairs G such that, for every E, G atones for E. The most familiar notion of atonement is of course derived from Christian thought, where incarnation and atonement are regarded as perhaps the greatest contingent goods.

---

[2] Compare Chapter 6, Section 2, for problems with the standard analysis of gratuitous evil.
[3] The "might" in this sentence and the preceding sentence is an epistemic might of the sort "might, for all we know."

Given the truth of Christian belief, however, there is also a contingent good-making characteristic of our world—one that isn't present in all worlds—that towers enormously above the rest of the contingent states of affairs included in our world: the unthinkably great good of divine incarnation and atonement. . . . God the Father, the first being of the whole universe, perfectly good and holy, all-powerful and all-knowing, was willing to permit his Son to undergo this suffering, and to undergo enormous suffering himself, in order to make it possible for us humans to be reconciled to him. And this in the face of the fact that we have turned our back upon God, have rejected him, are sunk in sin, indeed, are inclined to resent God and our neighbor. . . . [C]ould there be a good-making feature of a world to rival this?[4]

The Christian account of the response of God to vast amounts of moral and natural evil describes one important type of atonement. It describes the notion of freely given *divine atonement* for evil. But there is the possibility of non-divine responses to evil that also have the properties of atonement.

The value of free and non-divine, moral responsiveness to evil can atone for both moral and natural evil on a broader notion of atonement. For instance, the existence of moral and natural evil provides an occasion for instantiating acts of moral courage, charity, perseverance, hope, compassion, mercy, and generosity. These too are free responses to existing evil. Evil states of affairs also provide occasion to advance the goals of distributive, retributive, reparational, or compensatory justice.[5] The aim of non-divine atonement is to provide a response G to evil states of affairs E in such that way that G is not possible without E and the overall value of G & E is positive.

Compare, for instance, Plantinga's well-known example of someone (say, Smith) bearing up magnificently to his particular affliction.[6]

---

[4] Alvin Plantinga, "Superlapsarianism or 'O Felix Culpa'" in Peter van Inwagen (ed.) *Christian Faith and the Problem of Evil* (Grand Rapids: Wm. B. Eerdmans Publishing Co., 2004).

[5] Marilyn McCord Adams distinguishes between the global defeat of evil and local defeat of evil and argues against the possibility of the global justification of evil. See her "Horrendous Evils and Goodness of God" in M. Adams and R. Adams (eds.) *The Problem of Evil* (Oxford: Oxford University Press, 1990). My proposal is sympathetic to this view. But I argue that whether an instance of evil, even an instance of terrible or horrendous evil, has a point globally and to the individual that undergoes the evil depends on the moral responsiveness of that individual and many others. My proposal does depend on Adams's claim that the point of participation in some evils depends on its integration into one's relationship with God.

[6] It should be noted that Plantinga does not describe such acts as instances of atoning for evils.

Certain kinds of value and certain familiar sorts of good states of affairs, can't exist apart from evil of some sort. For example, there are people who display a sort of creative moral heroism in the face of suffering and adversity—a heroism that inspires others and creates a good situation out of a bad one. In a situation like this the evil, of course, remains evil; but the total state of affairs—someone's bearing up magnificently, for example—may be good. . . . But of course it is not possible that such a good state of affairs obtain unless some evil also obtain. It is a necessary truth that if someone bears pain magnificently, then someone is in pain.[7]

It is impossible to take that particular moral attitude to that particular affliction unless Smith actually endures the affliction. And it is possible for all to exercise their freedom in atonement for great evils in ways that instantiate exceptional moral value. It is possible for everyone to direct their moral attitudes to specific present or past evils E and to intend the actualization of a good state of affairs as compensation for E.[8] In general, for any evil E that occurs, there is a possible response G to E such that G is a free moral response to E, G is impossible in the absence of E, the overall moral value of G & E is positive. Call the denial of this position *moral defeatism*. Moral defeatism is the position that there exist some evil states of affairs E such that, no matter how anyone or anything, divine or non-divine responds, E cannot be redeemed.[9]

We know that, necessarily, there are worlds in which God can actualize a morally perfect world and God does not do so. But we do not know that, necessarily, God can actualize an unredeemed world. The actual world, it is reasonable to conclude, contains vast amounts of gratuitous evil. But that does not entail that the actual world contains even a single instance of unredeemed evil. So, of course, it does not entail that the actual world includes a single instance of irredeemable evil.

---

[7] See Alvin Plantinga, *God, Freedom, and Evil* (Grand Rapids: Wm. B. Eerdmans Publishing, 1974) 23 ff.

[8] It is possible for instance, for S to intend G specifically for the sake of evil E. The resulting state of affairs, *having brought about G in compensation for E*, is not possible in worlds where E does not occur. We can, for instance, act to ensure that a loved one did not die pointlessly by actualizing a great good intended to compensate for (or make meaningful) the otherwise senseless loss of that person.

[9] See Roderick Chisholm, "The Defeat of Good and Evil" in Marilyn McCord Adams and Robert Merrihew Adams (eds.) *The Problem of Evil* (Oxford: Oxford University Press, 1990).

# 8.1  Plantinga on Redeeming Worlds or Felix Culpa

Plantinga's most recent response to the problem of evil is a Christian informed theodicy that appeals, initially, to the value of worlds that include the existence of God.

First, any world in which God exists is enormously more valuable than any world in which he does not exist. According to the traditional doctrine of God's necessary existence, of course, God is concrete and necessarily existent, and the only being that displays both those characteristics. If this doctrine is correct, then there aren't any worlds in which God does not exist.... [H]ence this great-making character-istic, trivially, will be present in any world he chooses for actualization.[10]

On Plantinga's view God is unlimited or infinite in goodness, power, and knowledge and these properties are essential to him. And since God exists in every possible world—and certainly in every possible world that he could actualize—Plantinga concludes that every possible world is (at least) very good. But what, more exactly, does it mean to say that God's value is unlimited?

... consider a possible world W and then consider a state of affairs W- consisting just in the existence and properties of the free creatures W contains.... Now the way in which such a world W is unlimited is that W-, no matter how good, and no matter how many wonderful creatures with splendid properties it displays, is not as good as the state of affairs consisting in the existence of God.... No matter how much sin and suffering and evil W- contains, it is vastly outweighed by the goodness of God, so that W is a good world, and indeed a very good world. It follows, once more, that every possible world is a very good world.[11]

On this view, every world that includes God is very good, no matter how much disvalue it otherwise includes. There are, nonetheless, differences in overall positive value among possible worlds. Indeed, some worlds are much better than others.

Plantinga considers three distinct value hypotheses or value assumptions that might determine the ordering of the overall positive value of possible worlds. Each of the value hypotheses concerns the towering goods of the incarnation and atonement.

---

[10]  See Plantinga, "Superlapsarianism or 'O Felix Culpa'," op. cit. p. 7.
[11]  Ibid. p. 9.

For there is a second and enormously impressive good-making feature of our world, a feature to be found in some and not in all possible worlds. This is the towering and magnificent good of divine incarnation and atonement. . . . God was in no way obliged to provide a way of salvation for his erring creatures. It would have been consistent with his love, goodness and mercy not to institute this marvelous plan by which we sinful creatures can have life and be reconciled with God. Hence there are possible worlds in which there are free creatures who go wrong and in which there is no atonement.

. . . I believe that any world with incarnation and atonement is better than any world without it—or at any rate better than any world in which God does nothing comparable to incarnation and atonement.[12]

The initial value hypothesis is what Plantinga calls the *strong value assumption*.

> **Strong Value Assumption**: there is a level L of excellence or goodness among possible worlds such that all worlds at L or above contain incarnation and atonement.

According to the strong value assumption the value of incarnation and atonement is unrivaled by any other good-making feature of any world that lacks incarnation and atonement. There simply isn't any valuable state of affairs in any world distinct from incarnation and atonement that is comparable in value to it.

There is a weaker value hypothesis that refers to the pair-wise comparative value of worlds including incarnation and atonement.

> **Moderate Value Assumption**: for any two worlds W and W' that include the same creatures instantiated in the same maximal state of affairs T, if W is morally perfect and W' is morally imperfect, then if W' includes incarnation and atonement and W does not, then W' is better than W.

According to the moderate value assumption, for any morally perfect world that God might actualize and that does not include incarnation and atonement, there is a morally imperfect world that is better. Incarnation and atonement cover a multitude of sins. The moderate assumption does not imply that every world with incarnation and atonement is better than any world without incarnation and atonement. It does imply that for

---

[12] Ibid. pp. 9–10. Undeniably there are questionable claims in this passage concerning God's obligation to save those who have gone wrong and the consistency of divine love, goodness, and mercy with not instituting a plan for salvation.

every level of value among worlds there is some world with incarnation and atonement whose value is at or above that level.

The weakest value hypothesis simply claims that there are some very valuable worlds that include incarnation and atonement.

**Weak Value Assumption**: there are some worlds of great value that include incarnation and atonement.

The weak value assumption does not entail that the worlds including incarnation and atonement exceed in value any morally perfect worlds— even those morally perfect worlds that lack incarnation and atonement. Perhaps any morally perfect world is better than every morally imperfect world, no matter what else those imperfect worlds contain. The assumption entails only that some of the worlds that include incarnation and atonement are very valuable.

### 8.1.1 The Theodical Argument

The theodical argument Plantinga advances would succeed with the weak value hypothesis, though he in fact makes the strong value assumption. If the strong value assumption is true and God decides to actualize a really good possible world, then he will actualize a highly eligible world. Let the overall value of all and only highly eligible worlds be at least L and let all of the highly eligible worlds include incarnation and atonement.

But every world in which there is incarnation and atonement is a world in which there is sin and evil. Indeed, it is necessarily true that a world contains incarnation and atonement only if it contains sin and evil, and the suffering consequent upon them. So, there is no possible world whose value exceeds L that does not include sin and evil.

But then this gives us a very straightforward and simple response to the question "Why is there evil in the world?" The response is that God wanted to create a highly eligible world, wanted to actualize one of the best of all possible worlds; all of those worlds contain atonement, hence they all contain sin and evil. . . . But doesn't the above furnish us with an answer to the question "Why does God permit evil?" The answer is: because he wanted to actualize a possible world whose value was greater than L; but all of those possible worlds contain incarnation and atonement; hence all those worlds contain evil. So if a theodicy is an attempt to explain why God permits evil, what we have here is a theodicy—and, if I'm right, a successful theodicy.[13]

---

[13] Ibid. p. 12.

This theodicy also provides us with a defense of superlapsarianism on the order of God's decrees. According to Plantinga, God's fundamental intention is to actualize an extremely good possible world, a world whose overall value exceeds L. But every world whose value exceeds L includes incarnation and atonement, and so includes sin and evil. So the decree to provide incarnation and atonement—to actualize a world that includes incarnation and atonement—precedes the decree to permit creatures to fall into sin. God's ultimate aim is to actualize a world with great value. As a *means* of doing so, God must actualize a world that includes incarnation and atonement and therefore a world with sin and evil.

Suppose we try to reconstruct and clarify Plantinga's theodical argument as follows.

1. God actualizes a world whose overall value is L or greater.
2. Necessarily, God actualizes a world whose overall value is L or greater only if God actualizes a world that includes the incarnation and atonement.
3. God actualizes a world that includes the incarnation and atonement. (1), (2)
4. Necessarily, God actualizes a world that includes the incarnation and atonement only if God actualizes a world that includes sin, evil, and the suffering consequent on them.
5. God actualizes a world that includes sin, evil, and the suffering consequent on them. (3), (4).
6. Necessarily God actualizes a world whose overall value is L or greater only if God actualizes a world in which every evil state of affairs is atoned for and every human being is redeemed.
7. God actualized a world in which every evil state of affairs is atoned for and every human being is redeemed. (1), (6)
8. Necessarily, God actualizes a world in which every evil state of affairs is atoned for and every human being is redeemed only if God actualizes a world that contains no gratuitous evil.
9. God actualizes a world that contains no gratuitous evil. (7), (8)
10. Necessarily, God actualizes a world that contains no gratuitous evil only if there is no problem of evil.
11. There is no problem of evil. (9), (10).

The argument fails to distinguish between gratuitous evil and redeemable evil. Even if all of the evil in the world is redeemed or atoned for, for instance, it might nonetheless be true that all of the evil was gratuitous. Let E be all of the evil in the actual world prior to its atonement. It might be true that, for some world W such that W is better than the actual world, W does not include E. Since God might have prevented E altogether without any loss in overall value, E is gratuitous. Of course, if Plantinga is right about the value of incarnation and atonement, it might also be true that, once E is redeemed, there is no world $W'$ such that $W'$ is better than the actual world and E does not obtain at $W'$.

But the central problem for the theodical argument is premise (5). According to premise (5), God actualizes a world containing sin and evil and the suffering consequent on them *as a means* to achieving the ultimate aim in premise (1) to actualize a world whose overall value is L or greater. But it might reasonably be objected that God cannot use non-divine beings as a means to achieving even very good divine goals. Using non-divine beings as a means to achieving even the best world would (at least appear to) violate Kantian principles protecting individual autonomy. The objection is considered in Section 8.2.

It is also reasonably objected that God cannot intend to actualize an intrinsically evil state of affairs as a means to actualizing even the best possible world. Directly intending the actualization of an evil state of affairs as a means to achieving a good—even a very good—world would (at least appear to) violate the doctrine of double effect. This objection is considered in Sections 8.3 and 8.4 below. Additional reasons are adduced below for rejecting the Felix Culpa theodicy.

### 8.1.2 Non-Divine Redemptive Suffering?

According to Plantinga, evil states of affairs are those that result from free action in violation of moral law. Suffering is not intrinsically evil, even if suffering is intrinsically bad.

As I'm thinking of the matter, suffering encompasses any kind of pain or discomfort: pain or discomfort that results from disease, injury, oppression, overwork, old age, sorrow for one's sins, disappointment with oneself or with one's lot in life (or that of persons close to one)...I'm thinking of evil, on the other hand, as, fundamentally, a matter of free creatures doing what is wrong and/or displaying vicious character traits.[14]

---

[14] Ibid. p. 2.

But Plantinga takes the traditional position on suffering that both divine suffering and non-divine suffering is necessary to God's plan for redemption. It is through suffering that non-divine beings can be like Christ and participate in his redemptive activity. More precisely, for any eligible and redeemed world to be actualized, more is needed than the suffering of Christ. Every eligible world includes atonement, so every eligible world includes divine suffering and creaturely suffering.

> Creatures, therefore, can fill up what is lacking in regard to Christ's suffering in the following way: there is a necessary condition of the goodness of truly good (highly eligible) possible worlds that is not and cannot be satisfied by Christ's suffering; it requires creaturely suffering as well. It is in this sense that Paul as well as the rest of us can fill up what is lacking in regard to Christ's suffering.[15]

Non-divine beings partake in redemptive suffering only in the sense that their suffering is necessary to the actualization of a world that requires redemption. The suffering of non-divine beings does not contribute to the atonement of evil states of affairs.

Non-divine redemptive suffering, in this sense, is not—or at least not obviously—the possibility of non-divine responses to evil described in Section 8.0. We noted in Section 8.0 that the value of non-divine responsiveness can atone for both moral and natural evil in the broader notion of atonement. And certainly Plantinga would agree with this. The existence of moral and natural evil provide an occasion for instantiating acts of moral courage, charity, perseverance, hope, compassion, mercy, generosity, and the like. They also provide occasion to advance the goals of distributive, retributive, and reparational or compensatory justice. The aim of non-divine atonement is to provide a response G to evil states of affairs E in such a way that G is not possible without E and the overall value of G & E is positive. But the aim of redemptive suffering in Plantinga's sense seems to be to contribute to the actualization of a possible world containing a sufficient amount of sin, evil, and suffering to warrant divine redemption.

## 8.2  Kantian Problems and Wrecked Lives

In every world whose overall value is L or greater there is incarnation and atonement. In every incarnation and atonement world God deliberately

---

[15] Ibid. p. 14.

instantiates creaturely essences in circumstances where he knows they will act in seriously immoral ways. God instantiates creaturely essences in circumstances where he knows they will go wrong in order to satisfy a necessary condition for actualizing a world whose overall value is L or greater.

Intentionally instantiating creaturely essences in circumstances where they will go wrong in order to achieve the goal of actualizing a highly eligible world is at least a prima facie violation of individual autonomy. The second formulation of the categorical imperative requires that we act in such a way that we always treat humanity, whether in our own person or in the person of another, *never simply as a means*, but always at the same time as an end.[16] Since God deliberately chooses to instantiate creaturely essences in circumstances where he knows that they will act in ways ruinous to themselves and others in order to actualize an L-world, it is prima facie true that God is using creaturely essences as a mere means to divine goals. And that's a violation of individual autonomy.

Plantinga is aware of the problem that, prima facie, God is acting in ways that violate individual autonomy.

First, of course, God might, in perfect consonance with his love, permit me to suffer in order to benefit someone else or to achieve a highly eligible good world if I freely consent to [the suffering] and (like Christ) voluntarily accept the suffering.[17]

But of course, as Plantinga knows, those who endure the suffering necessary to the actualization of an L-world do *not* freely consent to the suffering.

But suppose that I don't voluntarily accept it: perhaps I am unable, for one reason or another, to make the decision whether or not to accept the suffering in question. . . . Well, of course we sometimes quite properly make important decisions for someone (in a coma, say) who can't make the decision for herself; we try to determine what the person in question would decide if she could make the decision herself.[18]

But, according to Plantinga, hypothetical consent is all we need. If she would have consented to the suffering if she could decide for herself, then God does not violate her autonomy in the imposition of suffering without her actual consent. But there are at least two serious problems with the

---

[16] See H. J. Paton (ed.) *Groundwork of the Metaphysics of Morals* (New York: Harper and Row Publishers, 1964) 69 ff. See also Roger Sullivan, *Immanuel Kant's Moral Theory* (Cambridge: Cambridge University Press, 1989) 149 ff.

[17] See Plantinga, "Superlapsarianism or 'O Felix Culpa'," op. cit. p. 24.

[18] Ibid. p. 24.

proposal that hypothetical consent is sufficient to obviate concerns about the violation of individual autonomy.

The primary concern is that, in cases where I would suffer immensely for the greater good of others or for the realization of an extremely valuable L-world, it is perfectly reasonable that I do not consent to the suffering. No one who appreciates the suffering incurred in severe child abuse, for example, would be considered unreasonable in not consenting to such abuse for the greater good of others or for the realization of an extremely valuable world. No one who appreciated the suffering incurred in the degradation, humiliation, and death in the Nazi death camps would be considered unreasonable in not consenting to such suffering for the greater good of others or for the realization of an extremely valuable world.[19]

Plantinga urges that decisions not to consent might be the result of ignorance or disordered affections.

> . . . but suppose God knows that this unwillingness on my part would be due only to ignorance: if I knew the relevant facts, then I would accept the suffering. In that case too, God's perfect love . . . would not preclude his permitting me to suffer. Finally suppose further yet that God knows that I would not accept the suffering in question, but only because of disordered affections; if I had the right affections (and also knew enough), then I would accept the suffering: in this case too . . . his being perfectly loving would not preclude his allowing me to suffer.

It is true that the decision not to consent might be the result of ignorance or disordered affections. But it is just not plausible to suppose that most decisions not to consent to suffering would be of that sort. Every person who endures any suffering knows that his particular suffering is not necessary to the actualization of an L-world. And even if a particular person's suffering were necessary to the actualization of an L-world, he might be perfectly reasonable—informed and psychologically ordered—in not consenting to it.

### 8.2.1 Should We Prevent Suffering?

There is a vast amount of suffering in the world and it seems obvious that we ought to prevent as much of it as we can, or at least as much as we *reasonably* can. We seem to have good reason to conclude that God should have permitted much less suffering and sin than he did. Plantinga disagrees.

---

[19] I certainly would not consider such individuals unreasonable. Some of the most heroic events of the era included efforts to prevent as much of that suffering as possible.

. . . for all we know, there is no minimum degree of suffering among these highly eligible worlds. Perhaps for every degree of sin and suffering contained in some highly eligible world, there is another highly eligible world with less.

This is compatible with the degree of sin and suffering in such worlds being bounded both above and below: perhaps there is a degree of suffering and evil $\mu$ such that every highly eligible world contains at least that much suffering and evil and a degree $\lambda$ such that no highly eligible world contains more than that amount of suffering and evil. Then it could also be that for any given evil, God could have actualized a highly eligible world without permitting that evil; it doesn't follow that he would be unjustified in permitting it.[20]

The supposition is not credible. Suppose the set of eligible worlds is bounded below by a world W that contains the degree of suffering and evil $\mu$. Every eligible world contains at least suffering and evil $\mu$ and W is an eligible world. Indeed it is the lowest bound on eligible worlds.[21] Plantinga's suggestion entails that it is impossible that any individual (say, Adam) in W commits a single sin or causes a single instance of suffering. Suppose Adam tells a single lie, for instance. Adam thereby actualizes a world W' that contains $\mu + \tau$ degree of suffering and sin such that there is some other world W' that contains the degree of sin $\xi$ such that $((\mu + \tau) > \xi > \mu)$. Adam cannot commit a single sin since, for any world W' that Adam actualizes in telling a lie, there must be infinitely many worlds between W' and W containing less and less sin and suffering than is contained in W'. Indeed, it must be true in W' that no matter how many instances of suffering and sin God prevents—even if he prevents infinitely many of them—he actualizes a world that is worse than W. That consequence is absurd.

But maybe the reply is that a single sin—say, the sin of the actual Adam—is infinitely evil. The suggestion is that there is a world W' that contains only finitely many more sins than W, but that contains infinitely more evil than W. But this reply is unsuccessful. Contrary to the conclusion Plantinga is after, this supposition entails that God might have

---

[20] See Plantinga, "Superlapsarianism or 'O Felix Culpa'," op. cit. p. 20. For a variety of reasons the argument here is not credible. See M. J. Almeida, "On Evil's Vague Necessity" in Jon Kvanvig (ed.) *Oxford Studies in Philosophy of Religion, Vol. II* (Oxford: Oxford University Press, 2009).

[21] I'm not entirely sure the quoted paragraph is coherent. The initial paragraph entails that the lower bound is not in the set of eligible worlds. The second paragraph entails that the lower bound is in the set of eligible worlds. But there are serious problems with the model either way.

prevented Adam's evil and actualized the eligible world on the lower bound of evil.

Suppose, then, contrary to the second paragraph quoted, that there is no degree of suffering and evil $\mu$ such that every highly eligible world contains at least that much suffering and evil. Suppose that every eligible world contains some degree of suffering and evil greater than $\mu$. The possible world containing the degree of suffering $\mu$ is on the lower bound, but worlds on the lower bound are not in the set of highly eligible worlds. The possible world containing the degree of suffering $\mu$ is such that, at precisely the level of suffering in $\mu$ it is metaphysically impossible that there should be incarnation and atonement. Nonetheless, it is true in this world that any additional (even infinitesimal) decrement in sin and suffering makes incarnation and atonement possible.[22] That consequence is also absurd. The transition between the degree of suffering and sin necessary for incarnation and atonement and the degree of suffering and sin unnecessary for incarnation and atonement is surely not discrete.

### 8.2.2 Informed Hypothetical Consent

According to Plantinga, if God has the hypothetical consent of instantiated essences that are informed and ordered in their affections, then he is permitted to use them to actualize an L-world. God does not use instantiated essences as a mere means under these circumstances, but treats them also as an end in themselves.

But there is a serious problem with the acquisition of hypothetical consent from significantly free instantiated essences. We know that significantly free instantiated essences are such that, for any world W and time t in W at which a fully informed and emotionally well-ordered significantly free essence consents to endure suffering for the sake of others (or for the sake of actualizing an L-world), there is a world W′ and time t such that W and W′ share the same past until t and the same fully informed and emotionally well-ordered, significantly free essence fails to consent to endure the suffering at t in W′.

God knows that, were he to instantiate the essence in W, he would receive an informed and well-ordered consent and God knows that, were he to instantiate the essence in W′, he would not receive an informed and

---

[22] Keep in mind that we are now assuming that evils are infinitely divisible.

well-ordered consent. It is not obvious which hypothetical reply matters to whether an instantiated essence has hypothetically consented. There is an informed and emotionally well-ordered consent world and there is also an informed and emotionally well-ordered non-consent world. The instantiated essence has hypothetically consented under ideal conditions and also failed to do so under ideal conditions.

But suppose each instantiated essence is such that he would consent to suffering for the actualization of an L-world no matter which hypothetical situation God considers. There is another serious concern for Plantinga's suggestion that God might acquire hypothetical consent from suffering instantiated essences. Instantiated essences that consent in every hypothetical situation in which they are given the opportunity are suffering from *transworld acquiescence*. Possibly, for every world in which God instantiates E, and E's instantiation $E_n$ is given the opportunity to consent, $E_n$ does consent to suffering for the sake of others or for the sake of actualizing an L-world. But it is difficult to see how the acquisition of hypothetical consent from an essence that is suffering from transworld acquiescence might constitute a good reason why God could allow $E_n$ to suffer as a means to actualizing an L-world.

Recall finally that the second formulation of the categorical imperative requires that we act in such a way that we always treat humanity, whether in *our own person* or in the person of another, never simply as a means, but always at the same time as an end. Our consent to be used in ways that does not respect ourselves as persons does not license God to use us in such ways. Marilyn Adams notes,

... persons who consent to be used in ways that are very likely to be degrading and depersonalizing, thereby furnish prima facie evidence that they do not really know what they are doing ... [23]

There are careers we cannot, consistent with the categorical imperative, consent to be chosen into. The lives of Hitler, Pol Pot. or Stalin, for instance, illustrate careers of wrecked or ruined agency.

... agency that is hardened or perverted (Hitler, Stalin, Pol Pot are only lurid examples), agency that is biochemically twisted (serial killers, child sex murderers, schizophrenics), agency that is biologically or psychologically too fragmented

---

[23] See Marilyn McCord Adams, "Plantinga on Felix Culpa: Analysis and Critique" *Faith and Philosophy* (2008) 123–40.

(whether by autism, or the traumas of child abuse and war) to be capable of wholehearted commitment to anything. Plantinga's Felix Culpa God chose for Pharaoh the career in which repeated heart-hardenings rain ruin on the land of Egypt; for Judas a career in which he betrays Christ . . .[24]

We cannot consent to be chosen into the career of Hitler or Stalin or Pol Pot, or the career of a child abuser or serial killer. Or, rather, consenting to such a career does not license anyone in choosing us into such a career. Consenting to careers such as these is not consistent with the categorical imperative. It is consenting to be used in ways that fail to respect our dignity as persons. The fact that someone might consent to be chosen into such a career does not license God in instantiating them in degrading and depersonalizing circumstances.

## 8.3  Double-Effect and Theodicy

On Plantinga's Felix Culpa theodicy God's primary intention is to actualize a highly eligible world. A highly eligible world is one in which there exist the towering goods of incarnation and atonement. According to this view, God intentionally instantiates individual essences and intentionally places them in circumstances where they will suffer severely, as a means to actualizing a highly eligible world. The theodical conclusion is that the total amount of suffering, evil, and sin in the world is justified by the great good of the incarnation and atonement.

But, as Plantinga admits, there is something peculiar about the idea of God intentionally instantiating just those essences that will go very wrong, and just those essences that will have to endure suffering, *in order that* God might save them. It is peculiar even under the false assumption that the instantiated essences consent to suffering terribly for the sake of the incarnation and atonement.

Isn't this a scenario for a cosmic Munchhausen syndrome by proxy? Isn't it too much like a father throws his child into the river so that he can then heroically rescue them, or a doctor who spreads a horrifying disease so that he can then display enormous virtue in fighting it in enormous disregard of his own safety and fatigue? Could we really think God would behave in this way? How could it be in character for God to riffle through the whole range of possible creatures he could create and the circumstances in which he could create them, to find some who would

---

[24] Ibid. p. 134.

freely sin, and then create them so that he could display his great love by saving them? How could he be so manipulative?[25]

But the main problem displayed here is not the manipulation of God's creatures. The main problem is that, on Plantinga's view, God is intentionally (and unnecessarily) actualizing a bad world for the purpose of redeeming it. God primarily intends to save at least some of the fallen. And since God needs some fallen individuals to save, he intends the intrinsically bad outcome that humanity fall into sin. But certainly God is not permitted to intend that something intrinsically bad occur as a means of producing something good, even something extremely good.

Suppose God instantiates Smith in circumstances where he intends for Smith to throw Jones into the path of a runaway trolley. It is wrong for God to do so even to keep the trolley from hitting five people on the track ahead. It is wrong for God to do so even as a means to actualizing the towering goods of incarnation and atonement. God would be intending to harm someone, or intending to have someone harmed, as a means to realizing an L-world.

Again, it is wrong for God to instantiate someone in circumstances where he intends for that person to murder millions. It is wrong, for instance, to instantiate Stalin, Hitler, or Pol Pot, in order to actualize a state of affairs in which millions of innocent victims are murdered and tortured. It is wrong that God knows that such a state of affairs would obtain and intends that such a state of affairs obtains even as a means to the towering goods of incarnation and atonement.

The main problem with Plantinga's Felix Culpa theodicy is not God's manipulation of his creatures. The main problem, as illustrated above, is God's obvious violation of the principle of double-effect. In the Felix Culpa theodicy God directly intends to actualize evil states of affairs and directly intends to actualize states of affairs in which many suffer terribly. These are intended as a means to actualizing a world with the towering goods of incarnation and atonement. But God cannot intend the actualization of an intrinsically evil state of affairs as a means to greater, even a much greater, good.

---

[25] See Plantinga, "Superlapsarianism or 'O Felix Culpa'," op. cit. p. 22.

## 8.4  Redeemed Worlds and Double-Effect

It is among the central aims of this book to establish that it is not possible
that, necessarily, God actualizes a morally perfect world or possible that,
necessarily, God actualizes the best world or even possible that, necessarily
he actualizes a good enough world. Among the conclusions of the impossibility arguments is that, necessarily, there are worlds in which it is true
that God can actualize a morally perfect world and God does not actualize
a morally perfect world. Indeed, necessarily, there are bad worlds in which
it is true that God can actualize a morally perfect world and he does not.

But in bad worlds God does not *intend* that anyone bring about evil states
of affairs or that anyone suffer terribly *as a means* to actualizing a world with
the towering goods of incarnation and atonement or *in order to* actualize
those towering goods. So God does not violate the principle of double
effect in actualizing a bad world. There must be bad worlds in which evil
states of affairs obtain and many people suffer, if God is permitted to
actualize the very best worlds. In bad worlds, God of course foresees that
many will bring about evil states of affairs and that many suffer terribly. And
in (at least) some bad worlds God responds to existing evil and suffering
redemptively. God's redemptive response to evil and suffering is *not* part of
a theodical account of evil and suffering. It is not the purpose for which
God allows evil and suffering. As we have noted there exist bad worlds as a
matter of necessity, since it is impossible that, necessarily, God actualizes a
morally perfect world. But there are not *unredeemed worlds* as a matter of
necessity. And as we have noted the redemption of bad worlds is the very
hard work of divine and non-divine atonement.

# 9

# Conclusions

## 9.0  On Dogmas in Philosophical Theology

It is part of the received wisdom in philosophical theology that, necessarily, God can actualize the best possible world only if God does actualize the best possible world. There is rarely an argument offered for this thesis. It is sometimes suggested that it follows in some obvious way from the Anselmian assumption that God is essentially perfectly good. Leibniz famously suggests that it is a moral necessity that God creates the best.

God is bound by a moral necessity to make things in such a manner that there can be nothing better: otherwise . . . he would not himself be satisfied with his work, he would blame himself for its imperfection; that conflicts with the supreme felicity of the divine nature.[1]

It is morally necessary that God creates the best possible world, if God can create the best possible world. It is metaphysically necessary that God would be lacking in goodness, wisdom, or power if he actualized a world that is less than the best. William Rowe also endorses a Leibnizian view.

An unsurpassably good, omniscient, omnipotent creator will create an unsurpassably good world. Indeed, unsurpassable goodness in an omnipotent, omniscient, world-creator is consistent only with the creation of an unsurpassably good world. For there is an impossibility in the idea both that there exists an infinite series of increasingly better creatable worlds and that there also exists a unsurpassably good, omnipotent, omniscient being who creates one of these worlds.[2]

But we have found that it is not a necessary truth that an unsurpassable being creates an unsurpassably good world. There cannot exist a best possible world unless there exist less than best possible worlds. Since

[1] Gottfried Leibniz, *Theodicy* (1710; LaSalle, Ill.: Open Court, 1985) 253.
[2] William Rowe, "Can God Be Free?" *Faith and Philosophy* 19 (2002) 405–24.

God exists in every possible world, God can actualize less than best possible worlds. Indeed, there cannot exist a best possible world unless there exist worlds that are very bad. The impossibility argument in Section 5.4 establishes an even stronger claim. Concede that, necessarily, God can actualize the best possible world. We have found that it is impossible that, necessarily, God does actualize the best possible world. It is necessarily true that there are worlds in which God can actualize the best possible world and God does not actualize the best possible world.

There is no credible argument that necessarily God can actualize the best possible world only if God does actualize the best possible world. And that's because the thesis is necessarily false. We also found that it is no more than philosophical dogma that, necessarily, God can actualize a morally perfect world only if God does actualize a morally perfect world. The impossibility argument in Section 5.2 shows that the thesis is necessarily false. The essential omnipotence, omniscience, and perfect goodness of God do not entail that, necessarily, God actualizes a morally perfect world. Indeed, it is a necessary truth that there exist worlds in which God can actualize a morally perfect world and God does not do so.

It is reasonable to suppose that God must actualize some member of a set of worlds which have a positive overall value at least as high as some minimum value N. We called the set of all worlds whose value is at least N the set S of good enough worlds. We made no other assumptions about the members of S. S might be the set of best worlds. S might include infinitely many worlds whose value is N or greater. It could be that S includes a set of infinitely improving worlds. There is no argument that, necessarily, God can actualize a good enough world only if God does actualize a morally perfect world. Indeed the impossibility argument in Section 5.5 shows that it is false that, necessarily, God actualizes a good enough world. The essential omnipotence, omniscience, and perfect goodness of God do not entail that, necessarily, God actualizes a good enough world.

The impossibility arguments together show that it is no more than philosophical dogma that, necessarily, an essentially omnipotent, omniscient, and perfectly good being can actualize the best possible world only if he does actualize the best possible world. Similarly it is no more than philosophical dogma that, necessarily, an essentially omnipotent, omniscient, and perfectly good being can actualize a morally perfect world or a good enough world only if he does actualize a morally perfect world or a good enough world. These conclusions are intrinsically interesting and important, since it is so commonly assumed that these dogmas are true. But, in addition, the proof that these theses are no more than philosophical dogmas provides a solution to many other difficult problems in philosophical theology.

## 9.1 Divine Predictions and the Logical Problem of Evil

In Chapter 4, Section 4.1, I showed that, necessarily, God can strongly actualize a maximal state of affairs T that includes God's having predicted or prophesied that an instantiated essence $E_n$ will perform an action A. God might utter such a prediction, for instance, prior to instantiating any individual essences or creating anything at all. But if God can predict that $E_n$ will perform A, then God can bring it about that $E_n$ performs A without causing $E_n$ to perform A. The predictions of (even) perfect predictors do not themselves cause the objects of their predictions to obtain or occur. But God can predict that any instantiated essence in any world will perform only morally right actions. We called such world actualization unrestricted actualization. Unrestricted actualization ensures that God can strongly actualize a maximal state of affairs T such that, necessarily, T obtains only if every essence instantiated in T always freely goes right. So God can unrestrictedly actualize a morally perfect world.

We argued that if God can unrestrictedly actualize a morally perfect world, then the thesis of universal transworld depravity is false. And John Mackie's logical problem of evil re-emerges in a much more serious form. Recall that Mackie reasoned as follows.

. . . God was not, then, faced with a choice between making innocent automata and making beings who, in acting freely, would sometimes go wrong; there was open to him the obviously better possibility of making beings who would act freely but always go right. Clearly his failure to avail himself of this possibility is inconsistent with his being omnipotent and wholly good.[3]

The fact that God can unrestrictedly actualize a morally perfect world suggests that Mackie was entirely right. God's omnipotence ensures that he can predict that every instantiated essence always goes right and God's

---

[3] See John Mackie, "Evil and Omnipotence" in Michael Rea and Louis Pojman (eds.) *Philosophy of Religion: An Anthology*, Fifth Edition (Belmont: Wadsworth, 2008).

omniscience ensures that his predictions are necessarily accurate. Necessarily, God can actualize a morally perfect world and Mackie urges—like so many others we have noted—if God can actualize a morally perfect world then God does actualize a morally perfect world.

The logical problem of evil redux is a proof that (1) and (2) are broadly, logically inconsistent. And the inconsistency cannot be resolved by rejecting the thesis that, necessarily, God can actualize a morally perfect world.

1. God is omnipotent, omniscient, and wholly good.
2. Evil exists.

Since, necessarily, it is within God's power to predict that every significantly free essence that he instantiates will always go right, it follows that (3) is true.

3. Necessarily, God can actualize a morally perfect world.

Mackie's observation is that God's omnipotence and perfect goodness are inconsistent with his failing to avail himself of the possibility of actualizing a morally perfect world.

4. Necessarily, God can actualize a morally perfect world only if God does actualize a morally perfect world.

Since (5) follows from (3) and (4), we have a contradiction. (5) and (2) cannot both be true: there are no evil states of affairs in morally perfect worlds.[4]

5. Necessarily God actualizes a morally perfect world.

The argument provides proof of Mackie's atheological conclusion. It is not possible that God is omnipotent, omniscience, and wholly good, and that evil exists. Obviously the problem cannot be resolved by appeal to the possibility of God's limited power to actualize a morally perfect world. It is necessarily true that God can actualize a morally perfect world. Just as obviously the problem cannot be resolved by appeal to God's limited

---

[4] I do not take a position on the question of whether natural evil is a species of moral evil. There is no question that God can actualize a naturally perfect world, so it's assumed throughout the argument that he does.

goodness in actualizing possible worlds. It is necessarily true that God is essentially perfectly good. Any solution to the logical problem of evil must be consistent with God's power to actualize a morally perfect world and God's perfect goodness in actualizing a possible world.

## 9.2 Resolving the Logical Problem of Evil Redux

In Chapter 5, Section 5.1, I showed that the logical problem of evil redux entails that one of the theses in (3.3)–(3.5) is true.[5]

3.3. Necessarily, an omnipotent, omniscient, wholly good being brings about *the best possible world* and the best possible world includes no evil states of affairs at all.

3.4. Necessarily, an omnipotent, omniscient, wholly good being brings about *the best actualizable world* and the best actualizable world includes no evil states of affairs.

3.5. Necessarily, an omnipotent, omniscient, wholly good being brings about *a good enough world* and a good enough actualizable world includes no evil states of affairs.

Theses (3.3)–(3.5) exhaust the sorts of possible worlds that might be morally perfect. The theses in (3.3)–(3.5) are of course independently intuitive and they have enjoyed broad endorsement. But we know that the first conjunct in each of (3.3)–(3.5) is false. The impossibility arguments in Sections 5.2–5.5 show that, possibly, God does not bring about a good enough world, and possibly, God does not bring about the best actualizable world and, finally, possibly, God does not bring about the best possible world. The logical problem of evil redux is therefore unsound. And this solution to the logical problem of evil redux is consistent with God's power to actualize a morally perfect world and God's perfect goodness in actualizing a possible world.

---

[5] Specifically premises (3) and (4), together with the assumption that God actualizes a naturally perfect world, in the logical problem of evil redux entails that one of the theses in (3.3)–(3.5) is true.

## 9.3  Resolving Other Problems in Philosophical Theology

The *Worst World Argument* aims to show that Anselmian assumptions about the nature of God entail the absurd conclusion that our world is a worst possible world. The central premise in the worst world argument states that, for each possible world W, we must (a) deny God's perfection at W or (b) hold that W is best or tied for best or (c) appeal to the free will defense to explain how W's not being the best is compatible with God's perfection. The argument urges that (a) and (c) are false, and so (b) is true.

But the impossibility arguments show that an essentially omnipotent, omniscient, and morally perfect being might actualize a world that is less than the best possible world. Indeed, an essentially omnipotent, omniscient, and morally perfect being might actualize a world that is less than the best possible world even under the assumption that, necessarily, an essentially omnipotent, omniscient, and morally perfect being *can* actualize the best possible world. So (a), (b), and (c) are all false.

According to Marilyn Adams there are horrendous evils and such evils cannot be justified by global goods. The fact that the world would be on balance better were I to participate in a horrendous evil does not justify God in permitting me to suffer that evil.

> . . . such an exercise fails to give satisfaction. Suppose for the sake of argument that horrendous evil could be included in maximally perfect world orders; its being partially constitutive of such an order would assign it that generic and global positive meaning. But would knowledge of such a fact, defeat for a mother the prima facie reason provided by her cannibalism of her own infant, to wish that she had never been born? Again, the aim of perfect retributive balance confers meaning on evils imposed. But would knowledge that the torturer was being tortured give the victim who broke down and turned traitor under pressure, any more reason to think his/her life worthwhile?[6]

Adams rejects the standard analysis of non-gratuitous evil. The fact that W is a best possible world and W includes a horrendously evil state of affairs E does not entail that E is justified. Not only do maximally good states of affairs fail to justify horrendous evils, it is difficult to imagine what sorts of reasons God might have to allow them.

---

[6]  Marilyn McCord Adams, "Horrendous Evils and Goodness of God" in M. Adams and R. Adams (eds.) *The Problem of Evil* (Oxford: Oxford University Press, 1990) 214.

Adams affirms that though we cannot so much as conceive of a candidate for the reason God might have for permitting horrendous evils there exist reasons why God allows such evil. We argued that Adams is mistaken on this score. In fact, things are just as they seem to be with regard to horrendous evils. There might be no reasons for horrendously evil states of affairs that serve to justify God in permitting those states of affairs. It is a bit of philosophical dogma that there is no world in which God exists and unjustified horrendous evil exists.

Of course there are superb possible worlds in which every significantly free instantiated essence satisfies the requirements of justice and beneficence. It is part of the moral value of superb worlds that significantly free beings observe the deep moral requirements prohibiting horrendous evils. But the impossibility arguments show that it simply could not be true that, necessarily, God actualizes such superb worlds. Indeed it is necessarily true that there are superb worlds only if there are possible worlds in which significantly free instantiated essences all violate the most serious and profound moral requirements. Those worlds in which significantly free essences all violate the most profound moral requirements are worlds in which there are horrendous evils. In those worlds God can prevent horrendous evils from occurring and it would be morally better if God did prevent horrendous evils. Nonetheless these are worlds in which God does not prevent the horrendous evils.

We found that the *Problem of Divine Freedom* poses two questions. First, was God free to refrain from creating any possible world? And, second, was God free to create other possible worlds instead of the possible world he did in fact create? Consider the second question.

According to William Rowe, among many others, the most perfect being must actualize the best possible world. And that is true, according to this view, whether or not it is a moral obligation to actualize the best possible world. Here again is Rowe.

And it appears to be inconceivable that a supremely perfect being would act to bring about less good than he can. On the assumption that God . . . exists and that there is a best, creatable world, we've reached the conclusion that God is neither free not to create a world nor free to create a world less than the best creatable world . . . [7]

But if God necessarily actualizes the best possible world, then God is not free. The world is necessitarian and God is not even compatibilist free. The

---

[7] Ibid. p. 410.

conclusion is extremely worrisome, but easily avoided. The impossibility arguments show that it is false that, necessarily, God actualizes the best possible world. There is some possible world at which it is true that God can actualize the best possible world and God does not actualize the best possible world. So, Rowe's argument against divine freedom is unsound.

The *Problem of No Best World* assumes that a perfectly good being fulfills every moral requirement and never does an action that is less good than another he could do instead. And so according to Rowe it is necessarily true that a perfectly good creator does not actualize a world that is less good than another world he could actualize. Rowe's *Principle B* expresses this moral restriction on perfectly good creators.

B. Necessarily if an omniscient and omnipotent being actualizes a world when there is a better world that it could have actualized, then that omniscient and omnipotent being is *not* essentially perfectly good.[8]

But of course we know that principle B is false. An unsurpassable being might fail to actualize a morally perfect world and fail to actualize a best world and even fail to actualize a good enough world. So an omniscient and omnipotent being that actualizes a world when there is a better world it could have actualized might well be perfectly good.

According to the *Evidential Argument from Evil* God would prevent the occurrence of any intense suffering it could, unless it could not do so without thereby losing some greater good or permitting some evil equally bad or worse. But we know that that's false. The impossibility arguments show that, necessarily, there are worlds in which God can actualize a morally perfect world and God does not actualize a morally perfect world. In those worlds there are evil states of affairs that God could prevent without thereby losing some greater good or permitting some evil equally bad or worse. It is also true that, necessarily, there are worlds in which God can actualize a naturally perfect world and does not. Necessarily, there are worlds in which naturally evil states of affairs obtain such that God could prevent them without thereby losing some greater good or permitting some evil equally bad or worse. So the evidential argument from evil is unsound.

---

[8] Rowe often presents B without explicitly stating that it is a necessary truth about all possible omniscient and omnipotent beings. But he does hold that it is necessary. See his "Can God Be Free?," op. cit. p. 416.

According to the *Darwinian Argument from Evil* it is necessarily true that God actualizes an evolutionarily perfect world. But it is true in these evolutionarily perfect worlds that most phenomenally conscious non-human animals have the essential property of possibly manifesting the disposition to suffer some pain. Indeed, the value of these evolutionarily perfect worlds depends on the modal fact that, possibly, every significantly free human and non-human animal goes radically wrong with respect to most or all of its morally significant actions. Worlds in which every significantly free human and non-human animal goes radically wrong with respect to most of its morally significant actions are, in many cases, worlds in which there is tremendous pain and suffering. The value of evolutionarily perfect worlds consists in significantly free human and non-human animals satisfying the prohibitions of justice and beneficence. There would be no such constraints were there no possible worlds in which the requirements of justice and beneficence were seriously violated.

Clearly there are evolutionarily perfect worlds in which no sentient being suffers pain and every significantly free human and non-human animal goes right with respect to every morally significant action. The existence of evolutionarily perfect worlds of this sort entails the existence of worlds in which every significantly free human and non-human animal goes radically wrong with respect to most or all of its morally significant actions. But then it is false that, necessarily, God actualizes an evolutionarily perfect world. Indeed, it is impossible that, necessarily, God actualizes an evolutionarily perfect world. The Darwinian argument from evil is unsound.

## 9.4  Redeeming Worlds

There are worlds in which God can actualize a morally perfect world and God does not do so. These are worlds in which God allows or permits gratuitous evil.[9] Gratuitously evil states of affairs are unredeemed states of affairs, but not in general unredeemable states of affairs. Evil states of affairs are gratuitous and redeemable relative to worlds. We specified conditions under which a state of affairs is redeemable in RE.

According to the conditions in RE evil states of affairs that are redeemed might nonetheless be gratuitous evils. A world $W'$ in which G atones for

---

[9]  Compare Chapter 6, Section 6.2, for problems with the standard analysis of gratuitous evil.

E might be such that, for some actualizable world W′, W′ does not include E and W′ > W′. We called worlds where every evil is redeemed, redeemed worlds. Redeemed worlds might not in general be as good, overall, as worlds including no gratuitous evil at all. Still, in redeemed worlds, there are no instances of unredeemed evil. On the other hand, some redeemed worlds might be better than worlds containing no gratuitous evil. It might be better that the gratuitous evil in W is redeemed than that the gratuitous evil in W is eliminated or prevented altogether.[10]

We noted in Chapter 8 that the most familiar notion of atonement is derived from Christian thought. But we noted that there is also the possibility of non-divine atonement. The aim of non-divine atonement is to provide a response G to evil states of affairs E in such a way that G is not possible without E and the overall value of G & E is positive. Plantinga offers a typical example of Smith bearing up magnificently to his particular affliction.[11]

It is impossible to take that particular moral attitude to that particular affliction unless Smith actually endures the affliction. Smith freely chooses to strongly actualize an, on balance, positive state of affairs that includes essentially the state of affairs of his suffering adversity. And it is possible for all of us to exercise our freedom in atonement for great evils in ways that instantiate exceptional moral value. In general, for any evil E that occurs, there is a possible response G to E such that G is a free moral response to E, G is impossible in the absence of E, and the overall moral value of G & E is positive. We called the denial of this position *moral defeatism*. Moral defeatism is the position that there exist some evil states of affairs E such that, no matter how anyone or anything, divine or non-divine responds, E cannot be redeemed.

It is a central aim of this book to establish that it is not possible that, necessarily, God actualizes a morally perfect world or the best world or even a good enough world. Indeed, necessarily, there are bad worlds in which it is true that God can actualize a morally perfect world and he does not. But, in bad worlds, God does not *intend* that anyone bring about evil states of affairs or that anyone suffer terribly *as a means* to actualizing a

---

[10] The "might" in this sentence and the preceding sentence is an epistemic might of the sort "might, for all we know."

[11] It should be noted that Plantinga does not describe such acts as instances of atoning for evils.

world with the towering goods of incarnation and atonement. So God does not violate the principle of double-effect in actualizing a bad world. It is a matter of necessity that there are mediocre worlds and bad worlds in which evil states of affairs obtain, if God is permitted to actualize the very best worlds. In bad worlds, God of course foresees that many will bring about evil states of affairs and that many will suffer terribly. And in (at least) some bad worlds God responds to existing evil and suffering redemptively. On the account of evil we have offered, God's redemptive response to evil and suffering is *not* part of a theodical account of evil and suffering. It is not the purpose for which God allows evil and suffering. It is rather the case, as we have emphasized, that God can actualize very good worlds and, as a matter of necessity, there exist good worlds only if there exist bad worlds. But there are not unredeemed worlds as a matter of necessity. But, as we have noted, the redemption of bad worlds is the very hard work of divine and non-divine atonement.

# Bibliography

Adams, M. M. (1990). Horrendous evils and goodness of God. In M. M. Adams and R. Adams (Eds.), *The Problem of Evil* (pp. 209–21). Oxford: Oxford University Press.

——(1999). *Horrendous Evils and Goodness of God*. Ithaca, NY: Cornell University Press.

——(2008). Plantinga on felix culpa: Analysis and critique. *Faith and Philosophy, 25,* 123–40.

Almeida, M. J. (2003). A paradox for significant freedom. *International Journal for Philosophy of Religion, 54,* 175–84.

——(2008). *The metaphysics of perfect beings*. London: Routledge.

——(2009). On evil's vague necessity. In J. Kvanvig (Ed.), *Oxford studies in philosophy of religion: Vol. II* (pp. 1–16). Oxford: Oxford University Press.

——(2010). O'Connor's permissive multiverse. *Philosophia Christi, 12,* 297–308.

——(manuscript). Transworld enablers.

——and Oppy, G. (2003). Sceptical theism and evidential arguments from evil. *Australasian Journal of Philosophy, 81,* 496–516.

Alston, W. P. (1989). *Epistemic Justification: Essays in the Theory of Knowledge*. Ithaca, NY: Cornell University Press.

Armstrong, D. (2004). *Truth and Truthmakers*. Cambridge: Cambridge University Press.

Bekoff, M. and Pierce, J. (2009). *Wild Justice: The Moral Lives of Animals*. Chicago, Ill.: University of Chicago Press.

Bergmann, M. (1996). Review of R. Douglas Geivett's *Evil and the Evidence for God: The Challenge of John Kick's Theodicy. Faith and Philosophy, 13,* 436–41.

——(1999). Might-counterfactuals, transworld untrustworthiness and Plantinga's free will defense. *Faith and Philosophy, 16,* 336–551.

——(2001). Skeptical theism and Rowe's new evidential argument from evil. *Noûs, 35,* 278–96.

Brogaard, B. and Salerno, J. (2007). Why counterpossibles are non-trivial. *The Reasoner, 1* (2), 5–6.

Cameron, R. (2009). What's metaphysical about metaphysical necessity? *Philosophy and Phenomenological Research, 79,* 1–16.

Chalmers, D. (1999). Materialism and the metaphysics of modality. *Philosophy and Phenomenological Research*. Oxford: Oxford University Press.

Chisholm, R. (1990). The defeat of good and evil. In M. M. Adams and R. M. Adams (Eds.), *The Problem of Evil* (pp. 53–68). Oxford: Oxford University Press.

Clarke, R. (2003). *Libertarian Accounts of Free Will.* New York: Oxford University Press.

Cohen, G. A. (2008). *Rescuing Justice and Equality.* Cambridge, Mass.: Harvard University Press.

Crisp, T. M. (2003). Presentism. In M. J. Loux and D. Zimmerman (Eds.), *The Oxford Handbook of Metaphysics* (pp. 211–45). Oxford: Oxford University Press.

Darwin, C. (1994). The origin of the moral sense. In P. Singer (Ed.), *Ethics* (pp. 43–7). Oxford: Oxford University Press.

Dawkins, R. (1996). *River out of Eden.* New York, NY: Harper Collins.

Deane, S. N. (1962). *St Anselm: Basic Writings.* Peru, Ill.: Open Court Publishing Company.

De Waal, F. (1994). Chimpanzee justice. In P. Singer (Ed.), *Ethics* (67–9). Oxford: Oxford University Press.

Edgington, D. (2004). Counterfactuals and the benefits of hindsight. In P. Dowe and P. Noordhof (Eds.), *Cause and Chance: Causation in an Indeterministic World* (pp. 12–27). London: Routledge.

Fine, K. (1995). Senses of essence. In W. Sinnott-Armstrong, D. Raffman, and N. Asher (Eds.), *Modality, Morality, and Belief: Essays in Honor of Ruth Barcan Marcus* (pp. 53–73). Cambridge: Cambridge University Press.

——(2005). Reference, essence, and identity. In *Modality and Tense: Philosophical Papers* (pp. 19–39). Oxford: Oxford University Press.

Flint, T. (1998). *Divine Providence: The Molinist Account.* Ithaca, NY: Cornell University Press.

Gauthier, D. (1987). *Morals by Agreement.* Oxford: Oxford University Press.

Geivett, D. (1993). *Evil and the Evidence for God: The Challenge of John Hick's Theodicy.* Philadelphia, PA: Temple University Press.

Goodall, J. (1986). *The Chimpanzees of Gombe.* Cambridge, Mass.: Harvard University Press.

Grim, P. (1988). Logic and the limits of knowledge and truth. *Noûs, 22,* 341–67.

——(2000). The being that knew too much. *International Journal for Philosophy of Religion, 47,* 141–54.

Guleserian, T. (1983). God and possible worlds: The modal problem of evil. *Noûs, 17,* 221–38.

Hajek, A. (2007). The reference class problem is your problem too. *Synthese, 156,* 563–85.

Handfield, T. (2008). Unfinkable dispositions. *Synthese, 160,* 297–308.

Hartshorne, C. (1941). *Man's Vision of God.* New York: Harper & Row Inc.

Hartshorne, C. (1965). The necessarily existent. In A. Plantinga (Ed.), *The Onto-logical Argument* (123–35). New York: Anchor Books.

Hasker, W. (1989). *God, Time, and Knowledge.* Ithaca, NY: Cornell University Press.

Hawthorne, J. (2004). *Knowledge and Lotteries.* Oxford: Oxford University Press.
——*see also* O'Leary-Hawthorne.

Heller, M. (2001). The worst of all worlds. *Philosophia, 28* (1–4), 255–68.

Hick J. (1978). *Evil and the God of Love* (Rev. ed.) San Francisco, CA: Harper and Row.

Hinchliff, M. (1996). The puzzle of change. In J. E. Tomberlin (Ed.), *Philosophical Perspectives: Vol. 10. Metaphysics* (pp. 119–36). Oxford: Blackwell.

Howard-Snyder, D. and Howard-Snyder, F. (1994). How an unsurpassable being might create a surpassable world. *Faith and Philosophy, 11,* 260–8.
————(1996). The real problem of no best world. *Faith and Philosophy,13,* 422–5.

Hudson, H. (2001). *A Materialistic Metaphysics of the Human Person.* Ithaca, NY: Cornell University Press.

Jordan, J. (2006). Does skeptical theism lead to moral skepticism? *Philosophy and Phenomenological Research, 72,* 403–17.

Kane, R. (2005). *A Contemporary Introduction to Free Will.* New York: Oxford University Press.

Kitcher, P. (2005). The many-sided conflict between science and religion. In W. Mann (Ed.), *Blackwell Guide to Philosophy of Religion* (pp. 266–82). Malden, Mass.: Blackwell Publishers.

Kretzmann, N. (1991). A particular problem of creation: Why would God create this world? In S. MacDonald (Ed.), *Being and Goodness: The Concept of the Good in Metaphysics and Philosophical Theology* (pp. 229–49). Ithaca, NY: Cornell University Press.

Kvanvig, J. (2002). On behalf of maverick Molinism. *Faith and Philosophy, 19,* 348–57.

Langtry, B. (2008). *God, the Best, and Evil.* Oxford: Oxford University Press.

Leibniz, G. (1985). *Theodicy.* A. Farrer (Ed.). LaSalle, Ill.: Open Court. (Original work published 1710).

Lewis, D. (1973). *Counterfactuals.* Cambridge, Mass.: Harvard University Press.
——(1984). Are we free to break laws? *Philosophical Papers II* (pp. 291–8). Oxford: Oxford University Press.
——(1986a). Counterfactual dependence and time's arrow. *Philosophical Papers: Vol. II* (pp. 32–51). Oxford: Oxford University Press.
——(1986b). *On the Plurality of Worlds.* Oxford: Blackwell.
——(1986c). The paradoxes of time travel. *Philosophical Papers: Vol. II* (67–80). Oxford: Oxford University Press.

——(1997). Finkish dispositions. *The Philosophical Quarterly, 47,* 143–58.

——(2000). Evil for freedom's sake? In *Papers in Ethics and Social Philosophy: Vol. III* (pp. 101–27). Cambridge: Cambridge University Press.

Mackie, J. L. (1955). Evil and omnipotence. *Mind, 64,* 200–12.

——(1982). *The Miracle of Theism.* Oxford: Clarendon Press.

Mackie, J. (2008). Evil and omnipotence. In M. Rea and L. Pojman (Eds.), *Philosophy of Religion: An Anthology* (5th ed.) (pp. 299–306). Belmont, CA: Wadsworth. pp. 173–81.

Malcolm, N. (1960). Anselm's ontological arguments. *Philosophical Review, 69,* 41–62.

Martin, C. B. (1994). Dispositions and conditionals. *The Philosophical Quarterly, 44,* 1–8.

Menzel, C. (2008). Actualism. In N. Zalta (Ed.), *The Stanford Encyclopedia of Philosophy.* Stanford, CA: Stanford University.

Merricks, T. (2009). Truth and freedom. *Philosophical Review, 118,* 29–57.

Mill, J. S. (1974). *Utilitarianism, One Liberty, Essay on Bentham.* M. Warnock (Ed.). New York: Penguin Books.

Morris, T. (1987). *Anselmian Explorations.* Notre Dame, Ind.: University of Notre Dame Press.

Murray, M. (2008). *Nature Red in Tooth and Claw: Theism and the Problem of Animal Suffering.* Oxford: Oxford University Press.

Nolan, D. (1997). Impossible worlds: A modest approach. *Notre Dame Journal of Formal Logic, 38,* 535–72.

Nozick, R. (1975). *Anarchy, State and Utopia.* New York: Basic Books.

O'Leary-Hawthorne, J. and Howard-Snyder, D. (1998). Transworld sanctity and Plantinga's free will defense. *International Journal for Philosophy of Religion, 44,* 1–21.

Otte, R. (2009). Transworld depravity and unobtainable worlds. *Philosophy and Phenomenological Research, 78,* 165–77.

Paton, H. J. (Ed.). (1964). *Groundwork of the Metaphysics of Morals.* New York: Harper and Row Publishers.

Pike, N. (1990). Hume on evil. In M. M. Adams and R. M. Adams (Eds.), *The Problem of Evil* (pp. 38–52). Oxford: Oxford University Press.

——(1998). Omnipotence and God's ability to sin. In L. Pojman (Ed.), *Philosophy of Religion: An Anthology* (pp. 283–93). Boston, Mass.: Wadsworth Publishing Co.

Plantinga, A. (1967). *God and Other Minds.* Ithaca, NY: Cornell University Press.

——(1973). Which worlds could God have created? *The Journal of Philosophy, 70,* 539–52.

——(1974). *God, Freedom, and Evil.* Grand Rapids, Mich.: Wm. B. Eerdmans Publishing.

——(1974). *The Nature of Necessity.* Oxford: Oxford University Press.

——(1979). De essential. *Grazer Philosophische Studien, 1,* 101–21.

Plantinga, A. (1986). On Ockham's way out. *Faith and Philosophy, 3,* 235–69.

——(1996). *Respondeo*. In J. Kvanvig (Ed.), *Warrant in Contemporary Epistemology Essays in Honor of Plantinga's Theory of Knowledge* (pp. 307–78). Lanham, MD: Rowman & Littlefield.

——(2004). Superlapsarianism or "O felix culpa." In P. van Inwagen (Ed.), *Christian Faith and the Problem of Evil* (pp. 1–25). Grand Rapids, Mich.: Wm. B. Eerdmans Publishing Co.

——(2009). Transworld depravity, transworld sanctity, and uncooperative essences. *Philosophy and Phenomenological Research, 78* (1), 178–91.

——and Grim, P. (1993). Truth, omniscience and Cantorian arguments: An exchange. *Philosophical Studies, 71,* 267–306.

Quinn, P. (1982). God, moral perfection and possible worlds. In F. Sontag and M. D. Bryant (Eds.), *God: The Contemporary Discussion* (pp. 197–216). New York: Rose of Sharon Press.

Rawls, J. (1975). *A Theory of Justice*. Cambridge, Mass.: Harvard University Press.

Rowe, W. (1996a). The evidential argument from evil: A second look. In D. Howard-Snyder (Ed.), *The Evidential Argument from Evil* (pp. 262–85). Bloomington: Indiana University Press.

——(1996b). The problem of evil and some varieties of atheism. In D. Howard-Snyder (Ed.), *The Evidential Argument from Evil* (pp. 1–11). Bloomington: Indiana University Press.

——(1998). In defense of "The free will defense." *International Journal for Philosophy of Religion, 44,* 115–20.

——(2001). Skeptical theism: A response to Bergmann. *Noûs, 35,* 297–303.

——(2002). Can God be free? *Faith and Philosophy, 19,* 405–24.

——(2004). *Can God be free?* Oxford: Oxford University Press.

——(2006). Friendly atheism, skeptical theism, and the problem of evil. *International Journal for Philosophy of Religion, 59,* 79–92.

Senor, T. (1991). God, supernatural kinds, and the Incarnation. *Religious Studies, 27,* 353–70.

——(2008). Defending divine freedom. In J. Kvanvig (Ed.), *Oxford Studies in the Philosophy of Religion: Vol 1* (pp. 168–95). Oxford: Oxford University Press.

Soames, S. (2006). The philosophical significance of the Kripkean necessary aposteriori. In E. Sosa and E. Villanueva (Eds.), *Philosophical Issues: Vol 16* (pp. 287–309). Malden, Mass.: Blackwell Publishing Co.

Sobel, J. H. (2004). *Logic and Theism: Arguments For and Against Beliefs in God*. Cambridge: Cambridge University Press.

Stalnaker, R. (1981). A theory of conditionals. In W. Haper, R. Stalnaker, and G. G. Pearce (Eds.), *Ifs*. Dordrecht-Holland: D. Reidel Publishing Company. 41–56.

——and Thomason, R. (1970). A semantic analysis of conditional logic. *Theoria, 36,* 23–32.

St Augustine. (2006). *Augustine: Confessions and enchiridion.* A. Outler (Trans.). Philadelphia, PA: Westminster John Knox Press.

Stone, J. (2009). CORNEA, skepticism, and evil. *Australasian Journal of Philosophy, 89,* 59–70.

Sullivan, M. (2012). Semantics for blasphemy. In J. Kvanig (Ed.), *Oxford Studies in the Philosophy of Religion: Vol. IV* (pp. 160–73). Oxford: Oxford University Press.

Sullivan, R. (1989). *Immanuel Kant's Moral Theory.* Cambridge, Mass.: Cambridge University Press.

Swinburne, R. (1998). *Providence and the Problem of Evil.* Oxford: Oxford University Press.

——(2004). *The Existence of God.* Oxford: Oxford University Press.

Talbott, T. (1986). On divine foreknowledge and bringing about the past. *Philosophy and Phenomenological Research, 46,* 455–69.

Taylor, R. (1992). *Metaphysics* (4th ed.). Englewood Cliffs, NJ: Prentice Hall.

Tichy, P. (1976). A counterexample to the Stalnaker–Lewis analysis of counter-factuals. *Philosophical Studies, 29,* 271–3.

Timpe, K. (2008). *Free Will: Sourcehood and its Alternatives.* New York: Continuum Publishing.

Tomberlin, J. E. and van Inwagen, P. (1985). *Profiles: Alvin Plantinga.* Dordrecht-Holland: D. Reidel Publishing Co.

Trivers, R. (1971). The evolution of reciprocal altruism. *Quarterly Review of Biology, 46,* 35–57.

van Inwagen, P. (1983). *An Essay on Free Will.* Oxford: Oxford University Press.

——(1995a). The magnitude, duration, and distribution of evil: A theodicy. *God, Knowledge and Mystery: Essays in Philosophical Theology* (pp. 96–124). Ithaca, NY: Cornell University Press.

——(1995b). The problem of evil, the problem of air, and the problem of silence. *God, Knowledge and Mystery: Essays in Philosophical Theology* (pp. 66–95). Ithaca, NY: Cornell University Press.

Vogel, J. (1990). Are There Counterexamples to the Closure Principle? In M. Ross and G. Ross (Eds.), *Doubting: Contemporary Perspectives on Skepticism.* Dordrecht-Holland: Kluwer.

Wainwright, W. (1988). *Philosophy of Religion.* Belmont, Calif.: Wadsworth Publishing Company.

Williamson, T. (2008). *The Philosophy of Philosophy.* Oxford: Blackwell.

——(2009a). Probability and danger. *The Amherst Lecture in Philosophy, 4,* 1–35.

——(2009b). Replies to my critics. In P. Greenough and D. Pritchard (Eds.), *Williamson on Knowledge* (pp. 279–304). Oxford: Oxford University Press.

Wisdom, J. (1935). God and evil. *Mind, 44* (173), 1–20.

Wykstra, S. (1984). The Humean obstacle to evidential arguments from suffering: On avoiding the evils of "appearance." *International Journal for Philosophy of Religion, 16,* 73–93.

—— (1996). Rowe's noseeum arguments from evil. In D. Howard-Snyder (Ed.), *The Evidential Argument from Evil* (pp. 126–50). Bloomington: Indiana University Press.

Yablo, S. (2008). Textbook Kripkeanism and the open texture of concepts. *Thoughts: Papers on Mind, Meaning, and Modality* (pp. 79–102). Oxford: Oxford University Press.

# Index